SIR DAVID MURRAY

METTLE

TRAGEDY, COURAGE AND TITLES

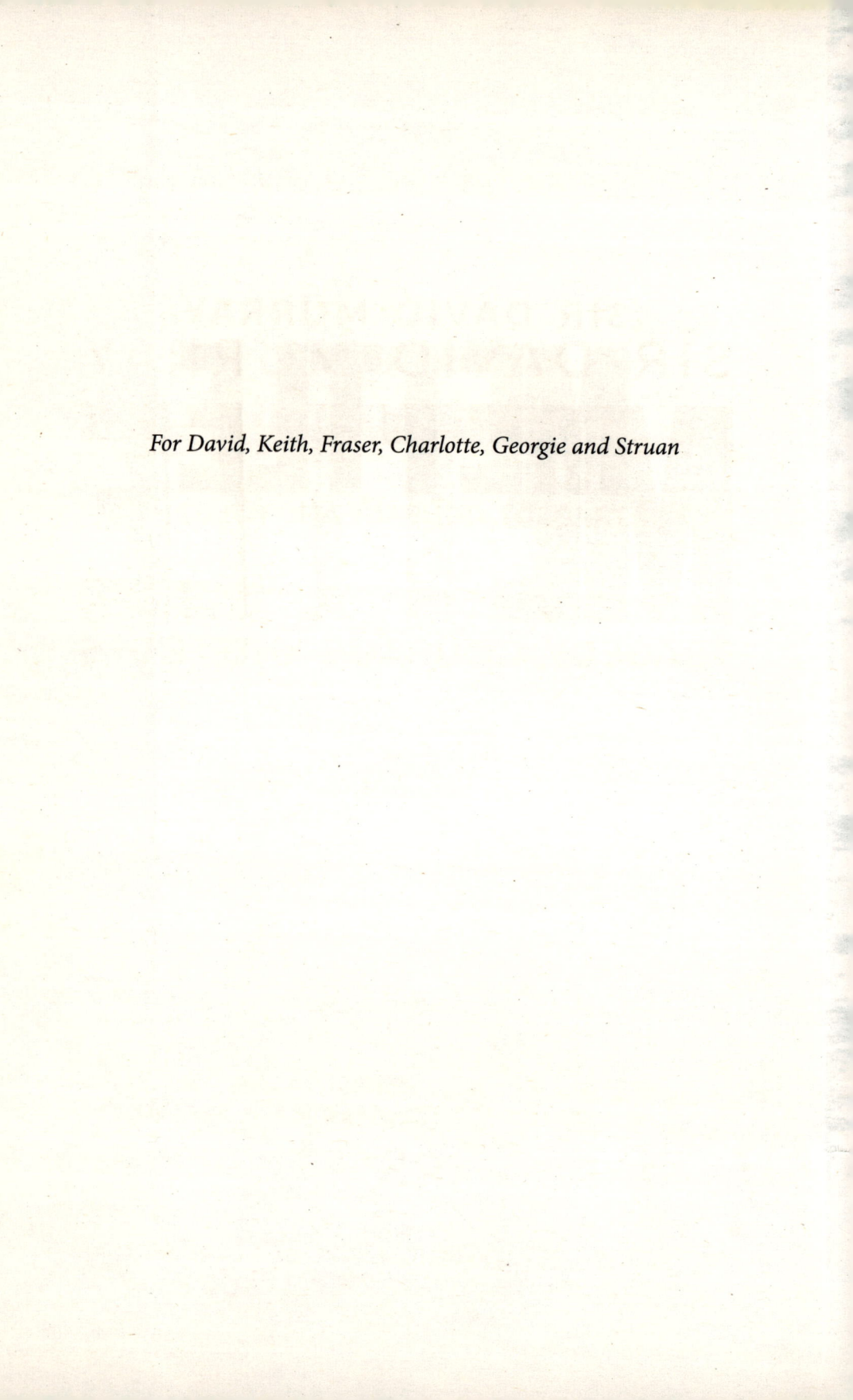

For David, Keith, Fraser, Charlotte, Georgie and Struan

SIR DAVID MURRAY

METTLE

TRAGEDY, COURAGE AND TITLES

Reach Sport

Reach Sport

www.reachsport.com

1

Written with Bruce Waddell

Published in Great Britain and Ireland in 2025 by Reach Sport.

www.reachsport.com
@Reach_Sport

Reach Sport is a part of Reach PLC.

Hardback ISBN: 9781916811263
eBook ISBN: 9781916811270

Photographic acknowledgements:
Sir David Murray collection, Mirrorpix, Alamy.

Every effort has been made to trace the copyright.
Any oversight will be rectified in future editions.

Editor: Simon Monk.
Production: Christine Costello, Roy Gilfoyle.
Cover Design: Chris Collins

Printed and bound by CPI Group (UK) Ltd,
Croydon, CR0 4YY.

MIX
Paper | Supporting
responsible forestry
FSC® C013604

CONTENTS

FOREWORD

By Graeme Souness

I HAVE KNOWN SIR DAVID MURRAY FOR 40 YEARS AND been in his company thousands of times, but I have only seen him show anything approaching self-pity over the loss of his legs once.

On that solitary occasion, we were together in an airport lounge and had too much wine. That was the only time he showed any disappointment over what happened to him.

David is an incredibly impressive man and there is no doubt that the way he refused to allow his accident to ruin his life provoked an immediate admiration on my part that soon flowered into a lasting friendship.

It has not impacted on him as it might have for many others because he is so mentally strong.

Despite having both his legs cut off above the knees, he is an action man. As a young businessman, there was no stopping him.

I would say he is the most competitive human being I have ever met. He still wants to compete in every waking moment.

I first met David soon after I became manager of Rangers. His basketball team, Murray International Metals, shared the same sponsor as I did – Adidas - and I went to watch it one night in Livingston due to this connection and met David for the first time.

They had a playmaker called Alton Byrd whose outstanding performance still sticks with me. After that, we started going for dinner together with our wives and it developed from there.

David has a very close-knit friendship group. He does not have lots of friends, but the ones he does have are close and trusted. We soon found that we had common ground and quickly hit it off.

He was a Rangers supporter from Ayrshire and said to me one day: 'I've got a chance to buy Ayr United, I am going to do it.' I replied, 'Where can you take that?' He said it was his hometown, where he grew up, and it was 'boy done good' buying the local football team, but I had a sneaky feeling that Rangers could be for sale, and my suspicion proved correct.

Lawrence Marlborough, the owner, was looking to invest in the USA and sell his UK assets and Rangers were part of that process.

I brokered the deal because I felt that David's business acumen and drive could take the club to another level again after my initial success at Ibrox as manager.

I loved being around that attitude because it was the same one that prevailed when I was a player at Liverpool.

You won the European Cup and they would say, 'yeah, but you didn't win the league this year' or 'you're a good player but we have had better before you lot.' David certainly had that. He was never happy with what he had and always wanted to improve, and that was the world I wanted to live in.

When you are managing Rangers in Scotland you must keep your counsel, you cannot be seen out in pubs gossiping or volunteering too much information to the wide world and we ran it together, the two of us.

I would leave Ibrox anywhere between two and three in the afternoons and go back along the motorway to Edinburgh and either pop into David's office or we would go out for an early supper together. We would see each other most days and speak to each other every day.

Louise, his gorgeous late wife, saw a lot less of her husband when he got involved at Ibrox but that is what Rangers does to you. You become obsessive and it takes over your life. We wanted to be successful, and it was all-consuming. We were a formidable team together at that time.

David was easily the best chairman I worked for because he knew his strengths. He would repeatedly say, 'football is your side of things but leave the business to me' and then quickly offer an opinion on a player!

We used to have lots of laughs and I can never remember us falling out. When I left Rangers, I thought, 'every job is like this,' but I had two unbelievably good chairmen. David Holmes was a decent man, who let me get on with it, and David Murray was the same, although I ran everything by him.

He turned out to be 100 per cent correct when he said I would regret leaving Rangers. We sat on a wall outside my flat in Edinburgh when I broke the news that I was leaving to manage Liverpool. I wanted to tell him first but he had already heard because keeping a secret in Scotland is exceedingly difficult. Having said no twice before to a return to Anfield as manager, I accepted the third time.

David tried to persuade me to stay, but I said, 'no, I have made up my mind.' I had a lot going on at that time. I was on the front pages of the papers as much as the back pages and it all got to me, but he was right when he said, 'you'll regret leaving.'

He told me to take a year or two out, to enjoy the fruits of our labour and he was 100 per cent right. I left Rangers when we were in great nick, it was the start of nine-in-a-row.

Since I stopped working in management and he stopped being chairman and owner of Rangers, we have seen more of each other again. We are still like two children. The banter is fierce between us. It is like being in a dressing-room again.

The higher up you go in football, the fiercer the banter, and David has loved all that since I have known him. When you analyse it, we cannot have a game of five-a-side or tennis together, so he wants to beat you with his mind. He is sharp as a tack and always has been.

I go up to stay at his house in Scotland and we end up drinking too much wine and talking absolute nonsense. He is great company but I have never seen him feel sorry for himself a second time.

Graeme Souness, February 2025

FOREWORD

By John Greig

WHAT DAVID MURRAY DID FOR RANGERS FOOTBALL Club must never be forgotten.

The titles and trophies alone won under his ownership makes him such a huge part of the club's history. But he brought something deeper than just being a winner – he created a special Rangers family during his time there.

I owe him so much and cannot express how much he has done for me personally.

When I joined Rangers early in my career I lived near Liberton in Edinburgh. I got a bus to Haymarket then got on the 8.30am train to Glasgow every morning, often with Sandy Jardine. I did that for 18 years. We would meet up with Willie Johnston and Willie Mathieson who came in from another station and Jim Baxter who arrived from Kirkcaldy. We all jumped on the 54 bus to Crookston and got off at Ibrox. Changed days but happy days.

I first met David through Graeme Souness who I obviously had come to know very well. I had managed the club and he was now the Rangers boss. One day Graeme said to me, "David would like to have a chat with you."

I really didn't know why. I had been working with the BBC at the time, as well as helping a travel agent who handled Rangers air tickets. That was probably my strongest remaining link with Ibrox. But I got the call to go and see David at his office in Edinburgh. What he said to me that day changed the rest of my life.

He asked me to come home to Ibrox. He will never truly know what that meant to me. He just said the club needed me and there was a job to be done. The job didn't even have a name but I didn't hesitate.

David really was an incredible man and, along with Graeme and then Walter, took the football club on to a different level that so many fans just took for granted at the time. I don't remember one single fan complaining. Some of the players that wore the jersey – Gascoigne, Laudrup, de Boer, Gattuso, van Bronckhurst – were genuinely world class. And he somehow kept adding to the list.

It was a golden era and I was effectively a club ambassador and part of that family. David also later made me a director and I helped Dick Advocaat settle into his job when he became the Rangers manager.

I have so many memorable moments from my playing career but in later years two particular events stood out for me – both instigated by David. Being voted the greatest Rangers player of all time in a fans' poll that had been commissioned was a massive honour but having a statue created and made part of a memorial to the victims of the Ibrox disaster was something that brought me to tears. All those names. I was lost for words.

The Rangers family bonds are strong and that will never change. I was truly sad and disappointed that David's time had to come to an end and he felt he had to go but we remain close friends.

FOREWORD

Looking back on the David Murray era, I feel privileged to have played a part as we enjoyed an outstanding period in the history of Glasgow Rangers.

He was a remarkable man and always so kind. Those memories will stay with me forever.

John Greig, 2025

FOREWORD

By David Dein

I FIRST MET DAVID WHEN HE BECAME CHAIRMAN OF Glasgow Rangers soon after I became vice-chairman of Arsenal in 1983. There was an immediate bonding between us because of his bubbly personality, quick wit and love for the beautiful game.

He has a vast knowledge of players in the UK and overseas and is never shy of voicing his opinion, invariably with good humour. David is incredibly astute and had a very successful career in the steel and property business. Despite having suffered an horrific injury losing his legs, he overcame his disability with extraordinary courage and mobility.

Although we only had one transfer between us which was Giovanni van Bronckhorst in 2001 for the princely sum of £8million, I remember he drove a very hard bargain – but it was fun!

Our real bonding came over the notorious debenture bond scheme. David personally pioneered the redevelopment of Ibrox

Park financing it through the scheme and his connections at Bank of Scotland. It went very well for them and he encouraged me to cut and paste the idea for Arsenal which I did. He introduced me to his bankers, financial advisors, marketing people and even a call centre for interested supporters and investors to buy the bonds.

Although initially I became public enemy number one as the fans had to buy their own seat, years later all the investors made a profit and we successfully developed Highbury.

David is never short of ideas and one day invited me up to Edinburgh to meet with his counterpart at Celtic, Dermot Desmond. Over a delightful dinner they hit me with the idea of Rangers and Celtic playing in the Premier League! After nearly choking on my vegetable soup, I thought about it and decided it was not as crazy as it seemed. It would certainly add salt and pepper to the meal and we all know that the two clubs could bring 10,000 plus singing fans with them to every game.

David is gregarious and very kind-hearted. I remember once telling him that I was coming with my wife to the Edinburgh Festival and he made sure that we stayed at his hotel as his guests. Football is poorer without his involvement and the names of Glasgow Rangers and David Murray will be intertwined forever.

David Dein, 2025

THE CAR CRASH THAT CHANGED MY LIFE

'I ADMIRE YOUR COURAGE'… FOUR WORDS THAT HAVE long had a bearing on so many aspects of my life. It became a blueprint. Four words that a doctor or a nurse at my bedside in the hospital might have been expected to utter and if they had, they might have been referring to the fact that I apparently had never cried. Not once.

The reason I have built so much of my life around those words is that they were conveyed to me – in a private letter – by a man who personified courage: Sir Douglas Bader.

Bader was a heroic World War Two pilot who lost both of his legs while attempting aerobatics, yet continued to fight in the cockpit of his Spitfire. Like millions of others I was only aware of him because of the 1956 British war film Reach For The Sky where Bader was played by Kenneth More.

In 1976, at the age of 24, I had just lost both of my legs – in a car crash – and was lying in hospital, a bi-lateral amputee, when the nurse delivered the letter that would act as a motivation throughout the rest of my life.

Dated 7 June, it read:

Dear David,
You will be surprised at receiving a letter from a complete stranger. The reason is that I lost both my legs many years ago at the age of 21. When your aunt, Mrs Beaumont, wrote to me at the end of March and told me that you had had the same ill luck, I felt that I would wait a few weeks then drop you a line.
I gather that you have got hold of the problem and decided to get on with life which is the only thing to do. Well done. That is the only attitude of mind to adopt. I am sure you will be all right as many others have been.
I just wanted to write to you and tell you how much I admire your courage and to wish you well.
Yours sincerely, Douglas Bader

I would later telephone the number he had left at the top of his letter to thank him for his encouragement and tell him exactly what it meant to me… and still does. It sits in a frame close to the front door.

Almost two months earlier, I had what Douglas Bader might enthusiastically have described as a rather miraculous escape. It was certainly life-changing. On an overcast Saturday afternoon on 13 March I drove my then two-year old son David to Musselburgh after gently persuading him that a nice thing to do would be to buy a bunch of flowers for his mum, Louise. It wasn't a special occasion but he was happy to go along.

THE CAR CRASH THAT CHANGED MY LIFE

I dropped him off back at home in Longniddry, East Lothian, then drove the 10 miles to play stand-off for Dalkeith against North Berwick. I scored nine points, three conversions, in a 16-9 victory and then began to make my way home.

The car – a purple Lotus Elite – had been serviced just 24 hours earlier and unbeknown to me at the time, the tyre pressures had been inflated to almost twice what they should have been. I also didn't put my seatbelt on – it wasn't a legal requirement back then.

As I made my way along a dual carriageway near Longniddry, in East Lothian, the front left tyre just blew. There was nothing I could have done. The car lurched to the side, I left the road and smashed headlong into a tree.

Revisiting the scene much, much later, I realised that just a few yards before the tree and a few yards after it, there was nothing but open fields.

How that tree is still standing I don't know, but remarkably it is. I recently stopped at the same spot again and nearly 50 years after the accident, there are still marks on the base of the tree. Equally amazingly, there are also still purple shards of the car's bodywork embedded in my upper leg.

Memories of the exact moment are hazy. The vehicle was made of fibreglass and the impact forced the engine block right through the facia and into the driver and passenger seat.

I was immediately shunted right through the door and lay unconscious and bleeding next to the wreckage. If I'd been wearing a seatbelt, I'd have been stuck in the car – things might have been much worse. A number of rugby supporters who had actually been at the game stopped their cars and raced to my side. There was lots of blood and they applied tourniquets with their ties to try to halt the flow.

They somehow kept me alive and even though I can remember

nothing about it, an ambulance was called and arrived quickly to take me 18 miles to Edinburgh Royal Infirmary.

That night, I lost 13 pints of blood and there was no option for surgeons but to immediately amputate parts of my mangled legs through the knees.

My wife Louise, of course, was frantic with worry yet somehow I'd managed to call her from a hospital payphone while lying on a trolley taking me back to the ward. I told her, "You have to come. I'm in a bad way." I have absolutely no recollection of this.

Louise, my family and friends took turns to sit by my bedside during the following days as I struggled to recover.

The anaesthetist Ned Trench and a surgeon fought to give me a better chance of a partial recovery, but five days after the accident they were finally defeated after an infection set in. I ended up having a further nine inches of my legs removed.

Following this I was finally transferred to the Princess Margaret Rose Hospital for 10 weeks of intensive care.

I must have spent days and hours wondering how I might cope with the rest of my life. I was still a young man, with a wife and young family and I was passionate about business and playing sports. I just felt numb but then that letter arrived and it made me so determined to carry on.

I know the accident and the aftermath was tough on my family, especially Louise. During an STV interview later she told the reporter, "Deep down, I just knew David would never give up."

In life, I never try to look back. We all have decisions to make – some of them big, reflective moments – and I am a great believer in the fact that you either turn left or you turn right.

If anyone I know is ever in trouble or facing adversity, I always tell them that every problem has a solution and to always look ahead.

Be decisive. Stay positive. I had no intention of quitting.

1

LIKE FATHERS, LIKE SONS

MY FATHER IAN MURRAY COULD ONLY BE DESCRIBED as 'charismatic'. He had a pencil-thin moustache and there was a vague resemblance to a slick, young David Niven.

He died, aged just 50, officially from renal failure but much of his poor health stemmed from chronic alcohol abuse. Gin was his thing. He was a giant of a man – a reckless gambler, a shrewd entrepreneur and even, at his lowest point, an unfairly-convicted fraudster, defended at his trial by Menzies Campbell MP and QC.

My mother Roma was permanently resilient… throughout her entire life. She needed to be.

She was born a Cockney and was educated in 13 different schools in the UK and at one point her father even moved the family to Chicago seeking work. They finally settled in Newington, Edinburgh, where he opened McEwan's Furniture Centre.

Ultimately, she was the glue that held our family together when I was young, even if it did eventually become unstuck.

She pointed all of her children in the right direction at critical points in their lives growing up and without her wisdom and strength I would never have achieved as much as I have.

It had been close to love at first sight in 1949 – four years after the end of World War Two. She was dressing a display at upmarket Jenners in Princes Street when she responded to a loud tap on the huge window. There was my father clowning around. He manoeuvred his way through the revolving doors, found her window and asked her out. Shortly afterwards, they married. He was still training, and hoping, to be a vet. I cannot imagine for one second how family life might have developed if he had qualified. As it transpired he went down the family business route.

They moved to Ayr and my father took over the family's established coal merchants, Murray Forest, which had been started in 1900 by my grandfather and a business partner. I still have the original brass plate hanging on a door in our home at Dunbarney in Perthshire.

And there is clearly something about entrepreneurial spirit that runs deep in our family. When my grandfather, also called David, died in 1942, his will left £26,820.12 – the equivalent of more than £1.6million today.

I was born in the Ayr Nursing Home on October 14, 1951 and christened in St Leonard's Parish Church on Christmas Day. My earliest single memory is sitting up in bed, aged four, at the Greystones nursing home where I had my tonsils taken out and was recovering with scoop after scoop of Cornish ice cream.

Our family lived in a grey sandstone villa, called Morelands in Southpark Road in Ayr where I had my own room, a large garden and a huge wall that would easily withstand the constant battering from the pounding of a leather football or a tennis ball. I would spend hours at that. There was always a ball.

My father instilled in me a lifelong love of sport. Aside from being an all-round sportsman he regularly took me to see Ayr United play at Somerset Park, he took me to Ibrox on European Cup nights, to Hampden Park in 1964 to see Alan Gilzean score the winner against England in front of 133,000 fans and months later he took me to a raucous Paisley Town Hall to see legendary World Middleweight champion Sugar Ray Robinson lose a non-title fight against Irishman Mick Leahy.

Before the age of 10, I was passionate about most sports – something that has continued throughout my life – and my father rarely missed a match that I was involved in from my time at Alloway Primary.

When I began showing an interest in golf at my first boarding school at Cambusdoon, near Ayr, a parcel arrived and inside was a golf bag. Inside the bag was one golf club – a five iron – one Dunlop golf ball and a tee. My father had written an accompanying letter which read, "The rest of the clubs will come only when you start practising and get better." I did and he was as good as his word.

The one sport that did divide us was horse racing. I had no interest in it – and never will have – yet it consumed him. At one point he owned 20 horses, two or three of them hugely successful and he counted top jockeys such as Scobie Breasley and Lester Piggott as close friends who rode in his colours. He won the Lincoln Handicap in 1961 with a horse called Hill Royal, ridden by Joe Sime. The odds had been 50/1 and some blokes working in our street had put money on the horse – they weren't seen for weeks afterwards.

If speed dialling had been around back then, after his family, button No2 would certainly have been the bookie. And not just one of them. On one memorable occasion in 1963 he put on a six-horse accumulator and had £500,000 – the equivalent of millions of pounds now – riding on the final race. It was a photo finish and he lost. We were on holiday in St Brelades Bay, Jersey at the time and his reaction? "Ce'st la vie," he said, before lighting a cigar and setting off for a long walk down the beach. Despite the fact I couldn't see his face or his reaction, I watched him for ages.

The *Daily Express* reported later the story of the man who had it all and lost it all.

It's probably no surprise that any entrepreneurial streak came from both my mother's and father's heritage. He was always looking for opportunities. I remember sitting in the passenger seat of his car one day and him driving his Jaguar down a bumpy countryside track. He parked the car and 15 minutes later came back to tell me that he had just bought a farm and the only reason he had done it was because the land would be crucial to the new Ayr by-pass.

He randomly bought a bar then he ploughed a lot of money into one of the country's first golf ranges at Prestwick. My mother continued to be understanding and protective of her children but life had begun to revolve around the next deal, the next horse race and – with almost hourly regularity – the next gin and tonic. His lifestyle had put an enormous strain on our family.

He had a runner for betting called Bobby Wylie from Ayr and my father was informed by someone in the TV industry that Come Dancing, the inter-regional dance competition, was recorded the night before it actually appeared on BBC. Bobby was dispatched, and somehow got into the studio and found out that Home Counties South had won, before driving back from Manchester with the news. My father then laid a substantial bet with John Banks, the infamous Glasgow bookmaker, and obviously won. In later years Banks approached me during a European night at Ibrox and relayed the story. Both of us had a great laugh at the sheer audacity of the man.

His betting became outrageous. He regularly gambled upwards of £10,000 on single races and on one occasion, a beleaguered bookie in Ayr threw a set of keys at him and said, "All yours. You now own my shop." Life was never dull. He bought the first Mark 10 Jaguar in Scotland and one day he arrived back at our family home with the American film actor Robert Mitchum in tow. They had previously met socially in London.

My parents finally split up in 1966. I was 15 and by then a senior pupil boarding at Fettes College in Edinburgh. My mother moved to the city with my two sisters and younger brother where she enjoyed a good life, and although I regularly spoke with my father – who continued to live in Ayr – he was on a tragic downward spiral.

At one point, one of his business transactions went disastrously wrong and he ended up taking the fall on his own, despite the fact, as our lawyers indicated, that others were primarily to blame.

He was convicted of a minor fraud and was sentenced to 12 months in prison. He was initially sent to Glasgow's Barlinnie jail and it was a daunting experience going there to visit him.

But within weeks, he had been transferred to Penninghame Open Prison near Newtown Stewart in south-west Scotland. It is now a splendid family home and there was an air of luxury about it even back in the 1970s. Before going in to see my father I vividly remember sitting outside and watching as one of the 'prisoners' entered the back seat of a Mercedes limousine where I later learned he was writing cheques – in effect running his business from jail.

My father struggled to recover from his experience there. One of my last memories of him was when my wife Louise and I had moved to Longniddry and he came to stay with us for the weekend. He went to the local hostelry but within a few hours, was worse for wear. I ended up driving him home to Ayr. It was so sad.

He died in Ballochmyle Hospital on September 20, 1975 at the age of just 50. I had driven from Edinburgh and was at his side. He is buried in Ayr cemetery in a family plot with his parents and grandparents. I visit his grave now and then, and often ponder what he might have achieved in later life. But then I always leave with a smile and the same thought: What a remarkable life he led.

My biggest regret is that he never saw what I went on to achieve and that he never got to properly know his grandsons David and Keith or their families.

He had told me more than once that the best career path for me was to try to get a job in London and join the Caledonian Club. He said I would meet influential people there that could help me climb the ladder.

I understood but by then I already had the entrepreneurial bug and was carving my own path.

Even from a young age I had been a confident boy – not cocky, but I knew what I wanted. I was passionate about history and geography, I was good with numbers but never truly enamoured by science.

At the age of 13 my parents were so proud that they had been able to send me to Fettes College in Edinburgh. On arrival there, I realised that it seemed to be full of children from England, so much so that my nickname became 'Jock'.

I quickly established myself in the rugby, boxing and cross-country teams – a huge advantage at a public school. I can remember so many boys who were deeply unhappy being away from their families but I actually thrived on it. At one point I won a medal for boxing.

My mother's resilience would once again keep our family together. Despite being left a series of debts by my father, she worked in her father's furniture shop during the day and took a job as a barmaid in the evenings. She bought a house in Craigleith Drive in Edinburgh and actually remained there, very happily, for many years.

She finally died in April 2013 – a few days after Margaret Thatcher passed away – and I spoke at her funeral at Mortonhall Crematorium.

I said, "Today we say goodbye to our mother, another true iron lady who has led an incredibly energetic life and had an effect on everyone and anyone who was close to her.

"Roma Murray was a proper Cockney, born in 1925 and I think we would all agree they just don't make them like that today. She left for Chicago with her parents at the age of one where her father Edward went to seek work just as the Great Depression was about to hit the country.

"After becoming homesick Edward and his wife Doris returned with Roma 12 months later. Over the next few years and after moving around Britain, working in different roles and Roma going to 13 different schools, they finally settled in Edinburgh where my grandfather opened McEwan's the furniture centre which was established as the family business.

"As a child my mother was in newspaper adverts for Pears Soap, and even had some small parts in several Alfred Hitchcock films.

"As a teenager she became a window dresser at the famous Jenners store in Princes Street, when a young veterinary student – my father Ian – tapped on the window and asked for a date. They were married at St Andrew's Church in Ravelston Dykes Road and settled in my father's hometown of Ayr where Sandra, Andrew, Katie and I were born.

"When Roma settled into family life, she had a passion for gardening and also spent more than 10 years assisting on a regular basis with disabled children at the Hansel village near here. She was thrilled to be asked, as recognition for this work, to attend the Queen's garden party at Holyrood but still decided to allow one of her team who had ailing health to take her place.

"While she had tried to create a loving family home for all of us, unfortunately my parents separated when I was 15. It was a difficult and emotional time for us. Moving to Edinburgh, our mother was the glue who held us together and, with a strong hand, pointed us all in the right direction and instilled the strongest of work ethics.

"I know that without her guidance I would not have achieved as much as I have in my life after the support given and sacrifices she made for us. She was never happier than chatting with us all at an event or at home, having a glass of wine and marking everyone's card. She had a special bond with so many and was working right into her 80s."

During my schooling, even mum's best endeavours – and there were so many – weren't quite enough to keep me at Fettes. In my fourth year, I went to nearby Broughton High School. At the time, there was probably significant embarrassment, certainly from my mother, that the fees couldn't be paid.

This was one of those significant left or right moments in my life. I was thrust into a new school, at a tricky age, and for the first time ever, I had to face up to a new reality – our family had financial problems.

Yes, my mum could still put food on the table but there were none of the luxuries that we had enjoyed a decade earlier. The Jaguar was long gone, holidays in Jersey were a thing of the past and I certainly didn't have the little extras that I had enjoyed at one of Scotland's finest schools.

The 'allowances' I had been given – the norm for most Fettes pupils – had instantly become pocket money at Broughton High and I had to earn that through hard work. So that's what I did.

I took a waiter's job at Bella Napoli in the city's Fountainbridge area working three evenings per week. It brought me £2 a night.

I also took my first steps at wheeling and dealing which ended rather badly. I bought 100 white shirts from a market trader then sold them on individually for a small profit. The quality was questionable – certainly a few threads short of the finest Egyptian cotton – and I can still remember the school janitor grabbing me on Monday morning to tell me that the shirt I had sold him, just out of the packet, had shed three buttons and had already begun fraying on its Saturday night debut.

It's probably quite telling that the 'close friends' I had made at Fettes literally vanished overnight. Not one of them from any of the classes I had been in or the teams I had been a part of made contact. Only in later years, when I began to have a more prominent profile, did a few of them re-emerge and attempt to reconnect.

At Broughton, the friends I made there in just two years remain close to this day. Many have worked with me and for me and one – a successful Edinburgh lawyer called Paul Clancy – was my best man.

I left school at the age of 16 with five O-Levels and no intention of going to university. Even at that age I knew I wanted to work. I had an uncle who worked in the metals business who would guide me to the next chapter of my life.

2

EARNING NOT LEARNING

I FREELY ADMIT THAT I WAS NEVER WHAT YOU MIGHT term a fine scholar.

I had a vague interest in sciences, a passable grasp of English and a healthy respect for geography and history. I also spent far too long on the sports fields, however, I knew from deep within that numbers were everything. Numbers made sense – and the right numbers made money.

When I decided to leave school with five O-Levels and without pursuing any higher exams I never once felt that I had let anyone down by not opting for university or further education. In the late 1960s only four per cent of school-leavers actually went to university.

At different sides of the country, both of my parents were in complete agreement that another year sitting in a classroom would serve no purpose for me and that I was ready to take my first steps into work and a career.

Through an uncle – Ken McLeod – I had gleaned bits and pieces about the metals business and went for a job interview with an established firm in Glasgow.

Although I would describe myself as confident, I was still riddled with nerves.

The manager of the business, Carmichaels, asked me why I wanted to focus on ferrous metals as opposed to non-ferrous and I vividly recall stumbling with my answer. The truth was that I didn't know. I just wanted to work. He stopped me almost immediately and told me that if I couldn't answer properly I wouldn't be getting any job. I was bitterly disappointed.

Ironically, 15 years later, the same gentleman – either very bravely or very remissly – applied to me for a job. If he'd been excited about landing an interview then any enthusiasm about a new start vanished quite quickly as he sat down and I immediately reminded him about our earlier encounter.

"No hard feelings," I said. "It was a long time ago." There was no Hollywood ending. He didn't get the job but I was fair about it, shook his hand as he left the room and jokingly told him, "At least your interview lasted 20 minutes longer than mine."

For me, the knock-back proved to be a minor one. Back in Edinburgh I applied for a role as a trainee aluminium salesman with a start-up company called Scotmet Alloys. Again, I was invited for an interview and this time I had borrowed a navy blue suit from a friend and sat down with the owner – David Tait. Within the hour I had become his first employee.

It was 1968. The salary was £7 per week, always paid on a Friday afternoon, £5 of which went to my mother and the remaining £2 was mine. I walked three miles every morning from home in Blackhall to the office in Trinity and then back again in the evening.

Hard-wearing new shoes were required every few months but in early 1971, Mr Tait gave me a small raise AND provided me with my first car – a brand new green Ford Escort, registration XSN 824J bought, ironically, from Ian Skelly in Dalmarnock who later became a Rangers director.

The thrill of any new car never leaves you and even now, 50 years later, I can proudly remember every single registration plate of every car I have owned.

Scotmet Alloys distributed aluminium sheet and sections for a huge variety of purposes, including general manufacturing and my role was fairly simple: I had to sell it.

Within days of starting I really was in my element. I mainly dealt with telephone inquiries and I made a promise to myself that I would never use the word 'No' to any customer.

The answer was always Yes. Yes…we could do anything a customer wanted, yes, of course we could provide anything… even if the answer should have been 'No'.

Within a few short months, Mr Tait was working almost entirely on cutting the metal and delivering it, both of which he was expert at. Meanwhile I was practically running the sales.

At this point, with my mother on a short holiday I held a party for friends and on a warm and sunny Friday evening in late August, I met Louise Violet Densley, the girl that would change my life.

Eight girls came along and Louise was one of them. Over the next few weeks she would often appear at my work in her James Gillespie's High School uniform.

I think I actually told her during one of our walks home that one day I would be a millionaire and she replied, "I know."

When the time came to ask her dad Raymond if I could marry his daughter it was a daunting prospect. I sat on a garden wall at the end of Craigleith Drive for an hour just wondering what the opening line was for one of the most durable men I had ever met. He was ex-navy, a World War Two chief wireless operator on merchant ships and he had survived three separate torpedo attacks. In the end, I blurted it out and he just laughed and nodded.

Louise and I married in Edinburgh's Prestonfield Church followed by a reception in Prestonfield House. Raymond paid for the whole day, which cost £114 for 60 guests. I still have the receipt.

We honeymooned in Craiglynne Hotel in Grantown on Spey where I had asked Louise not to let on we were just married to avoid causing a fuss. My Ford Escort had been upgraded to a yellow Ford Capri XL. However, my plan for a quiet entrance to the hotel fell apart instantly. As she opened the passenger door of the Capri, a gust of confetti blew out, straight in the hotel door and on to the reception floor.

Cue loud whooping and I don't think we had a minute's peace all weekend from that point on. We still had a memorable few days and went back there often over the next few years.

When we returned to Edinburgh I had the opportunity to clinch some business in Fife and Raymond let me borrow his purple Reliant Scimitar (AWS 25L) to look the part. Princess Anne had a Scimitar at the time and I felt like the king of the castle crossing the Forth Road Bridge and arriving in Burntisland. The deal was done within an hour.

Our first house was a new-build, three-bed detached home in Mitchell Street, Dalkeith. It cost us £6,800. At this point I was driving in to work in Easter Road Lane for an 8am start while Louise worked at her dad's post office in Greendykes.

I actually thought his job was a complicated one until one day,

Louise and her dad were both too ill to go in and they asked me to look after the place. Raymond said it was easy. All I had to do first thing in the morning was put out a huge bundle of *Daily Records* at one side of the counter and at the other side, put dozens of packets of Embassy-tipped cigarettes. Raymond was right. That really was all there was to it in Greendykes in the 1970s.

In 1973, when I was 22, North Sea Oil was about to come on stream and it took me no more than a few weeks – and one decent break – to know exactly where my future lay.

David Tait had sold out to Amari plc, a London-based aluminium stock holding company. I immediately clicked with their management team and they asked the question, "So what is it that you want to do?"

I replied, "Make money. I want to open my own business as a metal trader." They agreed to it immediately.

Murray International Metal Services (MIMS) was born, turning over £2million in the first year with a £100,000 net profit.

I became a client of the Bank of Scotland in 1971 at their branch at 141 Princes Street. It was a business relationship that would span four decades.

Initially I took calculated risks, just to try and establish myself. North Sea Oil was booming so there were two major problems. One was getting supplies and the second was the fact that I had no track record or credibility with steel mills and fabricators.

My first office was in Thistle House, at 22 Alva Street, where I employed three staff and a secretary.

Brown Brothers, who were a large Scottish engineering firm, made an inquiry to me about specialist steel plates for ship stabilisers. This was a yes-of-course-I-can-sort-it moment. I ended up making not a single penny profit on that deal but at least they now knew who I was and that I could deliver… most of the time.

I had to convince firms that I was legitimate, so I would simply telephone metal companies and ask if I could buy their goods. I had two or three other people in the office sitting right behind me who were taking orders, often for things that we didn't have.

However, if we didn't have it, we made sure that we would locate it and deliver it as quickly as possible. We effectively were just brokers at that stage.

The team I had built around me was outstanding and loyal. Ken Cockburn, the group managing director, was an old rugby opponent, Phil Sinclair was a classmate and close pal at Broughton High School and went on to have a great sporting career in basketball.

We went on to open businesses in Norway, in Sharjah in the United Arab Emirates and in Halifax, Nova Scotia.

Soon I was supplying major customers such as Highland Fabricators and McDermott. In 1982 there was a steel shortage. I had a warehouse and I was stocking steel. We had a business.

That same year turnover at MIM was £18million with £1.8million net profit, while the private Edinburgh bank Noble Grossart were arranging for five Scottish institutions to take a 10 per cent stake in the business for £1.5million.

Throughout this time we had diversified, launching Multi Metals and Premier Alloys and bought Austin Truman in 1988. At the time, the collective metal business was turning more than £200million a year, making a £22million net profit.

We were so successful in 1982 that I took the entire staff to The Majestic Hotel in Cannes for a celebration weekend after I sold 10 per cent of the business. I put receipts of the sale into the bank and with interest rates at that time got £3,000 a week.

EARNING NOT LEARNING

The late 1980s were a time of immense opportunity and in 1989, a fleeting visit to one of our businesses in Canada brought one of those life-changing moments.

In Halifax, Nova Scotia I was immediately struck by the fact that huge tracts of the area's major industrialisation were not centralised as it is in this country. Their plants' industrial estates were miles from the city centre.

It got me thinking about the contrast with home. Soon after returning I had taken Louise and my son Keith on a helicopter trip over Edinburgh and as we flew I realised that on my own patch there were very few development options within the city.

I realised east of Edinburgh was a non-starter so there was nowhere else to go or to build other than west.

Within a few weeks, I had visited and knocked on the door of a farmer called James Young and made him a good offer to buy 600 acres of his land around Edinburgh Airport. It cost me approximately £5million.

More than 30 years later, that land is now called the Edinburgh Garden District and is becoming one of the newest and biggest eco-friendly housing projects yet seen in Scotland.

Even to this day, I often drive around central Scotland weighing up potential areas for development but that short helicopter flight is where it began. It helped launch my foray into the property sector and it resonates with me to this day.

We formed a company called Murray Estates, in partnership with Bank of Scotland, and made many acquisitions in the property sector. A significant one was the purchase of Plumtree Court in the City of London for £97million but when the financial crash came in 2008, which included Bank of Scotland going bust and then being taken over by Lloyds, it left us in a no-win situation. Much more on this later!

All valuations were reduced and our whole portfolio was written down by a sum in the region of £400million. Plumtree Court was a prime example. The bank had it revalued at £47million which had to go through as a write down on our balance sheet.

We formed a work-out plan on this when the debt stood at £900million, primarily in property. Five years later Plumtree Court was sold to Goldman Sachs for £95million. Over a 10-year period Murray Estates bought, sold and built £800million of properties, industrial and commercial.

There are some people you meet throughout your life who just matter. One of them who meant a great deal to me was Jim McDonald. I first encountered him when he was the financial director for a firm of fabricators and engineers from Burntisland in Fife. They owed me £90,000 and trying to get Jim to square it off was a process I would never want to repeat. It annoyed me but it impressed me. He was a shrewd man.

I offered him a role of becoming our financial director which he instantly accepted and we really never looked back. For 25 years Jim managed the finances. He was measured, decisive, respected and he always told me exactly what he thought, even if I didn't always like it.

3

—

TESTING MY METAL

AS I EXPLAINED IN THE PREVIOUS CHAPTER, I STARTED Murray International Metal Services (MIMS) in 1974 when I was aged just 23. And at the time, I had two or three guys in the office sitting behind me who were taking orders, sometimes for material we just didn't have. We found the metal and then delivered it. We kept no stock at the time – we were just brokers.

But I really got my first steel break with a company called Brown Brothers in Edinburgh, a well-established business which had developed the Denny-Brown ship stabiliser used on many vessels including the QE2. I can remember it as if it was yesterday: they bought steel plate 3.6 metres, by 2.8 metres by 65 millimetres thick in a type of steel called Lloyds Grade D.

I received the enquiry from a buyer called Eric Clinch. I had earlier supplied him with bronze and aluminium. I asked him if he could mark my card on what price I should charge. He told me and I said I would match that price. In doing so I made no profit on that transaction but that was me into the steel business.

I was therefore able to buy ahead and stock it all, which enabled me to have a future margin on sales. If we ducked and dived and were completely flexible, I was convinced that we could make it.

We were competing against other businesses operating as intermediaries, working between the steel mills and fabricators on the one hand and the final users of the metals on the other.

Unlike other more established businesses I didn't have huge overheads; I was in a small office and I had no stockyard at that stage.

I would deal in small amounts and I would supply them very quickly. We simply had to find the metals, get them in the right quantities and at the right price and always at speed.

If someone wanted an aluminium bronze bar I would get a lorry to pick it up from places such as Columbia Metals in Camberwell, London. We knew exactly where to source the material.

Occasionally we would get caught out – but that's the way any business starts. Sometimes we let people down but we just had to take calculated risks.

Gradually I built up customers' trust. They might have a shopping list of five items and I would supply the five items even if I could make profit on only two of them and break even on the other three.

I had done a bit of training with ScotMet Alloys and I found I had a real knack for that side of the business. Eventually I started buying my own stock, when and where I could and keeping it in my own stockyard.

The steel strike in 1980 provided us with an opportunity. By that time we had established a facility at the Camps Industrial Estate in East Calder in West Lothian. We had good contacts within the industry including a steel plate mill called Fabrique de Fer, run by Louis Renard in the town of Charleroi, Belgium.

We had a fine relationship with Louis who ran the plant that rolled steel plates seven days a week. We took the steel plate we ordered by rail to Ghent in north-west Belgium where we had our own stocking facility working with an agent who did our shipping.

As far as I was concerned we had now reached the top of the game and were playing with the big boys. When the offshore business was booming, we were supplying the equivalent of Meccano sets in steel plates and beams, all cut and shaped ready to fabricate.

I would go down to London and negotiate a sale with an operator such as Bechtel or Conoco and they in turn would agree a contract with a fabricator in the north-east of England or north of Scotland. While they were negotiating, we would get the steel in place, mark it up and deliver it to the various sites in the United Kingdom, primarily in the north of Scotland which had become the centre of fabrication for the North Sea Oil industry.

My business was continuing to grow with the rise of North Sea Oil and the demand for metal it produced. It really was a boom time. By 1982 my turnover was £18million and £1.8million in net profit and had grown to that partly on the back of the steel strike.

By this time, I was supplying all the major fabricators such as Highland Fabricators and McDermott and RGC Methil.

In 1982, as an example, we supplied 8,000 tonnes of steel to the North West Hutton oil field, north-east of Shetland which was operated by Amoco – and that was for one project. That gives an idea of the scale in which we were operating. Almost without realising it, we had become the leaders for steel for the UK offshore industry sector.

When I think back it was a hell of a rise for a business that started being a trader – effectively a broker holding no stock – to one of that scale.

Our success was beginning to set tongues wagging and as I mentioned, I was approached by Edinburgh merchant bank Noble Grossart to buy 10 per cent of my business for a consortium that included Scottish Investment Trust, Northern Ventures and the Lothian Region Pension Fund plus others.

Together they clinched their 10 per cent for £1.2million which was a substantial amount of money in 1982. I put that in the bank at a time when interest rates were about 10 per cent, so I was getting roughly £3,000 a week in interest.

I then started to broaden my horizons. What I did with this first bit of money was to buy the Norton House Hotel in Newbridge, close to Edinburgh, for about £250,000. It was originally the Usher brewery family's home.

I spent about £1million on improvements. I kept it for a long time but 10 years later Richard Branson and I met at the hotel as part of a project called UK 2000 which then Prime Minister Margaret Thatcher had asked us to get involved in.

Out of the blue, Richard said that he liked the hotel and agreed to buy it from me for £2.2million, while I would retain the majority of the surrounding land.

The metals business continued to grow on the back of the demand from North Sea Oil. If you wanted offshore grade steel plate, the delivery time might be 10 to 12 weeks, beams might be 14 weeks and tubular seamless steel pipe was maybe 18 to 20 weeks.

I saw an opportunity there and so I bought steel ahead and laid it down so customers could order it one day and get it shortly thereafter. That was how we made our money.

By that time, I had lorries going up and down the A9 every day. The big accounts such as offshore fabricating company RGC, McDermotts and Highland Fabricators I dealt with myself to ensure that no competitor was getting in there and that we would continue to supply them.

When I reached the age of 30 I was really starting to motor, with the group turning well over £18million. Matt Goodwin of Hewden Stuart – which at its peak was reputed to be the biggest plant hire business in Europe – approached me to buy the Murray Group for a figure close to £20million and for me to become the managing director.

I mulled it over and vividly remember being with my family in Turnberry Hotel, Ayrshire. David and Keith were about seven and five. We were out playing the pitch and putt course and David looked up at me and said, "What's wrong, Dad?" I said, "I've got a big decision to make, boys." David said, "What's that?" I then told them I had been made an offer to buy our business. One of the boys said, "But where will we work when we're big boys?" That was all it took. No deal. I was not selling the business.

I was galvanised and continued to expand, setting up subsidiary companies. I brought in Phil Sinclair who was at school with me at Broughton High. At that time he was a qualified gym teacher but agreed to start a company called Premier Alloys. I employed Ken Cockburn whom I had played rugby against, and who then went on to successfully run the metals group.

Then, in 1978, we set up Multi Metals which supplied aluminium sheet in sections. I was diversifying in metals with people I simply trusted, some of whom knew nothing about the metals business but were just such strong characters.

One thing I remain happy about is that most of the team who came with me on the journey have all made a pretty good living. I never had any problem with them making money, providing, of course, I made more because I was the founder, the funder and the one who invariably made the big deals. But we fought for every penny and we played hard.

We did some entertaining across the north of Scotland but I knew we were capable of expanding a little further so I decided I would have a look at Canada. Using the same logic and pure instinct that we had used to build our business, I sent for Alan Baillie, an American player in our MIM basketball team.

He was a bit stunned at first but eventually shook my hand on it and we opened an office in Halifax, Nova Scotia, a major business city on Canada's eastern seaboard. I was over there eight times in 18 months going round all of the shipyards. We got some work there but we were a bit surprised that the offshore sector never really took off.

We also opened in Sharjah, the third biggest city in the UAE. Ken Cockburn went there to represent us. He later went on to Stavanger in Norway, which was another city that had grown, like Aberdeen, on the back of the oil industry.

One of Ken's children was, in fact, born there. We eventually opened an office in Singapore, continuing to diversify and spread geographically to look for opportunities. Murray International Metals was indeed living up to its name and was core to launching all the other areas of our work. We eventually had seven different metals businesses.

The peak of our metals business would arrive in late 2007 and early in 2008, when, through all our companies, we sold 400,000 tonnes of steel beams in one year – that's a lot of material. In total we sold about 550,000 tonnes of steel and to put that into perspective the Forth Rail Bridge is close to 50,000 tonnes, so imagine the equivalent of 11 of those.

We built the steel business up and that became our beating heart. It made us money and allowed us to diversify into so many other areas. That included businesses in different sectors and locations.

One of my customers in the mid-80s was a gruff but likeable old character called John Strachan, who had started a company in Paisley called Quality Metal Fabrication. One of its customers was computer giant IBM which had one of the biggest personal computer plants in Europe at Spango Valley near Greenock in the West of Scotland. I saw the potential in John's business and decided to back it. In 1984 that business moved to Livingston, a new town not far from Edinburgh, and was renamed Mimtec.

The company was awarded an IBM contract for the sub-assembly of personal computers. No-one knew that the IBM contract was in the offing but it meant the timing of my investment was almost perfect.

The contract was a game-changer for the business and a new Mimtec plant was built at Gourock near the IBM plant which cost £20million and employed 400 people and was opened by the Duchess of Kent in 1994. By that time, we owned 88 per cent of the Mimtec business with John owning the remaining 12 per cent.

In 1987 I bought a New Zealand electronic retail business after Roger Sutherland, a guy who I had been to school with and played rugby with at Edinburgh Colts, had invited me out there. We bought Bond & Bond, the New Zealand retail business that was their equivalent of Comet or Curry's.

By 1996 the chain had 38 stores and a turnover of £55million. That year it merged with a rival operator Noel Leeming with the deal giving us a 40 per cent stake in the enlarged business which was called the Pacific Retail Group.

In 1997 we were offered the chance to take a majority stake in the Pacific Retail Group. Singapore-owned Rosebury Holdings which offered us a 21 per cent stake in PRG for £4million. I thought it was too good an opportunity to pass up. It effectively gave us control of a group with a turnover of £95million a year and which had 100 retail outlets and about 900 staff. Less than a year later we sold our 58 per cent stake to Cullen Investments.

We just didn't rein it in and we never stopped looking for new opportunities. I then met a man called Alex McDonald when he came to sell me something. Alex had his own business and when he wanted to set up another one he came to me to back him. Dial Office Holdings began in premises at Newbridge on the M8 motorway with us owning 60 per cent and Alex 40 per cent.

Dial's main business was renting photocopiers and fax machines but later set up a subsidiary called Russell Office Systems. By 1993 Dial had a turnover of £10.5million and employed 200 people but by then it was not profitable, reporting a loss that year of £350,000. We sold the photocopier arm of Dial, including Russell Office Systems, to Danka UK for £1.7million.

Dial was a perfect example of a path I trod many, many times. It went a bit like this: Meet the person who will run the business, provide financial backing and advice, leave the day-to-day running to them, allow time for the profits to build up and then pick the right time to sell.

Meanwhile the core business, Murray International Metals, was still making money most years but in 1986 there was an unexpected and terrible slump. The price of steel collapsed. I had steel in stock double the height of a house and I couldn't shift it.

We had supplied drill pipe for offshore companies: 24-inch, 28-inch, 30-inch, and 38-inch for downhole drilling. In my warehouse I had 28-inch pipe that would cover a vast area and I honestly didn't know what I was going to do with it.

I immediately came up with an off-the-wall idea that I

would build an office block in the Gyle area on the outskirts of Edinburgh which was part of the land I had bought. I asked the architect, "Could you design it round that 28-inch pipe?" He did.

Now if you were to look at the Prison Scotland, Sports Council and Blyth & Blyth offices there – they are all made out of 28-inch steel pipe. It was quite innovative.

I had seen the opportunity that North Sea Oil would bring to the metals market and almost overnight I saw the potential that there was in property. A business that had begun in a single Edinburgh office trading in metals with no stock was about to move in a whole new direction.

4

CRASHING DOWN TO EARTH

IN MARCH 1976, WHEN I WAS AGED JUST 24, I WAS involved in the car crash that changed my life. I was driving home from playing a rugby match when the front tyre of my Lotus Elite blew on a dual carriageway near Longniddry, in East Lothian. The car smashed headlong into a tree, and I was lucky to survive.

I've already gone into the details of the crash in the prologue to this book. It was a terrible incident and an experience that will never leave me. But as horrific as the accident itself was, the aftermath presented challenges which in their own way, were just as tough.

While my love of sport has never once diminished, after the accident I spent months facing up to the fact that I would never kick a ball, make a tackle or swing a bat again. I had been 24 and still playing competitively two or three times a week so this new reality was absolutely devastating.

Looking back I was in a shocking physical and confused

mental state but somewhere, deep down, I realised the injuries and the aftermath could either consume me or I could actually accept my lot, unimaginable as it was, and do something about it. Thankfully, with the help of the brilliant NHS in Scotland, and something deep in my core, it was a fight that I was up for. I never forgot the work that the brilliant surgeon Jim Christie did on my legs and years later I thanked him by sending him a special case of wine.

I asked myself – and answered – a lot of questions during that hellish post-operation recovery in Edinburgh's Princess Margaret Rose Orthopaedic Hospital where they had given me a heroin derivative for four days to dull the pain. I hallucinated constantly but I do vividly remember a man in the next bed to me who was paralysed following a fall on rocks during a work trip.

For weeks after it happened, his mum, his wife and their young children would faithfully come in every day between 2pm and 3pm and again between 7pm and 8pm during visiting hours. But one evening a few weeks later his mum appeared during visiting time to tell him that his wife and kids wouldn't be coming to see him again. She had left Scotland for Australia and would never be coming back. She told the mother that she just couldn't face a life looking after him.

I had shared some difficult times with the man in hospital and could only look away as he suddenly began sobbing his heart out as his mum held him. It was grim and it brought home the enormity of what had happened. It also made me realise the mammoth challenges that I would have to overcome just to try to 'be normal' and live a life that everyone takes for granted.

As I lay in the hospital, I lived for the daily visits from my family and close friends.

Then, one day, a familiar yet surprising face appeared at the end of my bed. It was Ian McLauchlan, a Scottish rugby legend, with the nickname Mighty Mouse. I knew him through us both being born in Ayr and from the sporting business world as well.

I asked him what the hell HE was doing there and he replied, "I've got something for you."

At this point he produced a fairly battered rugby ball which a few days earlier had been used in the Lansdowne Road Five Nations match between Ireland and Scotland.

It was signed by every single Irish and Scottish player. Scotland had won the match 15-6 and Andy Irvine scored four penalties, which made the gift extra special because Andy and I had played together at Edinburgh Colts on the back pitches at Murrayfield where we shared kicking duties.

When I finally did get home following numerous operations a brilliant young physiotherapist called Laura Penney began the slow process of turning my situation around. She told me, 'You really need to get going. You can do this. It will be painful and you won't enjoy much about it but I will help you.' And boy, did she. I listened to her and, I suppose, for once in my life, I just did as I was told.

She told me that the most important thing in my physical rehabilitation was balance.

If the accident had happened now, the outcome, I know, would have been vastly different. The advances in technology have just been astonishing over the past two decades and nowadays I might have been fitted with a lightweight titanium frame and computerised knees. No crutches. A world-class German company called Ottobock produces incredible prosthetics and pieces of mobility equipment.

I'm not sure I would even need hand controls on cars now, given what is available and I have explored the possibility of updating but in reality it's too late for me. It would require a complete resetting of everything I have learned and been used to for nearly five decades.

One very simple recent innovation for me has been the advent of flexible rubber shock absorbers on the end of my crutches. They help me negotiate some difficult surfaces, including marble floors and wet pavements.

But back in the late 1970s, Laura began the process by asking me to balance on two small rocking pylon legs. Every day for weeks on end I perched on those and did exercises and every day I told myself that if you put a smock over my head, I probably was the spitting image of French artist Henri de Toulouse-Lautrec, well known for his under-sized legs due to injury and a rare medical condition.

It hurt, every sinew and tendon was sore, everything chafed, I felt phantom pain where there were no legs and the start of recovery was gruelling. I also spent the rest of the physio time heaving myself up and down on parallel bars and building my upper body strength. All of it was designed to give me balance. Without that, I would simply have keeled over. I had to keep going, too. If I took a couple of days off and then went back, my stumps throbbed.

But I had passed a mental milestone. I had a purpose. My wife and sons were relying on me. I had a staff and a business who needed me. I grew stronger and stronger as each day passed and I began tasking myself with making 500 movements every day, some of them press-ups. Laura told me that the effort I required to walk a few steps was akin to anyone else running up a full flight of stairs.

She also taught me how to fall. If I was going to topple I had to learn how to roll and not take the weight. This was fine and

I managed for years without having to deploy it until one night at the Champany Inn, near Linlithgow, West Lothian, I went to what was a fairly cramped toilet, slipped on a wet tile and face-planted far too close to the urinal. I still had a few grazes and if someone hadn't come in right behind me, I might still be there. Approaching 50 years since my accident, I totally rely on my artificial legs and the maintenance and fitting done by the team at the Astley Ainslie Hospital and my prosthetist Murray Noble.

———

Meanwhile, with all of this trauma going on I found my business was under threat too. Luck inevitably plays a role, big or small, somewhere or other in all entrepreneurial success stories and in this respect mine is no different.

As I lay in my hospital bed following a second operation, my business partner Amari PLC ruthlessly decided to exercise their option under the partnership agreement which had established Murray International Metal Services in the first place.

Amari had been given the option to purchase 40 per cent of the company's share capital, consisting of one thousand £1 shares, exactly the same as when the company was founded.

However, Murray International had grown rapidly since launch and Amari really had played an insignificant secondary role, leaving its entire running to me.

I had spent a great deal of time and effort cementing some of the key business ties that would underpin our future. One major example was the relationship with the Bank of Scotland. I came to know Ken Faulkner, manager at the Bank of Scotland's Princes Street branch, closely and a good business relationship had been forged.

Turnover at Murray International was already several million pounds so exercising this option at a price of £1 per share – a total of £4,000 – would have represented an incredibly lucrative deal for Amari and, of course, a staggering loss for me.

But as it turned out I had a stroke of luck. Tom Coleman was the financial director of the Amari group at the time that the partnership with me had been established. Later, I invited Tom to leave and join me at Murray International and my offer was accepted. Then a week before receiving formal notification that Amari intended to exercise their option, Tom alerted me to what was coming down the line.

This gave me time to increase the share capital from one thousand £1 shares to one million penny shares, which we were perfectly entitled to do.

When Amari smugly arrived with the cheque for £4,000, the bank said, 'No, we don't think so. Here's the situation now. Have you got the additional £396,000 to exercise your option?'

They were stunned and of course, totally unwilling to pay this amount and that's the reason I was able to keep Murray International Metal Services private and securely under my control.

I changed its name to Murray International Metals and the company went from strength to strength.

———

Back in hospital, the day I had my 100 stitches taken out is one I'll never forget. I smoked 30 full-strength Gold Leaf cigarettes hanging out my window next to the hospital bed.

A week later one of the men I worked with came in to visit and gave me a lift home to Longniddry in his large Volvo estate.

It was pouring with rain and 20 minutes after leaving the hospital, we stopped just outside Musselburgh to pick up a poor soul who was soaked to the skin and thumbing a lift. We pulled over and he got in. I asked him, "Where are you headed?" And he replied, "Anywhere's fine."

I then asked him what he was doing out there and he replied, "I've just escaped from Saughton." Saughton, of course, was HM Prison, Edinburgh. He certainly didn't seem dangerous but from the back seat I looked at my friend's eyes in the rear view mirror and exchanged a few knowing looks. We took an instant detour to the A1 before finally letting him out far, far away from where I lived.

Meanwhile my work with Laura Penney was starting to pay off. She kept telling me I had to start becoming mobile again and start learning to walk with a frame. Instead, I think I shocked her by telling her that what I really needed was to get back to work. I had a business to run with people relying on me.

So we reached a compromise. Just 12 weeks after the accident, I returned to my desk in Alva Street in the centre of Edinburgh but every afternoon I would attend the Princess Margaret Rose Hospital and she would help me learn how to walk on a set of what were called pylon legs.

On reflection, it probably sounds quite daunting that I would contemplate driving again, particularly with no legs, but in July, I bought a Jaguar XJ6 from a dealer and sent it to a specialist in Dutch Corner, Glasgow, for conversion to hand controls, which were completely new to me. I can still remember the thrill of being able to drive back home on my own.

I also received the letter I mentioned earlier, from World War Two pilot and fellow amputee Sir Douglas Bader, urging me to keep going.

The letter was not only a personal get well soon card – it held a far greater purpose. In those difficult days I had decided to create my own Murray Foundation for amputees – just like Douglas Bader's – to help people whose lives had been affected by amputation. It later won a Queen's Award.

Through incessant hard work and endeavour, and with unwavering support from family and staff, within five years I had won the Young Businessman Of The Year award during a ceremony at Prestonfield House.

5

FIRST STEPS TOWARDS GLASGOW RANGERS

DESPITE FORGING AHEAD IN BUSINESS AND BECOMING a bi-lateral amputee, my genuine passion for sport had never gone away and I became involved in sponsoring a number of teams in basketball, hockey, volleyball and rugby.

From the age of eight until the age of 24, not one week would go by without me playing a competitive sport, usually cricket or rugby, but show me any kind of ball back then and I'd have had a good idea what to do with it.

Just because I couldn't play any more, it didn't mean I couldn't be involved and I wanted my boys David and Keith to go along and feel exactly the same way as I did.

I recently worked out that – aside from from my 25 years with Rangers – the Murray family have invested almost £30million in today's value in sports outwith football in Scotland. I would never call any sport minor. The players who won basketball and hockey and volleyball trophies were utterly dedicated to their sport and gave pleasure to so many.

Surprisingly, the sport that was to become the main focus of my attention was football. It would be a 23-year-long roller coaster of highs and lows. It would challenge me every day. It would sometimes bring me out in a cold sweat. It would bring joy and heartache but between 1988 and 2011 it would utterly dominate my life. I worked out that 80 per cent of my time was devoted to running the club. That had a major impact on my life and business.

As I explained earlier I had bought the Norton House Hotel before selling to Richard Branson and at a dinner there in 1986, I first met Graeme Souness through an Adidas director called Robin Money. Of course, I was well aware of his legendary attributes as a player for Liverpool, Sampdoria, Middlesbrough and Scotland.

But he was at the beginning of a new career as a player/ manager. Graeme was by then boss of Rangers and during the event that evening, he told me he was hoping to sign the former England defender Terry Butcher.

I invited him to watch a Murray International Metals basketball match at Meadowbank and over the next weeks and months we quickly became good pals and he asked me and Louise to Ibrox as his guests on a number of occasions. She had become friends with Graeme's wife Danielle. The atmosphere at these games was never anything other than electric.

Oddly, I recently rewatched a 1987 UEFA Champions League game of Rangers v Dynamo Kyiv – 14 months before I even met with Lawrence Marlborough and became involved with the club – and our Murray Group and its subsidiaries had every advertising board at the front of the Govan stand. Maybe it was always meant to be.

But the first game I went to as Graeme's guest in October 1987 was something quite extraordinary. It was later dubbed the Old Firm shame game – a fiery 2-2 draw with red cards for Chris Woods and Frank McAvennie. Both later got charged and fined for conduct likely to invoke a breach of the peace. Talk about a baptism of fire. I never forgot it.

It is certainly not the case in the 2020s that football fans across Scotland follow what you might call a wee team and a big team – and maybe an English team too – but I did. Ayr United was my hometown club and I also had an affinity with Rangers. When I was young my dad frequently took me to Ibrox for midweek European games and I can still remember standing outside The Sportsman's pub in Govan after match-nights waiting on my dad having a quick drink with pals and getting fleeting glimpses through the swing doors as Jim Baxter held court inside. Baxter owned the bar.

Jim was a club legend but rarely seen around Ibrox so after I later bought Rangers I personally invited him back to be part of the corporate hospitality team. He was a great storyteller and did his job brilliantly for years.

I have never forgotten that on the day he was buried in April 2001, the funeral cortege stopped outside the stadium and his son and his father took time to come across and shake my hand.

Anyway, I had decided that I wanted to be more involved in football and assumed that Ayr United would be interested in a cash investment. It was my team growing up, my grandfather had been a director in 1938, as well as president of the Ayrshire Football Federation and my dad was a lifelong supporter.

How wrong was I? After an initial discussion with highly-enthusiastic club chairman George Smith, I spoke with then owner Bill Barr and offered a £350,000 injection to the club. However, what I had not anticipated was Mr Smith then being approached by veteran and legendary manager Ally MacLeod who said that if I was allowed to take ownership of the club, then he would leave immediately. By a slight majority, the board agreed to reject my offer. I was both surprised and disappointed.

I am often asked the question: Where would Ayr United be now if you had taken over? I would, of course, like to believe that the club would be in the Premiership and that Somerset Park would be a 15,000 capacity, state-of-the art stadium packed to the rafters every second week. It is still the first result I look for on a Saturday. I'll already know the Rangers score by that time.

I remember meeting with George Smith years later when Rangers were playing Ayr United in the Scottish Cup at Somerset. He was an extremely kind man and had been in favour of the deal and as I sat in the directors' box at half-time he handed me a cup of tea at which point we both heard a wag from the terrace shout, "Too bloody late talking to him now, Smith…!" Rangers won 1-0 with Ally McCoist scoring the winner.

———

The life-changing call in November 1988 came from Graeme Souness. It was brief. He said to me, "The Lawrence Group wants out of Rangers – they want to sell the club."

It's often said that I paid £6million for Rangers, but I also took on almost the same again in debt. It was obvious the Lawrence Group weren't doing so well and, if you looked at their balance sheet, Rangers had debts. There was an overdraft of £5million and I am not sure it was sustainable. The club had been buying houses for players, which wasn't cheap.

There was some pressure to get the deal done quickly because of interest from Robert Maxwell. He had a connection to Lawrence Marlborough's brother, who was a lawyer in Livingston, and had plans to buy Rangers through the brother, so I moved quickly and got it done right away.

It was different days in banking then. I remember phoning Gavin Masterton, who was then in charge of entrepreneurs for the Bank of Scotland and later went to Dunfermline Athletic, and said, "Gav, I wonder if you could lend me £6million please?"

He asked what it was for, and I replied, "I'd like to buy Rangers."

"No problem," came the response. I phoned him an hour later and said, "That's it done" and he replied, "Oh no, what have you done?"

Jim McDonald, meanwhile, took a cautious line and asked me, "Are you absolutely sure about this? Do you know what you are taking on?"

The truth is that I didn't but there was no halting the process at that stage. I met with the Rangers chairman David Holmes for an initial discussion then met Lawrence Marlborough in a quiet room during the first half of a home game.

He didn't know much about me but I had done my homework and quickly pointed out the fact that we had been to the same school – Cambusdoon in Alloway. I quietly left the stadium at half-time with a handshake and the deal confirmed.

I say quietly but as I stood on my crutches outside the main stand doors someone shouted from across the road, "Ho. Did Terry Butcher get ye, pal?"

We completed on November 22, 1988 and at the age of 37 I took my seat in the directors' box on Saturday, November 26 for a home match against Aberdeen, which we won 1-0 thanks to a goal by Richard Gough.

Seven days later Dundee Utd came to Ibrox and won 1-0. We then lost 2-0 at Tynecastle and I was wondering what I'd just done. However, beating Celtic 4-1 at Ibrox the following week reminded me exactly why I had bought the club.

Graeme gave me one good bit of advice following the takeover. He urged me not to become chairman straight away and get the lie of the land first, so I asked David Holmes to remain in place for six months, which he was happy to do. However, I still found the first two years all-consuming. I owned a house in Jersey by then and tried to spend any spare time I had with Louise and the boys there.

Football still has the capacity to shock and amaze every week and one telephone call just weeks after I had bought the club still astounds me to this day.

My son Keith came racing through to where I was sitting at home and said, "Daddy, a man is on the phone wanting to speak to you." I asked him who it was and he said, "Robert Maxwell."

Maxwell still owned Oxford United and Derby County at the time and had a stake in Reading so I assumed he was on to talk about a player. But when I picked up the phone the voice boomed down the line, "David, it's Robert Maxwell… I want to buy Rangers from you and then I want to buy Celtic and merge the clubs."

I checked my watch to see if it was happy hour. I can't remember my exact response but it was fairly terse.

I remembered that he had tried to do something similar with Reading and Oxford United and a planned team called the Thames Valley Royals.

Needless to say, we had no further contact.

It goes without saying that I revelled in a memorable 23 years as the chairman and owner of Glasgow Rangers Football Club.

FIRST STEPS TOWARDS GLASGOW RANGERS

During my tenure we played 1,124 matches, we had 771 victories, with 244 games drawn and 109 defeats. We won 35 trophies.

And although my legacy is obviously up for debate, the history books will always show that Rangers were a hugely successful club during my time in charge.

6

SOUNESS AND ME

I AM PROUD TO SAY THAT MY FRIENDSHIP WITH Graeme Souness has stood the test of time. We are as close now, in our 70s, as we were when we were running Rangers together in the late 1980s and early 90s.

I speak to Graeme most weeks and he regularly comes to stay at my home in Scotland. If either of us makes a slip with our words when we are talking about life or watching football on television together, the other one will waste no time in pointing it out, suggesting that senility has set in.

We take the p*** out of each other or give each other 'laldy,' as we say in Scotland. It's the same sense of humour we shared from the start, one of the reasons we hit it off immediately and that our friendship has lasted so long. I've even finally forgiven Graeme for leaving Rangers for Liverpool in 1991 – almost.

As I've said, our friendship started before Graeme became Rangers' manager in 1986.

Although I didn't buy Rangers until November 1988, I was involved in the signing that started Graeme's revolution at Ibrox.

When he was trying to buy Terry Butcher from Ipswich Town immediately after the 1986 World Cup, he asked, "Do you mind coming along with me to meet him?" I had nothing to do with the club at that time, but I agreed, and the three of us had dinner together at Norton House. Terry asked me about Rangers, and I said they were a huge club with great potential and that was the start of Rangers buying half the England team.

I suppose, looking back now, it was also the first example of Graeme and I working together to rebuild Rangers. We had a short chain of command and a clear division of duties. We weren't running a bowling club, after all. We'd agree who was doing a deal and from then on it was one singer, one song, in terms of representing Rangers in the negotiations.

I was a complete novice in football, so left it mostly to Graeme and trusted his judgement and vice versa with the business side of things. When he later decided to get rid of important players including Graham Roberts and big Terry, it was entirely his call.

That was Graeme's side of the business. I am not passing the buck but when Graeme makes his mind up about something he's determined to do it.

Later on, Graeme and Terry Butcher weren't getting on very well. Terry had broken Graeme's ban on speaking to STV, which came about after the broadcaster filmed Graeme standing in the tunnel while he was suspended by the SFA, but maybe Graeme also saw something on the training ground that I didn't.

Terry went to Coventry City in 1990 and played six games in two years. He was struggling to come back from a serious injury and maybe Graeme was getting frustrated by that. Later, Terry went to Sunderland and played 38 games, so he maybe took two or three years to get over the injury – sometimes we don't see that side of things.

In football or business, I take the view that you are in the trenches with somebody and you are all on the same side. When you are a manager or a chairman you are not going to get all the decisions right, but you are still better making decisions than not making decisions. That was something else that Graeme and I had in common.

Don't put it off. If it's on your list to do today, do it today. You must make decisions, or it festers.

In management of anything, if you don't make decisions, it builds up into a bigger problem. It doesn't go away if you duck dealing with it. You must have some rationale, take the facts into consideration, digest them and make your decision. If you don't, you don't sleep at night and I have slept soundly for most of my life.

Graeme identified the players. The only time I 'signed' a player for Rangers was when Terry Hurlock joined us from Millwall in August 1990. I'd seen him playing on television and said, "That Terry Hurlock's a tough bastard, he would sort a few out". Graeme said, "You think so?" I replied, "I do, go on."

Every great team has someone in midfield to win the battles and I thought he would be good going to Parkhead, Pittodrie and places like that and, as it happens, he was.

I always felt it was important to freshen the team every year. You had to sell season tickets and change the menu to make it more interesting for supporters, but we would start that process at Christmas and by the summer most of our deals were already done for the following season.

———

Anyway, Graeme and I were of similar age and both self-made men with similar interests, although I wasn't as much into the Versace gear as Graeme was at that time. His upbringing was a prefab council house in Saughton in Edinburgh, then to Tottenham, Middlesbrough and you know the story from there.

I was born into a well-to-do family, but my father goes bust, so I couldn't afford to fail. Then, at 24, I have my car accident, my father dies, my second son is born, and I had to succeed. Failure was simply not an option for me with a young family to support.

As I've explained, sport had always played a large part in my life. From the age of eight to 24, I'd played it, whether it was cricket or rugby at school, so I was a reasonable sportsman. I could kick a rugby ball and use a cricket bat, but I also went to watch my share of football.

Every second Saturday, from when I was eight or nine, I'd go for a haircut then walk to Somerset Park to see Ayr United. For away games, we used to meet in Ayr and get a Western Scottish bus and go to places like Arbroath, East Stirlingshire and Forfar.

A clear childhood memory is going to Hampden to see Scotland, where Alan Gilzean scored a header and we beat England 1-0 in 1964. There was 133,000 there and four of us going to the game. My dad said, "I have two stand tickets and two ground tickets", and I said, "I'll just go in the ground with my pal." You wouldn't risk putting your kid into that size of crowd today, would you?

Denis Law, who died recently, was the most talented Scottish player for me, and I was so pleased to meet him at the UEFA Cup final in 2008. He didn't have shoes as a kid and went to Huddersfield when he had to get an operation because he was cross-eyed. He was tough, too, and who can forget his famous back-heel for Manchester City against Manchester United?

In my early 20s, if I didn't have a rugby game, I would drive down south and watch a football match. I went to see Sunderland at Roker Park just before they beat Leeds United in the 1973 FA

Cup final. The reason was their right-back was a guy called Dick Malone, who came from Ayr United.

My dad would take me to big European games at Rangers and I remember players like Davie Wilson, Ralph Brand – people that I would later get to work with us at the club. It was me that brought Jim Baxter and John Greig back to Rangers. John was working at the BBC at the time, and I am very close to John to this day.

I went to Rangers, with Louise, when we were both about 18. Rangers were playing Everton in a pre-season friendly in August 1971, and I remember big Brian Labone, Everton's centre-half, running out and he was like a Clydesdale horse. Rangers won 2-1 and it was that week that the Rangers News was launched.

———

Graeme warned me Rangers would take over my life and wouldn't be like any of my other businesses and the impact was even greater than that on reflection now. I didn't realise the enormity of what I was taking on. I'd go to corporate days and senior businessmen would come up and say, "Nice to meet you, Mr Chairman" and I thought, 'What have I done here?' It was quite a big thing.

Lawrence Marlborough said 10 years is long enough in football in an interview, and maybe he was right, but the fans do influence you to make decisions that you would not normally make.

A current SPL chairman whose club was going through a difficult time recently asked me for advice and I told them this, "Enjoy the good days but you will fail eventually." Managers do, chairman do. In politics, public life or football... 95 per cent of those at the top will fail, unless of course you are perhaps The King or Sir Alex Ferguson.

I was friendly with Jeff Randall, an experienced business journalist at The *Sunday Times*, and he said sensible, successful business people leave their brains at the door when they go into football and that's probably true, too.

———

When I took over, Rangers had just won the Skol (League) Cup against Aberdeen, but the previous year Butcher broke his leg, and they lost the League and Scottish Cup double to Celtic. I always remember the Dundee United game early on in my tenure because Jim McLean, United's great manager, growled at me, even though I'd never met him before. I was sitting in the back row, and he called me 'son', I think he was trying to put a shot across my bow of the 'who do you think you are?' variety.

That was an era of Wallace Mercer at Hearts and Dick Donald at Aberdeen, fellow chairmen who I had total respect for. I remember winning a trophy and Dick, a class act, congratulated me. I replied, "I hope I am half as successful as you" in front of people from both clubs. There was a bit of comradeship but obviously competition, too, particularly between us and Celtic.

My gruff 'welcome' from Jim McLean was positively friendly, compared to the one waiting for me at Celtic in my first visit there as Rangers' owner and chairman. A fan shouted, "You dirty, Orange, cripple, ba*****". When Graeme asked me about it, I told him it just made me more determined. It was a case of 'I'll show you'. That's just me. I never think about the past or the accident, it's other people who bring up things like that. Why have negativity?

Mostly, though, I loved the banter and camaraderie of football. You needed a thick skin at times, but I had always had that type of personality anyway. It was all new to me and it was fun. They always used to play Bon Jovi on the bus from Ibrox to Parkhead, 'shot to the heart, but you're too late', to get the team going. The supporters' buses were double deckers and when they saw the team bus, I thought they would topple over because everybody ran to the windows on one side.

I was a hands-on chairman. If we were in a bit of bother, I would speak out. I would do an interview and speak to the press. I always believed you were better trying to influence it. The story is the story, but you were always better getting some input was my view.

Modern chairmen don't put their heads above the parapet as much. In many cases, they don't stand a chance now because, with social media, the article is already written. If you look through the UK, directors of clubs like Sheffield Wednesday, Reading, Scunthorpe have had their lives threatened, so I can understand the reasons for the change in approach, but I do think chairmen are not up front as much as they were in my time – but do have to face up to a different era with social media.

———

Graeme and I were like pals in the trenches together. You defended each other. You supported each other. You were one. We never had a cross word because we were so tuned in to each other. That came from spending a lot of time together, we would go on trips where we got to know what made each other tick.

I remember one mini-break mid-season where we left Edinburgh and flew to Heathrow. Graeme asked where we were going next and I said, "New Zealand". I'd spoken to Walter Smith, and he was going to take charge for a few days while we were away. We stayed in the Shangri-La hotel in Singapore. The suite was so big that Graeme could train by running round it.

We flew on to New Zealand for a Burns Supper, where the haggis was terrible, then went to a vineyard. That was the sort of thing that bonded us, talking about life together on those trips.

There was a growth potential at Rangers, which had been

started, but where I got it wrong was thinking that it might have helped my business. That was neutral overall because some people didn't want to do business with you because of Rangers and others did. One big company in Northern Ireland, for example, stopped dealing with us because of the Rangers connection.

Graeme would phone me on his way into the club in the mornings, then on his way home in the afternoons and we would compare notes. I liked to eat early, and we would often make big decisions regarding Rangers over dinner together at Raffaelli's, an Italian restaurant in Edinburgh.

Graeme thought he was an Italian but he really could eat for Scotland. It was not unusual for him to have a single fish as an appetiser before sitting down to a meal in a restaurant. I'd never seen people have spinach with garlic and Parmesan cheese on the top and I thought, 'where did this come from?'. He only played 70 games for Sampdoria, but it influenced him a lot. At Liverpool, it had been cans of lager on the bus and fish suppers and they seemed to do alright with it. I have never seen anybody eat like Graeme but he trains and works hard. Too hard, I sometimes tell him as his pal, because we are both that bit older now.

These dinners together were like management meetings but in a restaurant and less formal. Sometimes friends of Graeme's from football would join us, such as Mark Lawrenson, his former teammate at Liverpool. We'd dine together like this regularly for a couple of years even before I bought the club. Graeme was just one of these guys you meet and get on with. It was the same with Sean Connery, we got on right away. I still have pals I knew at school in Ayr and at Broughton School, too. I'd like to think I am loyal to my friends – and they are loyal to me.

———

Everything was kept inside, nothing leaked out. If it leaked, whoever leaked it was out. The one exception to that rule was the most controversial transfer we did together for Rangers, signing Maurice Johnston after Celtic thought they had the deal done. And that was only because we had to make extra security arrangements and someone tipped off a journalist.

All the talk was of Johnston joining Celtic, but Graeme came to me and said, "Apparently he's not signed, the paperwork's not done, we can get him." I asked for a day to think about it, phoned him and said, "Yes, I think we should do it for numerous reasons – for football reasons and to remove an area where we can be criticised for not signing Catholic players. And why not make it the best one, who can come in and contribute?", even though at that time Mark Hateley and Ally McCoist were the strikers and had an excellent partnership.

Finally, just 24 hours before we were due to unveil the player, we took a call from a young journalist at *The Sun* in Scotland ahead of a story being published. It was blindingly obvious that someone had leaked the name.

On July 10, 1989 *The Sun* ran half of its front page with the simple headline MO JOINS GERS. It certainly didn't spoil the unveiling. If anything, it ramped up the tension.

At Ibrox the press conference was packed full of journalists from across Britain and Alex Cameron from the *Daily Record* still seemed to be in denial. He sidled up to me before we took our seats and asked quietly, probably more in hope, "Is it John Sheridan?"

There was still a collective gasp when the announcement came.

———

At another meeting before the Johnston deal was completed, Maurice was in Edinburgh in the dining room of my house in

Murrayfield with Walter, Bill McMurdo, and Graeme. There were golfers walking past the window looking in and probably saying to themselves, 'no, it can't be'. Even at the signing conference there were still some veteran sportswriters, who knew their stuff, coming up to me and asking if it was true Rangers were 'actually going to sign a Catholic'.

The strategy afterwards was to get Maurice straight to our training camp in Italy. I said to my late wife Louise, "You need to get the boys away here, this could either go badly or brilliantly." I was concerned about their safety in the event of a backlash. Everyone went to Glasgow Airport but I arranged for a small private plane to come to Edinburgh instead. Mo's agent Bill McMurdo, Maurice, Graeme and I were on it.

They dropped me off in Jersey and then went on to Italy, where Jimmy Bell, the kitman, set up a big, long table for the players and then a table in the corner for one to welcome Maurice into the club. Mo took the joke well, of course.

The final paperwork was done by Alan Montgomery, our then chief executive, in the back of a taxi going round the Peripherique ring road in Paris, with Francois, the taxi driver, as a witness. Alan did a decent job but Graeme didn't get on with him, so he eventually had to go.

We were creating quite a big business and I felt it needed a chief executive. Alan was a Rangers fan and very sensible at STV, but suddenly he was putting out the corner flags and turning up in the kit. Graeme said, "what are you doing?" and Walter was also unhappy at one stage. It was eventually a case of Graeme saying "It's either me or him." I felt for Alan because he came in with good intentions but it brought out the fan in him too much. At one AGM, he suddenly started talking about Catholic schools, when we wanted to focus on the football.

A lot of people questioned whether I'd done the right thing signing Johnston. We had a board meeting in Edinburgh and Jim McDonald, my trusted right-hand man, was concerned it could be damaging commercially and a lot of people were thinking that. Jack Gillespie, who was a big supporter of mine, was not 100 per cent either but came round.

Hugh Adam and I never got on because he gave the money from the Rangers Pools to buy Richard Gough before I arrived, and all his money was getting drained away and I think he thought he could be in charge one day. McMurdo made a lot of money from that deal and never tired of talking about it, but he was never an agent that I warmed to or trusted.

Graeme and I both received numerous death threats. Phone calls saying, "You're getting it" and all that stuff, that's why I got my family away in the aftermath, but, long-term, we took the view that if you went through life worrying about everything you would never do anything. It wasn't our first attempt to sign a Catholic player.

People have said that signing set Celtic back 10 years, but I don't think it was just that, we were getting the upper hand anyway, and they were in a financial mess until Fergus McCann arrived to sort them out.

Fergus must be the only man who has come into football, made money and then left before losing any of it. I got on alright with him. People still bring up that I said I'd spend £10 for every £5 Celtic did, but it's true – I did spend double what Fergus did.

I got to know Maurice because he lived in Edinburgh to avoid any aggro in Glasgow. He was a good guy who did his bit for Rangers, ended that taboo, then went to Everton. He scored an important late winner against Celtic in November 1989 to win over most, if not all, of the fans, beating Paddy Bonner low down, but Ally McCoist was stronger than Johnston. I met Willie Miller one day and he said, "Don't underestimate how tough McCoist is." I never thought of him like that, but Willie said he would back into you and you would know all about it.

It wasn't just Celtic we were beating to players in those days, but also the leading English clubs. People sometimes forget that we signed Trevor Steven from Everton the same summer we signed Maurice, seeing off Sir Alex Ferguson to do so. In those days we could outbid Manchester United. Sir Philip Carter, who was chairman of Everton, was pushing him to United, but I always felt if I could get the player in person to either the stadium or to my house in France, we stood a chance and so it proved with Trevor and so many others.

The signings and success kept coming, but so did the scrutiny and strain on Graeme as the high-profile manager of Rangers. The problem at Rangers and Celtic is you are feeding this big beast of a football club with the expectations of supporters. As his friend, I knew it was taking a toll, but I also knew it went with the territory and was what we had both signed up for.

We also both knew that he could still be sacked as manager if the success suddenly stopped. It was two separate things. Buying the club was a business transaction, an introductory offer if you like because he had supported me to do so, but that didn't mean he was immune from the sack like any other manager.

I could see Graeme was starting to get agitated and Donald Cruickshank, the doctor, was concerned about his health. Donald was a great man for counselling and opinion. There were 2,000 people at my first AGM at Rangers, aged 37. I came out shellshocked and he said, "It's alright being in business David, but you are at Glasgow Rangers now" and that stuck with me.

I'd been 100 per cent my own man, but at Rangers you had a responsibility to thousands.

When we were playing Hearts and Hibs in the early days, it would be Graeme, Walter, Doc Cruickshank and I who would have had dinner together when the team stayed at the Roxburghe Hotel. What's crucial about the team doctor is that he is a catalyst, that he has contacts to the correct surgeons. He might not be a specialist, but he knows a man who is.

The players need to have the confidence that he will identify the injury and the person to treat it. Also, for foreign players for their wives and families to have a contact if their children are not well. The doctor is a crucial part of the team, and Rangers were very lucky with Donald, and later Iain McGuinness, Paul Jackson and Gert Goudswaard, who came with Dick Advocaat.

———

Graeme was taking painkillers all the time, his marriage had broken up and he was being followed about by the tabloids. He was outspoken and I suppose some of the press think you are a target because of that. They were hounding him, and he felt a lot of guilt about his kids.

When Kenny Dalglish stepped down as Liverpool manager, it was natural they would target their former captain, now a successful manager in his own right at Rangers, to take over. The first time they tried to tap Graeme, immediately after Dalglish left, I managed to persuade him to stay but then they came back towards the end of the same season. I remember going to his house, sitting on the wall and saying, "What do you want to do? You can't go mid-season. I can understand the attraction to go back to Liverpool, but you're not going now."

Then Graeme came back to me with four or five games to go and told me he'd accepted the Liverpool job. I said, "Oh have you, let me think about this, you can go now. Leave now and take that Boersma with you. Where is he anyway? Over at the gym?"

That was just a joke between us because I knew Phil Boersma, his pal and physio/coach, would be part of the deal.

We'd had dinner at Raffaelli's as usual, and I could sense something wasn't right. I took the view, without speaking to any of the other directors, although I then brought them into the discussions and Richard Gough, the captain, that it was no-win situation for me as chairman.

If I let Graeme leave and he wins the league, it would come back on me as 'why did you let him go?' But if I let him stay and we lost the title to Aberdeen, who were pushing us hard that season, then I would be blamed.

It's true I told Graeme he'd regret returning to Liverpool, but I took no pleasure in being proved right in that respect. There was clearly an attraction going back to where he had great success as a footballer, but that doesn't guarantee success as a manager and that's how it turned out.

If I remember correctly, a lot of players at Liverpool were coming to the end of their careers. Kenny Dalglish had largely signed well, but towards the end there were a few who weren't up to the usual Liverpool standards, and there was also Graeme's health to factor in – he had the heart operation as well.

We were still close. You can have a disagreement; it doesn't mean you don't remain friends. I visited him in the hospital in Liverpool after his heart bypass and he came out in his dressing gown. He'd just met Karen, who became his wife and who he recently celebrated 30 years of marriage to. We never fell out. I never fell out with any manager, but we have become much closer again in the last decade, since I have not been busy running Rangers.

SOUNESS AND ME

The press wrote that I wanted a big-name manager to replace Graeme and George Graham, who had been successful at Arsenal, was mentioned, but in my mind, right away, there was only one option for continuity, which is what I thought we needed at the time: Walter Smith.

7

A SEASON LIKE
NO OTHER

I SUPPOSE I CAN PUT IT DOWN TO THE EXUBERANCE OF Rangers winning the league during that first season as owner but the remainder of 1989 was to contain more drama and intrigue at Ibrox than a BBC six-part series.

The team had totalled 56 points, six more than runners-up Aberdeen and had beaten third-placed Celtic 4-1 and 5-1 at home but lost the Scottish Cup final to them 1-0, denying us a domestic treble.

And the Mo Johnston saga seemed to dominate for the entire season and reverberated far beyond the confines of Scottish football. I've got so many vivid memories of what would turn out to be historic days.

Looking back, that Hampden cup final that we lost to Celtic in May 1989 was actually to prove quite significant. Celtic's fans had been chanting throughout the 90 minutes, "Mo, Mo, Super Mo" in anticipation of him signing for them to which Rangers supporters sang back, "Mo, Mo, f*** your Mo." If only they had known.

———

By now, I was confident in the steel business that we had built, and equally comfortable in my role as Rangers chairman as well as owner.

I had taken Graeme's advice to listen and learn before taking over the chairman's role. Those who know me well know I am an astute observer and a keen listener. That, coupled with the knowledge and support of the outgoing David Holmes, had proved invaluable and made the process so much easier than I might have anticipated.

All of the sports and business journalists had my telephone numbers, I was comfortable talking to them and rarely an evening went by without at least one phone call asking about a potential transfer or deal. Perhaps in hindsight, I should have been a little less available.

Friday nights between 7pm and 10pm were usually the busiest – that's when the Saturday newspaper deadlines were almost past and the eager Sunday newspaper sportswriters didn't have to worry about being scooped by their daily rivals. I don't think that has changed.

I still find it mystifying that one or two extremely senior Scottish journalists chose not to phone me at all throughout their entire careers. I'm sure they had their reasons.

Whether it's 1989 or 2025, football will always have the propensity to stir emotions like no other sport and make you believe that what seems impossible can somehow be achieved. What happened back then seems almost unimaginable now.

As my second season at Ibrox was beginning I received an intriguing telephone call to my office in Edinburgh's Gyle from an old friend. "Are you interested in owning a slice of Manchester United?" I replied, "Of course."

It may seem odd to say this but in 1989, Rangers were probably a bigger club than Manchester United. The English Premier League had not been launched, we had outbid them for the England international Trevor Steven and Alex Ferguson was endeavouring to establish himself following his fantastic success at Aberdeen.

The so-called golden generation of youngsters that they had – Beckham, Scholes, Giggs, Butt and the Nevilles – were a few years away from reaching the first team. Manchester United were not regular title contenders and Liverpool were the recognised force in English football.

I always like to remind myself that I was only 38 years old at this time.

On August 19 that year a man, one year younger than me, had strutted onto the Old Trafford pitch before the first game of the new English First Division league campaign.

In full United training kit, a virtual unknown called Michael Knighton performed a bit of keep-uppy with a ball before firing it into an empty net. He then stood in front of the Stretford End, soaking up the adulation.

On the previous day, Knighton had announced what was considered a sensational £10million deal to purchase 50 per cent of this global footballing institution. He was the prospective new owner showing off to the loyal fans of the club that could soon be his.

But there was one major snag. Michael Knighton's MK Trafford Holdings didn't actually have the full amount required to purchase the stake in the club that was on offer from United chairman Martin Edwards.

And that's where I came in. Suddenly I was being offered the opportunity to come up with half of the £10million for a 25 per cent equity in Manchester United. I spoke with Graeme and we formed a plan. Timing was everything. We would play our way in, then attempt to take the major stake in Manchester United. I had never met Alex Ferguson at this point but the plan was straightforward enough. Graeme – whose family hadn't properly settled in Scotland – would consider becoming manager and Walter Smith would take over as manager of Rangers.

I had yet to work out the mechanics of how I might manage these huge cross-border roles but we were all set to give it a go.

On September 15, I had written the following letter to Michael Knighton.

Dear Michael,
Further to our discussions I confirm that the Murray International Group would like to support you in your acquisition of a controlling interest in The Manchester United Football Club.
My understanding of the present position is that you personally or your company MK Trafford Holdings Ltd have an irrevocable option granted by Martin Edwards or his family to purchase the 50% of issued share capital which he owns or controls.
The price is £20 per share. If you exercise the option, you then also have to offer to buy from the other shareholders all the remaining shares in issue at the same price.
Assuming this is correct we are prepared to offer the following:
1. The availability of cash equal to 50% of what you ultimately have to pay to Mr Edwards and the other shareholders under the option and the public offer.
2. The introduction to our bankers who will fund your own stake i.e. the per centage which we don't provide.

3. *The availability of the same bankers to take over the banking facility and requirements of the club.*

4. *The introduction to experienced merchant bankers who will carry through the Public Offer to the other shareholders.*

5. *The availability of management advice and expertise from the Rangers Football Club plc to whatever extent you reasonably require.*

6. *Availability of financial advice in areas including costs trimming and maximisation of existing potential based on our own experience at Rangers.*

7. *Any other advice and access to any of her personnel as you may reasonably require.*

This offer is made subject to the following provisos:

A. *Your being able to satisfy our bankers that you have adequate security – free assets to the extent of not less than £5million as collateral to cover the funding of your own equity stake.*

B. *My being satisfied that either I personally or Murray International Holdings Ltd or any subsidiary can properly take either an interest in the management of the club or a directorship or an equity stake given my existing board appointment in the Rangers Football Club plc, in which we, Murray International hold a controlling interest.*

C. *Your undertaking irrevocably that in the event of you (or MK Trafford Holdings Ltd or any other company in which you or your family directly or indirectly hold a controlling interest) succeeding to acquire a controlling interest in the issued share capital of the club, you will transfer (at no more than £20 per share) (free of any security encumbrance) 50% of that interest to Murray International Holdings Ltd or a person to be nominated by us.*

Your maintaining total confidentiality on the content or existence of this letter until I direct otherwise.

If by close of business on 29th September, 1989 the provisos is in paragraphs (a) and (b) above have not been satisfied then at my action only we can treat this letter as having been withdrawn and your undertaking as of no effect.

In the unlikely event of a dispute ever arising between us Scots law would apply to this letter and the undertaking we are asking you to grant. You are of course free to take separate advice before signing the docket below.

It was firstly signed by me then fully accepted and signed by Michael Knighton.

This plan was so advanced that we had reached the stage where a commercial "merger" plan was produced by our marketing team detailing exactly where United and Rangers could jointly benefit.

It was detailed and much of it made perfect sense. This is what was proposed in a commercial sense:

A. Generally increased bargaining power in negotiations with third parties.

B. Subject to completion of existing commitments of Manchester United and Rangers, potential for advertisers and sponsors to "double up" e.g. trackside advertising and shirt sponsorship. This should be good for all concerned in that it offers increased exposure to advertisers and sponsors and should allow Manchester United and Rangers to secure better financial return.

C. Reduced administration costs. By merging certain administrative, accounting and banking facilities, overheads could be significantly pruned. This is an extremely important issue not only in the present climate of high interest rates but also having regard to the constantly spiralling costs which seem to attach to a football club without necessarily having an immediate benefit to management player or supporter.

D. Virtually limitless marketing and product potential. Manchester United and Rangers are already two of the best-known and best-supported clubs in the world. By joining forces on a marketing front this already strong position could be further exploited. Areas which could be looked at include television/satellite/video rights, publishing and official merchandise (including sports and leisurewear, not just memorabilia). By using each club's existing contacts and agents, and expanding thereafter, there would be an opportunity to substantially increase sales and a worldwide market, while at the same time almost halving the overall administrative costs. A further advantage would hopefully be a greater control of this area of activity would assist in the fight against pirating of goods bearing the name of Manchester United or Rangers.

E. Opportunity to improve player 'perks' without additional cost to clubs. Extra volume (and exposure) produced by effectively doubling number of players for commercial purposes should produce better deals on, for example, cars.

F. The ability to swap notes. Two clubs of the stature and experience of Manchester United and Rangers should be able to assist the other in a variety of commercial areas without prejudice in each other's independence on the playing side.

On the footballing side we also identified a number of areas that we thought could interlink. Our team produced the following:

A. Improved health and fitness facilities for players and local communities. Both clubs already have impressive equipment, medical and physiotherapy services. By sharing capital costs on the very best equipment, which might otherwise be prohibitive, Manchester

United and Rangers could offer its players an independent, in-house fitness facility which would be second to none. In addition to helping with the players' personal fitness there would, of course, be the added advantage in some cases of shortening the healing time on certain injuries. Rangers already have plans at a fairly advanced stage for offering a form of sports medical facilities to the local community and an expanded version of this could be offered by Manchester United and Rangers and could even form a platform for a concentrated move into the leisure industry, with particular emphasis on local community family participation in the club.

B. Reverting to the subject of healthcare it should have proved possible to negotiate improved terms on permanent health and other insurance premiums for player care. It is a duty of major clubs to take a leading role in the reasonable, responsible approach to players with long-term injuries.

C. Whilst the formation of a power base could not be the main objective of any merger it is an inescapable fact that a unified voice presented by Manchester United and Rangers would be a powerful one at home and in Europe.

D. On a perhaps altruistic note the merger could genuinely be good for football in general if other clubs see Manchester United and Rangers taking an innovative role in various areas of activity. They may feel a need or obligation to their supporters perhaps to do the same and this could only be of benefit to the game in the long-term.

E. Increased revenue on a commercial level would be channelled into a number of areas none-the-least of which would be ground improvements, spectator safety and comfort.

F. Improved revenue should generate extra funds to buy new players with a view to bringing greater success to each club. Equally importantly, however, greater resources could be devoted to widening the scouting system, improving youth policy and strengthening *integration of schools and local community level. The way forward is to place major clubs in the position of focal point of a community, not simply Saturday afternoon attractions. By adopting the foregoing approach and moving forward from the steps already taken by both clubs this objective could be achieved.*

And that was how we saw the future – two global institutions intertwined.

———

Negotiations were in full swing and we introduced Knighton's people to our bankers in Scotland who said they would help him fund the proposed acquisition.

We immediately came up with our £5million.

However, the bank demanded to see signs of his assets. He certainly owned a small castle in Girvan, a nursing home and a house in Edinburgh's Great King Street but it was obvious from the first sweep of his assets, carried out by surveyors DM Hall, that he just didn't have the necessary collateral to merit a £5million loan. His grand plan was off the table.

We continued weighing up the possibilities, holding several exhausting meetings with legal advisor Andrew Cubie in the offices of Edinburgh firm Bird Semple Fyfe Ireland. One of the sessions even dragged on all night and I can remember Graeme and I pitching up back at my house in Murrayfield and Louise making us egg and chips with mugs of tea at 3am.

Eventually, it was clear that Michael Knighton would NOT be able to fulfil his dream of taking over the world's most famous football club – but that meant I could.

For seven days I was in pole position to make the acquisition but by then I had to make contact with the Scottish Football Association to clarify our position.

Two men would make that decision for me by delving into their famous rule books – Ernie Walker and Jim Farry (both of whom I actually respected as senior custodians of Scottish football and both of whom I sincerely wish were still around our game). In effect they told me that cross-border dual ownership was entirely unacceptable. It broke their rules and they didn't even require a magnifying glass on the small print. It was just a big no-no. The deal was dead and the dream was over before it had begun.

In hindsight, I'm sure millions of Manchester United fans throughout the world might look back over the 1990s and beyond and shout from the rooftops, 'Thank God that never happened.' For the same decade, Rangers fans might have said exactly the same for different reasons.

Graeme was obviously involved in the inner workings of the potential deal right from the off and years later, he wrote, "David Murray said he was going to give Knighton the money – so he'd have owned both Rangers and Man United.

"They actually shook hands and I went to bed believing I was going to go down there to manage Manchester United and Walter would manage Rangers.

"I don't think Fergie had won a trophy for years. I honestly don't know how it would have worked out – an ex-Liverpool player at Old Trafford. I was pretty fearless in those days, though."

Alex Ferguson never raised it with me and l later on I went on to have a good relationship with him and I have enormous admiration for what he has achieved in football and in life.

As for Michael Knighton, now an avid art collector, he was quoted years later in a BBC interview saying, "Of course I loved it. Who wouldn't? Despite how it all turned out, I don't regret going on that pitch and if I had the money to buy Manchester

United today, I would do exactly the same again. I was fulfilling every schoolboy dream in the world."

And for me, if I was given the opportunity to take any stake in Manchester United again, we'd certainly be talking billions, not millions.

8

A PROPHET AND A PROFIT

I'M QUITE PROUD OF THE FACT THAT I HAVE BEEN IN business for 51 years and in 44 of them I have made a profit.

After a financial downturn in 1986 had taken it out of all of us I had left Ken Cockburn to concentrate on the core metals business while I focused my attention on property.

I saw the need to diversify for business reasons, but I was getting stale as well. I had been doing the same thing for far too long and to be honest I was a little bored.

What really got me into property was what I saw in Canada. While our attempts to enter an offshore market that was just not there began stalling, what I really noticed was how Halifax itself was growing. It seemed to me that one business family, the Irvings, owned everything there – they owned the shipyards, the oil companies, everything. As I went back and forward, I saw the development that was happening around the airport there. I remember thinking to myself, 'Wait a bloody minute!'

I saw the developments at Halifax and Toronto Airports. I saw how they were building up industrial sites around the airport's periphery with new office complexes and business parks.

Earlier I had seen the opportunity that North Sea offshore development would bring to the metals market and now I saw a similar potential in property.

As I mentioned earlier in the book, when I was back in Scotland after my Nova Scotia trip, my late wife Louise and Keith, my youngest, and I went up in a helicopter around Edinburgh airport and I saw there was a gap with no development in the Sighthill area of the city. I thought 'development has to happen there'.

I remember flying above the Gyle, what would become the location for Edinburgh's largest shopping centre and business park, and I saw a road come to a dead end with all the open ground around.

Soon afterwards I bought that 500 acres from the farmer, which we still own to this day. Our biggest property development to date will be based on part of that site.

I ended up using that first move into property as a template. I bought some extra ground which I built offices on. We had our head office there and I built a mini complex of offices now used by the Scottish Sports Council, the Scottish Prison Service and the university grants office. Eventually I sold that site for £20million to the Prudential and that was the foundation of the property business.

By the late 1980s the business was more complex than it had ever been. The core metals business was continuing to grow, and we were using the profits and borrowing more money to expand further. The profits we made in metals would help fund other businesses, but it was funding from the Bank of Scotland that helped create the property business. I was one of probably half a dozen serious entrepreneurs in Scotland who were backed by the Bank of Scotland, which along with The Royal Bank of Scotland, was one of this country's two major banks and indeed biggest companies. The bank had been involved with the business right back to the time of the first deal I did with Ken Faulkner, the manager of the bank's branch at 141 Princes Street in Edinburgh.

In 1987 I came to an agreement with Gavin Masterson and his colleagues at the Bank of Scotland to establish a property joint venture, Murray BS, of which Murray International Holdings owned 80 per cent.

It grew from that first land deal in 1988 where we bought 3,000 acres including 600 acres near Edinburgh Airport. The deal to buy the Roxburghe Hotel for £9million followed in 1990.

———

Our growing property business took a major reverse in the early 1990s as recession hit and the bottom fell out of the property market. The *Scotsman* newspaper would later refer to this period as Murray International's "dark days of the early 1990s."

While the metals division of the business was still profitable, our electronics division was significantly underperforming. Taken together it was a loss-making position. For the year to 1991 we reported losses of £4.2million, with the picture being even worse the following year when we reported losses of £5.5million. By 1993 we had hauled back some of the ground, but we still had to report an annual loss of £1.5million.

As I said at the time, "Property does pull the group down, short term. But we have to live with the market as it is. It's my only area of concern in the group. We are sitting on some property gems but we'll take steps if we need to."

When your business hits troubled times like this there is a huge advantage in being private. We did not have the daily distraction of looking at a falling share price and we did not have external shareholders breathing down our necks. It meant that we could look and think long term.

The newspapers would report our annual figures but that didn't have the immediate, negative impact as it did on publicly quoted businesses. As a private group we had invested heavily in assets that would yield over the long term rather than a shorter one.

In 1992 we made the decision to separate our property interests out from the rest of the business. We put them in a wholly owned subsidiary called the Premier Property Group (PPG). I made Ian Tudhope, MIH's lawyer, managing director of PPG.

This move meant that £37million worth of property-related debt could be taken off the MIH balance sheet, making it look immediately healthier. Through the Bank of Scotland, we formed a joint venture called Propco and refinanced Murray BS.

Separating out the property interests into PPG, careful trading and the gradual improvement of property prices over the next few years meant that we clawed our way out of the position we were in and the financial position for the group began to improve.

By 1996 the property interests were making a positive contribution to the group's performance. That year Murray International recorded its best ever results due largely to the restructuring that we had done in response to the dark days of the early 1990s. That year I reported in my chairman's statement that "we have consolidated our interests in our main areas of activity, particularly steel, electronics, property and sport."

A key part in the success was in reducing the group's debt burden. In 1997 I announced, "Our group's financial performance has been very satisfying indeed. The success of our programme of debt reduction is reflected in the results. By removing our exposure to non-core activities, we have improved the quality of our earnings."

It was through my interest in sport that that year I made a business introduction that would lead to a £20million deal and a long-term business relationship that would prove key in the development of a business empire.

I had taken a group of friends and contacts out to Turin where Rangers were playing Juventus in the Champions League at the fantastic Delle Alpi stadium. My friend and fellow entrepreneur Tom Hunter was there and asked if I could introduce him to Gavin Masterton of the Bank of Scotland. I said of course and asked why. He told me that he and Philip Green wanted to buy Olympus Sports. I introduced Tom to Gavin on that trip and he and Philip Green bought equipment company Olympus Sports for £20million and that was the start of Tom's significant sporting business. That was the sort of support that Bank of Scotland was offering.

As well as Gavin and Tom, the group that I had taken on that trip included Sean Connery and Angus Grossart. It was a great trip but we got thumped 4-1 on the pitch. One key memory from that trip was meeting the late, great Gianluca Vialli. I talked to him for ages and thought I had persuaded him to come to Rangers, but he later changed his mind and went to Chelsea.

In 1996 the ENIC investment group was looking to build up their football portfolio, which at that point included AEK Athens, FC Basel, Slavia Prague, Vicenza and Tottenham Hotspur.

So, led by London billionaire trader Joe Lewis, they invested £40million in Rangers for 20 per cent of the club, which valued us at £200million.

In the process Daniel Levy and Howard Stanton joined the

Ibrox board but it became apparent very quickly that there would be regular disagreements over transfer spending.

They wanted to run it very differently but in the end it didn't matter. UEFA ruled that multi-ownership was not permitted so they had to get out. Stanton resigned in May 1999.

And the relationship concluded in 2004 when Daniel Levy resigned and the 20 per cent stake was bought by Murray International Holdings for £8.27million.

The conclusion of the arrangement was swift. Joe Lewis berthed his £100million yacht at Eden Roc at Cap d'Antibes, walked through the reception of the Hotel Du Cap where I picked him up.

We drove less than a mile to my house where he stayed for exactly 18 minutes and signed the necessary paperwork. It was what I would call a factual exchange.

9

FAMILY TRAGEDY

MY WIFE LOUISE REGRETFULLY RARELY ENJOYED GOOD health. She was what some might describe as delicate and I knew early on in our relationship that she was having problems.

At the age of 17 we had gone to North Berwick for the day and after a short run around a park she was utterly exhausted, which indicated there was an underlying medical issue. Within 24 hours she had visited the doctor and had been diagnosed with asthma.

Over the next two decades she dealt with a number of troubling problems, including, at the age of 30, collapsing at Turnberry Hotel in Ayrshire before being taken to Irvine Royal Hospital for an ectopic pregnancy and surgery.

This was followed later in the year by a full hysterectomy on Christmas Day in Edinburgh. Then, in early 1992, Louise had gone on a short winter holiday with Keith to our home in New Zealand.

She felt seriously unwell on their return and following a few visits to her doctor she required a small stomach operation due to peritonitis. That was in March and it was the beginning of what would be a truly horrendous time for our family.

Despite the immediate success of the op, her condition seemed to deteriorate further and there was only one MRI scanner in Scotland at that time – at Ross Hall Hospital in Glasgow. We both needed to know what Louise might be facing and we managed to fix an appointment. It was a Saturday in July.

I went to Ross Hall and, despite me wanting to remain at her side, I was advised to leave her with the medical team and return in three hours. I drove to a deserted Ibrox, parked my car and sat alone in an office in the main stand. My mind was churning.

On Tuesday of the following week, we were asked by our consultant Mr MacPherson to go into the Murrayfield Hospital in Edinburgh to discuss the results.

We were both dreading the visit because we knew deep down that what came next could not be good. The news, when it came, was still crushing. The oncologist told us that Louise had advanced liver cancer and it was spreading rapidly. We had both asked the specialist to be completely up front about what was about to happen and he was. She was given three months to live.

We both sat there too shocked to say anything. We were both thinking about our boys, how they would react, how they would cope and what the future might look like for them.

The doctor told us that, in his opinion, it would be best if we sat down with David and Keith and told them everything. We did exactly that. They hugged their mum and they cried.

I had been through what I thought was the toughest time of my life after my crash but it really was nothing compared to the anguish of seeing my teenage sons trying to come to terms with a future without their mum in it.

Her bravery over the next months stunned me. She just tried

to carry on as normal. It was heart-wrenching. I vividly recall her sitting in the bedroom putting on make-up and getting dressed for a dinner appointment with friends from New Zealand who had arrived in Scotland in September. We arrived at the Norton House Hotel and she was in such good form.

She was anything but normal, of course. She was exhausted. She was fighting to just stay alive.

During the autumn months, her condition deteriorated to such an extent that she was struggling to stay awake. She had constant 24-hour home care.

On November 28, 1992, Louise died at home, aged just 39. It was 6.20am. I was with her and so were her beloved sons, one aged 18 and the other 16. Much later, we found in a desk drawer individual letters to the boys with her hopes and dreams about how their lives would turn out and how she wanted them to always look after each other.

They have both done her proud. On November 28 every year, we visit her grave at Mortonhall in Edinburgh where she is buried alongside her parents and we reflect on what she instilled in all of us.

She was old-fashioned. It was family first and family last. She once gave an interview to STV where she told the reporter that all that mattered to her was making sure that I was looked after and able to look after her and her sons.

Her constant support helped me build Murray International, particularly after the accident and she never complained when I was travelling the world and trying to win new business. It was for her and the family.

She was always inspired by the style and the fashion of France, particularly Princess Grace of Monaco, and Louise's love of all things French has since proved to have an impact on all of our lives. During the early 1980s we both fell in love with Saint-Jean-Cap-Ferat, a lovely town on the Cote d'Azur, and ended up buying a beautiful flat overlooking the harbour. It cost us £180,000. One of my abiding memories was watching the renowned actor David Niven, who lived in a beautiful sea-front villa, walk to the local cafe every morning and greet everyone with a polite "Hello there."

Louise also created a wonderful home in Jersey which became an all-year round holiday haven for the family. We would often just decamp there for eight weeks during school summer breaks.

After Louise died my only concern was David and Keith. The football took a back seat and so did the metals business. These boys had just lost their mum at a critical juncture in their lives and I needed to help them through it.

We spoke a lot in the weeks following the funeral and I felt it was important to give them time and space to deal with it.

David, who earlier that year had learned a few tough lessons helping to tar roads with Wimpy Construction up in Inverness-shire, has my nature. Over the rest of that year he was stoic in how he processed what had happened.

From that point on, he never looked back and went on to complete a degree at Heriot-Watt University. He travelled too, working for two years with IMG and the Thai Football Association, then a summer stint at the David Leadbetter Golf Academy in the States. He also spent time working in New Zealand.

He studied at the LSE and Harvard, worked in the corporate graduate scheme for Bank of Scotland and when he came into the Murray Group, he brought two vital things to the boardroom table – a far better education than I ever had and a life-long belief in our family business.

He is now a successful managing director of Murray Capital but with a very different style to me. I went big. I took risks. He is a thoughtful and pragmatic co-investor, taking positions in different companies and his goal is to create a legacy business.

Keith was different. He has his mum's nature. Just like David, he was at Merchiston Castle School in Edinburgh but he didn't want to follow in his dad's footsteps.

We discussed his options and although I had maybe envisaged him going into the property sector, perhaps as a quantity surveyor, he was honest enough to admit that the course he was on at Napier University just wasn't for him and he had his own ideas.

He had enjoyed a couple of jobs, one in particular at the Caledonian Hotel and he wanted to be part of that industry. Eventually he ended up going to Robert Gordon University to complete a degree in hospitality management.

Keith was a grafter and at one point worked as a chef at Langan's Brasserie in London for three years. It served him well.

He now manages our successful wine business in Routas, France as well as a number of wine businesses in the UK. He is also a director of the Murray Group and is helping to establish the family name across the globe.

My sons are very different but I'm so content that I am able to pass on my business to them knowing that – unlike in so many other family businesses – there is no conflict because they have individual and completely separate roles.

When I was young and starting out in business it really was all about money but over the years, financial security and planning for the future generation has become my priority.

And I can take comfort from the fact that money is not my sons' be all and end all. For them, they define our business in terms of family, unity and the next generation. Much of that is down to preparation, experience and a family council initiated by David 10 years ago and led at all times by an independent chairman.

That and, of course, the standards set by their mum Louise.

10

A PLANE DRAMA
(OR TWO)

I HAVE NEVER BEEN WHAT YOU MIGHT CALL A comfortable flyer. Given the choice I probably prefer a road trip but given what I do, that is a rare occasion.

I tend to use private aircraft only because trying to navigate a packed airport terminal and security on crutches is nigh on impossible.

And even boarding any plane can often be a three-act play given my disability. However, I still fly regularly to France and the Middle East and the whole experience has become more routine.

It wasn't always that way.

Following my accident and exit from hospital and getting the business moving in a positive direction thanks to an expanding oil industry, I had taken our entire staff of 12 to Tenerife for a short holiday in May 1977.

We flew from Glasgow Airport and it was one of only two times that I have ever used a wheelchair. The other was a spur-of-the-moment decision when I just flopped into an airport wheelchair to help me beat one of the longest queues I have ever seen at Newark in the United States in 2003 during a trip with David and Keith.

The travel to the Canaries was a monumental hassle from start to finish, from going through the airport to boarding the plane and disembarking. There was a grim sight to greet us as we flew into Los Rodeos. Just a few weeks earlier two 747s – one from KLM and one from Pan Am – had collided, killing 583. The debris was still lying at the side of the runway.

I was just not comfortable in a wheelchair, then to cap it all during one of the evenings out after we got to the Botanic Hotel in Puerto de la Cruz, a couple of my team got a bit worse for wear and started racing in it.

I vowed there and then that I would rather stand tall and a few years later I was in the fortunate position of being able to finally buy my own private jet.

It was a Learjet 35a, purchased in 1998 from a New York antique dealer and it was managed by Northern Executive, a company operating out of Manchester. It could seat seven and reach speeds of 545mph. Edinburgh to Jersey, where I had a house, took exactly one hour. Our family and friends used it often.

In April 2000, we were waving off friends back to Scotland at the airport in Jersey and I spotted my plane getting towed round to the terminus. Something was clearly amiss and after immediately making inquiries I was told that it had a 'minor technical problem'.

With the technology involved in a modern small jet, you can't exactly nip into Kwik Fit for a new part. I was spooked – enough for me to decide there and then to sell it and join leasing specialist NetJets. They had a worldwide fleet of bigger planes which I regularly used for the following decade.

My LearJet, tail registration G-MURI, was subsequently put on the market and it continued doing occasional charter flights.

On Tuesday May 2, 2000, I was in Scotland and took a call from Northern Executive managing director David Antrobus. He opened the conversation by saying, "I have terrible news". He then told me that the LearJet, which was still in the process of being sold, had crash-landed in Lyon, France.

The aircraft had left London Farnborough bound for Nice but tragedy struck 90 minutes into the flight. Both pilots, David Saunders and Dan Worley, had been killed instantly but what David said next stunned me. He said that Formula One driver David Coulthard, his fiancee at the time Heidi Wichlinski and David's fitness trainer Andy Matthews were the passengers and had all walked out of the wreckage. A small dog also survived.

I knew David and bizarrely his father Duncan had recently walked up to me in the Seacrest Hotel in Jersey to thank me for being the only person to actually reply to his plea for financial assistance as he tried to help his son achieve his motor racing dreams.

I got in touch with David as soon as I could and we spoke at length about what had happened. He told me that after escaping the wreckage he had even gone back to see if he could help the pilots but there was nothing he could do.

David had told journalists, "We had time to prepare ourselves for the landing in the brace position. When the plane finally came to rest, the front of the cockpit had snapped free from the fuselage. The only way out for us was through the front of the aircraft."

He later described his feelings in a Motor Sport interview and said, "I probably should be dead. You can't have a situation like that which brings you so close to the realities of how fragile we are on this earth and not change in some way.

"I have an increased sense of how lucky I am, how lucky I am in my life and what I have. I don't live in the real world being a Grand Prix driver. It's made me realise the importance of family and friends."

As the official owner of the plane I was later sent the accident report and it made for fairly grim reading.

According to testimony from David, Heidi and Andy the flight was going normally until the left engine started making noise then juddering. The pilot then pulled the left red T-handle at the top of the control panel and then shut down the left throttle. There were no unusual smells or smoke in the cabin before or after the engine stopped.

The speed-brakes were used during descent and then stowed when approaching the ground. The co-pilot had told the passengers that they were going to be landing in Lyon because of an engine problem.

The approach seemed normal and, a few metres from the ground, the pilot placed his hand on the right thrust lever. The nose went up a little at the same time as the aircraft turned to the left then the left wing dropped and touched the ground. One passenger stated they felt the aircraft accelerating a short time before the wing touched the ground. Another stated that the aircraft veered to the left while the right engine was accelerating. Either way, the effect was devastating. A few seconds later the aircraft stopped; the cockpit was missing and the right side of the aircraft was on fire.

I later asked myself, 'What if?' Could I have survived like David did? He was such a fit athlete with incredible reflexes and not afraid of risk. Incredibly a few days later, David had shaken off any after-effects from the crash and he drove brilliantly for a podium finish at the Catalonia Grand Prix in Barcelona.

Now most people go through their life and experience maybe a couple of what you might call 'bad flights'… a bit of turbulence, a bumpy landing. But my experience of private jets continued to be enjoyable… right up until Sunday, February 18, 2024.

I had decided to fly to Cannes in the south of France where I was due to attend a business meeting. One of my team was accompanying me.

Our flight – a Dassault Falcon 2000 owned by a friend – left Edinburgh at noon and as we climbed through the clouds, the air steward opened a bottle of Chablis and we sat back and relaxed, reading through documents and preparing for the meeting with lawyers early the next day.

We had just reached 36,000ft and were crossing the border at Carlisle when there was a sudden bang.

"What was that?" I asked the steward. She didn't know but was convinced it had just been a bag at the back of the plane dropping to the floor.

The aircraft juddered and then the oxygen masks immediately dropped down.

It was terrifying and surreal at the same time. I felt a bit ridiculous with a glass of white wine in one hand, and the other making sure I had put the mask on properly. You are literally helpless, entirely in the hands of two experienced pilots who, although you know they are experts and will do their utmost to get you back on the ground, still leave you asking yourself the questions, 'What the hell was the bang? Do these guys know how bad this is and are afraid to tell me? Is it going to catch fire? Can we get down safely?'

The reality of our situation was no less comforting when we learned what had actually happened. The stewardess relayed to us from the pilots that the cabin was depressurising and we had to get down as quickly as possible. The pilots had donned special masks, different to ours (think Biggles) and the descent was rapid. We had to get below 14,000ft and quickly. Priority was getting a landing slot at the nearest airport. Manchester was our first hope but they couldn't accommodate us. Liverpool's John Lennon Airport was available.

By the time we were on the approach to the runway I had calmed down slightly, only to see a slew of emergency vehicles ready, lights flashing.

Well, rapid doesn't start to describe our descent. We were on the ground within 13 minutes.

On the Tarmac we then sat on the plane for two hours. One of the pilots told me that at one point there had been smoke coming out of the instrument panel.

We were then offered the opportunity of waiting until a replacement aircraft could be sourced and dispatched to take us to Cannes. Honestly, I just couldn't. The thought of getting back on a similar jet was too much. Not that day and not for a while, anyway.

A car took us from Liverpool back over the border and home to Perthshire. However, I had a problem. I needed to be in France for business. I grabbed a few hours' sleep then got in the car and drove… all the way to the south of France. And then all the way back again a few days later. It had taken far longer than I had anticipated.

I found out a couple of things a few days later – both pilots had a commendable 12,000 flying hours under their belts and nothing like this had ever happened to either of them, and we had approximately six minutes of oxygen left when we landed. Thank goodness we were over land and not over the ocean.

I never asked 'What if', in that instance, but I'm sure they would have had a solution.

And has it put me off flying forever? Not a chance.

11

MAN OF PROPERTY

FROM THE YEAR 2000 ONWARDS, WE DID A SPATE OF deals following a decision the year before to divide our property activities 50:50 between development and investment.

Part of the strategy behind this was to spread our risk in what we had seen first-hand was a notoriously cyclical property market.

The moves were also a response to market opportunity – following the global stock market crash in March 2000 as the dot.com bubble burst.

We bought 55 Strand in London for £8million in a joint venture with Iain Wotherspoon's Kilmartin Property Group. We bought it from building society group Halifax plc which took out a 25-year lease on the ground and lower ground floors at a rental of £290,000 a year.

We refurbished the upper floors to provide 24,000 sq ft of high spec offices.

As part of the joint venture with the Bank of Scotland we acquired the Scottish property portfolio of P&O for £70million in the year 2000. The portfolio was made up of 19 office and retail properties mainly in the West of Scotland including Farnborough House, Colville House and The Grosvenor in central Glasgow as well as properties in Edinburgh, including Apex House and in Inverness.

Overnight we became landlords to a list of tenants that included Scottish Enterprise, The Secretary of State for the Environment, the Department of Work and Pensions, Scottish & Newcastle Breweries and a range of High Street retailers.

We didn't have the funds ourselves to do deals such as buying the £70million P&O property portfolio. Our banking facility went up from £100million to £300million – we were getting access to funds readily.

We bought the ABC Cinema complex in Edinburgh in a joint venture with J. Sainsbury Developments, in a deal that involved redeveloping the complex, adding 57,000 sq ft of Grade A office accommodation.

In the same 2000-2001 financial period we bought the Kingsgate Shopping Centre in Dunfermline, Fife from Scottish Widows Investment Partnership for £37million. The centre had 110,000 sq ft devoted to retail businesses with tenants including Safeway, Dixons, Etam and the Arcadia Group.

That year we also bought Excel House in the heart of The Exchange, Edinburgh's financial district, in order to develop it. In a back-to-the-future deal, we also bought the 35,000 sq ft Westpoint in South Gyle, which had formerly been the Murray International Holdings HQ, to redevelop it.

We later sold it to Prudential. A further deal that financial year was the joint development with CGM (Edinburgh) of City Point in the Haymarket area in Edinburgh's West End to create offices.

In 2002 we bought 6 South Gyle Crescent on the outskirts of

Edinburgh from BAE Systems and developed the site to provide 190,000 sq ft of office space. And the following year we bought 10 and 11 Charlotte Square, properties adjacent to our headquarters at number nine in a deal worth £2.75million.

In 2004 Ian Tudhope said to me he would like us to buy the International Press Centre in London. He and I flew down to London for the day. He gave me the numbers. It cost £40million. We looked at it together and analysed it.

He asked me what I thought. My response? "It's a no-brainer."

We did the same thing with Cloth Hall Court in the centre of Leeds where the existing tenants included the then accountancy giant Ernst & Young (now EY) and corporate law firm Eversheds. We bought the 100,000 sq ft of office space for £21million.

With deals like these, Premier Property Group grew to become one of the 30 largest property businesses in the UK and one of the largest privately-owned ones.

I had a rule of thumb when it came to property deals. When I was buying major developments, I always looked to see if the rents from the existing tenants would cover the interest on the funding taken out to finance the deal.

For major properties I would get the bank to put in 70 per cent and us 30 per cent. The rent ensures that there is income coming in on the property with it mostly covering the interest on what was borrowed and then longer term you have to ensure that you have a gain on your investment when you sell the property on.

In those days when we were deciding whether to buy a property we would look carefully at the local market and particularly at the potential for increasing rents. You should look at the financial track record of the tenants and you look at refurbishing the property to improve it.

The tenants may have rent reviews coming up in a year or two

– we would try and get a justified rent increase. For example, if you can spend £1million on a shopping centre, improving the entrance, improving the marketing, getting the foot traffic up, then you'll get a better rental. With a stronger rental you can sell it with a better future income, a better yield and make a profit.

It does perhaps sound quite ruthless but you have to be hard-headed when you're looking at rentals coming in when you buy the property. In 90 per cent of cases the interest you have to pay is covered by rents from the tenants. That protects your downside.

But there has to be the potential for rental growth. If there's no rental growth then there's no appreciation in value and there's no earn-out (a provision written into some financial transactions whereby the seller of a business will receive additional payments based on the future performance of the business sold). There has to be an earn-out.

We ask questions. Can we handle the downside? Is the debt covered? Do we have financially stable tenants? Is there income potential? Is there growth? It's not rocket science and without fail your gut tells you if a deal is right or not.

On example: you buy a property for £10million and you cover £2million of that from your own funds. The remaining £8million you borrow from a bank which might cost you around £450,000 a year in interest payments. If you assume that your property has an eight per cent yield, then you will be getting £800,000 in rents.

That is a margin of £350,000 on your £2million outlay – that's an example of the no-brainer that I mentioned to Ian during our London trip.

A key factor for us became our sheer scale as a property business. Not everybody has £30million or £100million to do a deal or can raise that kind of money but we had a good track record. We had been doing it for a long time and had been highly successful.

But while property has been a major strand of the group's business for decades, it was my involvement in property that led to two of my biggest mistakes. I just got too heavily into property, accepting too much debt from the Bank of Scotland to fund it.

Then when the property business was making all that money – one year we made £50million – what dividend did I take out? Nothing. If I had taken out £30million, no-one would have batted an eye.

Those errors of judgement were to prove very costly.

12

THE FAN WHO WOULD BE KING

"I'VE NEVER ACTUALLY WATCHED ALL OF DR NO before," he said. If the words had been spoken by anyone else, particularly from my generation, I might have raised an eyebrow. It was, after all, one of the most iconic films of all-time, but the fact they had been uttered by Sean Connery left me more than a little surprised.

A few close friends were mulling around in the darkened cinema room at my vineyard, Chateau Routas in Provence, after a quiet dinner and I suggested we put on the movie. He was quite laid back, shrugged and said, "Sure."

I think I was probably expecting him to regale us with some amazing inside stories about his James Bond co-stars, maybe a bit about the cars, the gadgets and definitely some tales about the exotic locations.

Instead, it transpired that I knew the plot and the lines pretty well – in fact, we all did – and his abiding memory was of an IWC

Steel watch he wore during the film that he hadn't clapped eyes on for decades. Eventually, after much cajoling, he did finally tell us that HIS favourite Bond film was *From Russia With Love*.

Sean Connery was a special man, a fine actor, a passionate Scot and across three decades, he became one of my closest friends that I would frequently turn to for counsel. He also sought my advice on a number of business deals that he was involved in.

Late in his life, his wife Micheline gave me a book of her pictures and paintings and signed it, 'To David. Sean's best friend'. That meant a lot to me because we had shared so many incredible days together.

Sean had that rare gift of being knowledgeable about so many things that mattered and, exactly as you might expect, both women and men just adored him.

When I first saw him in the flesh it was actually from my back garden in Barnton Avenue West in Edinburgh. He was playing in a Pro-am golf tournament at the Royal Burgess Golf Club and one of the greens was right at the bottom of my garden. I took my boys David and Keith to the fence and we all waved at Sean and the comedian Ronnie Corbett as they walked to the next tee.

I wouldn't meet the man properly until 1990. During a black tie dinner at the Balmoral Hotel in July, organised by an Edinburgh *Evening News* sports journalist called Craigie Veitch, we sat down together on the top table and being an avid sports fan, we just seemed to hit it off straight away.

At the end of the event, I said to him, "If you ever want to come to a Rangers game as my guest, please let me know." He would take me up on the offer much quicker than I had imagined.

Three weeks later, Rangers were playing at Celtic Park and a flustered Sean called me out of the blue. The conversation was a surprising one. I had assumed that, as Scotland's most famous man, he would just be able to pick up the telephone to Celtic Park and they would, of course, welcome him with open arms.

Not on this occasion. Sean told me he had rung the number he had been given by a Celtic official and asked about acquiring a ticket for the Old Firm match.

The woman in the ticket office who picked up the phone said, "Who's calling?" and Sean replied, not surprisingly, "It's Sean Connery," to which the woman replied, "Aye, right. So it is. Away and bile yer heid," before promptly hanging up.

I laughed and told him to forget it and that he would come to the game as my guest. He was staying at The New Club in Edinburgh and I picked him up outside the nearby Roxburghe Hotel in Charlotte Square, which I owned at the time, and we travelled through to Glasgow for the match in my car.

When we exited the car outside Celtic Park, there were quite a few raised eyebrows. As for me telling Sean to forget the ticket snub, he did nothing of the sort. Celtic had just asked him to do the voice-over for an upcoming club video. He subsequently declined.

I think folklore would dictate that Sean was a diehard Celtic fan who somehow became a Rangers fan but that's not true. He was certainly in awe of Jock Stein and the great Celtic team of the late 60s but, if anything, Sean was originally a Hearts supporter. He grew up in Fountainbridge and was a regular at Tynecastle in his teenage years.

Just over 20 years ago I got a telephone call from a tradesman who knew that I'd become close to Sean. His workmen were pulling down a number of Edinburgh tenements around the area and he wondered if I wanted to buy the original street sign 'Fountainbridge' where Sean had grown up and perhaps send it to him in the Bahamas.

I paid £20 for what seemed like a fantastic piece of nostalgia and sent it to him. Sean was thrilled. Ironically, he had already set up a production company called Fountainbridge Films.

Sean was also a decent football player and turned out for Bonnyrigg Rose in the East Region juniors. He told me that he had once been for a trial in front of Matt Busby at Manchester United. It came to nothing and that was as close as he got to playing in the big time.

But it certainly wasn't the last time he got to mix it with top players.

On a number of occasions, I would go into the dressing room before big European nights and Sean would be right at my side, geeing on our team. A last-minute pep talk from 007 was definitely something that gave them an edge and had the boys talking for days afterwards.

It certainly worked brilliantly in Copenhagen in 2003 as we tried to qualify for the group stages of the Champions League, which at that time was hugely important for us in both football and financial terms.

It had been a strange old day. We landed in the city and immediately went to the famous Tivoli Gardens for lunch but twice during the next few hours Sean was screwing up his face and asking the same question, "What the hell is this?" The first was when someone put down a plate of cold, raw fish and the second was when we bizarrely got ushered on to a kids' train just to get back out of the gardens and meet our driver who was taking us to the stadium.

Aside from Sean's dressing room appearance, the game was a memorable one, Shota Arveladze scoring the winner in the 90th minute.

For years, Sean and I would share a catch-up call every

weekend to chat through the football and we would inevitably kick off with Rangers.

After all, he had put £1million into the club which no one knew about at the time or even since. I was raising £50million in 2004 and Sean asked if he could invest.

I told him that it was football, that there were no guarantees and he should get professional advice but he was adamant. He wanted in. Needless to say he never did get the money back but he understood completely. Football was, is and always will be a risky business.

He also had a huge interest in Manchester United and the English Premier League. If one of the teams had a Scot, he would know.

Sean followed our national team avidly and always wanted to speak to the managers whenever they had time. I think that other than my extraordinary times with Rangers, one of my most abiding memories of the game is sitting between Sean Connery and King Juan Carlos of Spain at Hampden Park watching Zinedine Zidane score one of the finest-ever European goals in the 2002 Champions League final. I was a proud man that evening while Sean and I were just blown away by the occasion.

Our friendship continued not only across football but across the continent as well, initially in Jersey where I had a home and in particular, France.

In Jersey I vividly recall Sean arriving after he had filmed Entrapment with Catherine Zeta-Jones. He was utterly exhausted, feeling travel-sick and when he dropped his bags inside the front door, he could barely speak. He just turned around and headed for the beach. He wanted fresh sea air and he stayed out there for hours.

Gradually he relaxed and by the end of the week he was in great spirits. We went to a fine Portuguese restaurant in St Brelades on the Friday evening and the waiter discreetly asked if Sean would mind having his picture taken but only after the meal, which at the time I thought was a polite and reasonable request.

Sean, of course, agreed and the waiter said he would just quickly go home to get his camera.

However, when dinner ended and we went outside to get into the car, Sean turned round to find the waiter with a top-of-the-range cine camera... and a very professional-looking tripod. Sean stared at him and jokingly growled, "Oh, c'mon. Really? Who do you think you are? Cecil B. De f***** Mille?"

Sean winked at me but he still let the camera roll.

He had a large villa overlooking the Bay of Nice which several years ago was put up for sale at €20million and described in all of the brochures as 'the house where James Bond lived'. It was stunning. We visited it once and the interior was truly spectacular, however, Sean told me it wasn't his favourite and he didn't live in it at all...not even for one single night.

But he did love France. For nearly 15 years, we would spend time in our family homes Villa Madonna in Juan-les-Pins or at Chateau Routas. He described the Chateau as a haven for him where he could just be himself, read books, drink his favourite red wine and think.

He had this amazing routine, where every morning he would rise at 7.30am, put on his dressing gown, put a heavy, old-fashioned camera around his neck to ensure he would stand upright and force himself to think about his posture. He would then go outside and walk the same mile and a half route through the vines before returning for a porridge breakfast on the terrace.

This was all well and good, until the day the paparazzi took to the skies in a helicopter and they weren't even chasing him. My next door neighbours on one side – perhaps half a mile away – were at this time Brad Pitt and Angelina Jolie. The photographers were desperate for any snaps of the pair and the copter began swooping and diving.

Sean, of course, was clocked by the pilot who came round for a closer look and that was enough. Sean beat a hasty retreat back to the chateau and the pre-breakfast routine immediately came to a halt.

One of my favourite holidays in France with Sean was during the 2010 World Cup in South Africa.

It had begun in Edinburgh. Sean and Micheline had been due to attend a special Edinburgh Film Festival showing of his film The Man Who Would Be King.

I was flying to France on the same evening and said that if he wanted a lift to Nice then he would have to be on the runway at a certain time. I sat on the jet with another close friend and we both had our doubts over whether he would make it.

Well, he did attend the screening but almost as soon as the lights were dimmed, Sean and Micheline were tip-toeing out of the back row and into his waiting limo. He made the flight with five minutes to spare.

Micheline departed for the week to visit her daughter and for seven days, the three of us hunkered down in Juan-les-Pins, drank wine, ate pizza and watched football... lots of it. On the one evening we all finally decided to drag ourselves away from the screen, we drove around Cannes and our car was mobbed by fans at every set of traffic lights. He was weeks away from his 80th birthday and I can't think of any other stars of that age who could still elicit such a reaction.

The same frenzy happened during another Champions League match. Rangers were in Turin on October 18, 1995 to play a star-studded Juventus side with a line-up that included Fabrizio Ravanelli, Alessandro Del Piero, Didier Deschamps and Antonio Conte. Another of the Juventus players that night was Sergio Porrini who we ended up signing.

Sean had been so desperate to be there that he had hired a taxi all the way from Rome. A squad of us had booked into a hotel where – not known to us at the time of the booking – the Italian Secretary Of The Year final was being held. When Sean suddenly appeared at the event, the screaming was reminiscent of a Beatles concert.

On the afternoon of the game, Juventus owner Giovanni Agnelli, who also owned Fiat and Ferrari, had called Sean and told him that he was looking forward to meeting him at the game later.

I jokingly whispered to Sean, "Ask him when my blue Ferrari will be ready." I had actually bought one 12 months earlier and was still waiting on delivery. Sean then asked Agnelli who replied, "Tell David he is third on the list... and definitely behind the Sultan of Brunei."

I didn't feel too bad about being relegated to No3 – the Sultan of Brunei is, of course, a car fanatic and his collection is incredible. The result that night did make me feel bad, however. We ended up losing 4-1.

That blue Ferrari, meanwhile, was my pride and joy – I drove it for 90,000 miles.

———

Sean often stayed at our family home in Perthshire. He would pitch up with his good friend Murray Grigor and he would happily spend days wandering around the estate soaking up the peace and quiet and the fresh air, just glad he was in his beloved Scotland.

When I actually came to buy Dunbarney House in 1999 Sean and Micheline came along with me. For days I had been talking about gutting the place, getting rid of everything inside it and she said to me, "No, David…You must buy everything. You cannot replace these pieces of furniture. This is history."

She told me later that if I hadn't bought the estate then she and Sean would have. I know she wasn't kidding.

Sean was certainly thrifty and managed his money well. He told me that when he stayed at one of the five-star hotels in Monaco, where he had previously owned a home, he would always buy a new pair of socks every day rather than pay the exorbitant bills for his worn ones to be laundered.

We rarely spoke about politics – he was an ardent and vocal nationalist and I have always been in favour of the union – but we somehow kept getting invited together to dinners or events at the First Minister's residence, Bute House, by Alex Salmond.

My office was just yards away and Sean used it often for calls or meetings with people from the film or arts world.

One day, on May 7, 1999, he asked me if he could borrow the boardroom for an hour. I said, "Of course." It transpired that Alex Salmond had asked him if he could give a pep talk and some pointers to his protege, Nicola Sturgeon.

Sean duly obliged and there is a famous picture of him leaving my office right after the session.

He said afterwards, "I just gave her some advice and it will remain private."

Sean was often criticised by sections of the UK media for being an arms-length Scot… always happy to pontificate on issues back home from his home in the Bahamas. But that was so unfair.

He and a number of prominent Scots, including Sean's friend Sir Jackie Stewart, set up the Scottish International Education

Trust (SIET) in 1971. To help kick it off, he donated his entire fee from Diamonds Are Forever and the SIET is still active. Sir Chris Hoy and Kirsty Wark are currently patrons. Sean also provided extensive funding for medical research in Dundee.

To me he was always a wise and trusted confidante and advisor. He was interested – always asking questions, and was never afraid to tell me I might be wrong.

He visited me not long after the Dunblane massacre in 1996 and asked me if I would drive him there. He had no immediate connection to the place but was shocked and upset that something as horrific as that could happen in Scotland.

We stopped on the way and he bought flowers. When we arrived in Dunblane, he made his way quietly to the primary school gates and placed them beside the thousands of bouquets and teddy bears which had been left. He stood with his head bowed for a long time and on the drive home, we spoke very little and were both hit by an overwhelming sadness.

One of my regrets in later life is that I never got the chance to visit him at his home in the Bahamas. We had driven to see him at his place in Gstaad in Switzerland, but he had been asking me for years to travel to the Caribbean.

Finally, I decided to make the trip. I booked the flight and had packed my case before a brief phone call from Micheline.

"I don't think you should come, David. The weather is not so good and Sean is not feeling so well."

I was deeply disappointed but told Micheline that I understood. That was the point I realised that I might never see my old friend and mentor again. He was well into his 80s, travelling far less frequently apart from medical treatments in Miami and he had stopped playing golf, which he had always been passionate about. His health, I knew, was failing and I felt a huge sadness.

The weekly phone calls had become monthly phone calls and football was rarely the starting topic. He never forgot my birthday. On my 50th, he sent a Swarovski telescope and on my 60th it was a Tiffany gold clock which still has pride of place in our company's boardroom.

When he died, on October 31 2020, I sat silently for so long before poring over photos, books and trying to etch every memory into my brain. Nearly five years later I still miss him and our weekend chats.

I speak to a lot of people and most of them would tell you that they've lived a bit. None of us even came close to what Sean Connery experienced.

13

BUYING AND SELLING

I WAS ALWAYS LOOKING FOR NEW OPPORTUNITIES, whether ones that sprung up from our contacts in the metals business or others that I was approached about.

In 2004 an opportunity came about in the shape of one of the most important customers of our Multi Metals business. TransBus, a coach manufacturing company with its headquarters in Camelon, Falkirk – slap bang in between Glasgow and Edinburgh – bought aluminium from Multi Metals for coach bodies and interior fittings.

The company's plant in Guildford made the chassis, which were transported up to Falkirk for bodies to be added.

TransBus International Bus Body and Chassis, which was the UK's largest bus builder, had been so named after being bought by the Mayflower Group in 1995. It was a major business with an annual turnover in 2004 of more than £200million with more than 1,400 single and double-decker buses produced in Falkirk and more than 1,200 chassis made in Guildford. We had built up a great position with the company, providing stock for all of the buses they produced and all their components. We were virtually the only aluminium supplier for the business. We received a printout from them at the start of the week detailing what material was required for their buses and we would make two or three deliveries a day, five or six days a week.

We had done a good job selling to Mayflower and no-one else could get in the door. Of course, we had the advantage of being nearby. Nobody else was local enough to give them that service – you could hardly send three lorries a day from a plant in Birmingham. We had been supplying to them for 20 years.

But all that changed in one fell swoop in 2004 when the Mayflower Group collapsed after a £17million accounting hole was discovered in its accounts. It was a potential disaster for jobs in Scotland and for the company's manufacturing base.

Then I got a phone call from Angus Grossart of the Noble Grossart investment bank, which was, of course, a shareholder in Murray International Holdings. He asked me if I wanted to come in on a deal to buy the TransBus business with him and Brian Souter, co-founder of major bus and train company Stagecoach. I said, "Let's meet."

The three of us sat down in the lounge at Dunbarney and we agreed that we'd buy it. They asked me how I thought we should split it. I said we should divide it according to the time, effort and benefit we were going to bring to the company. I explained, "I'm going to bring the metal at competitive prices, which is important. Brian, I presume you can help in the sale of buses (he had to be careful as Stagecoach was a plc) and Angus, you are going to raise the money. Why don't we do it 30 to Angus, 30 to me and 40 to Brian."

We shook hands on it there and then and that's exactly how it panned out. Actually doing the deal took seven days, when our legal teams got involved and it was concluded at four in the morning, finally buying the company from the administrator Deloitte.

Angus and I had 30 per cent each and Brian and his sister Anne Gloag had 40 per cent. Angus raised £80million with Peter Cummings from Bank of Scotland. I supplied the metal, and the business, which in the end was renamed the Alexander Dennis Group, became a great Scottish success story.

In preparing the deal we took advice from Bill Cameron, a former TransBus chief executive, who became chairman of Alexander Dennis with Jim Hastie – a former professional footballer with Hibs – becoming chief executive, followed by Colin Robertson who with his previous experience ran the business successfully through to the buyout by the Canadian Group NFI.

For Murray Metals our 30 per cent stake in Alexander Dennis secured the position of our Multi Metals business as the main supplier of aluminium.

Angus Grossart called the deal "a very interesting example of how Scotland, as a country, can benefit from cohesion. We were a very co-ordinated group which was capable of being very decisive."

If we hadn't done the deal the business would have fallen into the hands of a venture capital company and jobs would have gone. In fact, the deal meant the saving of 1,300 jobs – something that is worth underlining because of what happened a bit more than a decade later with Scottish steel plants.

The Alexander Dennis deal was to be followed 18 months later by another one that surprised many people, even some of those who knew me very well. That deal was a result of the telephone call from Angus, this came about following a surprise approach from an American private equity group.

Jeffries Capital Partners offered to buy Murray International Metals, my original start-up business and one that had been at the heart of the growing group, providing profits that were to finance so many other business opportunities.

While the approach came out of the blue, I could easily understand the reasons for it because of the then performance of the Murray International Metals business. As I reported in my chairman's statement of November 2005, group turnover increased by 58 per cent from £233million to £369million, while operating profit almost doubled to £37.3million from £18.7million. I said then that I was particularly encouraged by the increase as it was the sixth consecutive year of growth.

The Murrays Metals Group, I reported, "experienced its strongest ever year on the back of a rising steel market". I also reported that we had bought Ireland Alloys on August 5, 2004, which helped improve the performance of MIM even more.

In 2005 Murray International Metals made a key contribution to the performance of the Murray Metals Group – it contributed £172million to the group, 28 per cent of the overall group's total, making a pre-tax profit of £21.9million, up from £5.5million the previous year.

It had been the core of everything – we grew the whole group on the back of the metals business and its performance in the early days of North Sea Oil. So why then did I sell it?

The deal surprised people but the fact is, I thought that the business had peaked. I got offered £110million for it and I took it to buy other things. Thinking back to that moment now, it does sound like I'm a bit of a business junkie.

I still had Austin Trumanns, the specialist steel stockholding business which had started in the English Midlands in 1948. Austin Trumanns was turning over £150million but I thought the trade that Murray Metals was in had peaked and I wasn't far wrong.

Trading in the business had pretty much collapsed in 1986 and then it came back again. When I got the offer, I thought, 'Wait a minute, we're back again but maybe this is the time to get out because it could collapse again.' I put my efforts into Austin Trumanns and developing the other metals businesses.

Murray International Metals customers were in offshore and energy while Austin Trumanns was general construction. What was particularly good about the deal was that all the boys who made it got a few quid, Ken Cockburn, Pat Boyle, Willie Hamilton; all the boys that without doubt helped me build it up in different places – Paddy in America, Willie in the Middle East and Ken in Norway. When we sold it, they all got weighed in and rightly so.

It was a huge moment. We had sold the business to American private equity group Jeffries Capital Partners for £110million.

They then sold it on to the Japanese group Sumitomo who have since lost a fortune on it. They closed the premises I built at Newbridge as a warehouse. That business has now closed having lost £40million in its last three years.

Ultimately what happened is that I started up again and I have taken many of our original customers back. We got out at the top of the game and we and the key management team all reaped the benefits.

14

THE OLD FIRM

SCOTLAND HAS BEEN RIVEN WITH DIVISION FOR AS long as I can remember – East v West, Labour v SNP, Edinburgh v Glasgow and Protestant v Catholic, usually and correctly highlighted by the permanently negative rivalry that is Rangers v Celtic.

As I began navigating my way through the minefield that can be Scottish football I never wanted to accept the premise that the Old Firm fixture was the epicentre of sheer hatred. It was, however, a few red lines further up the mercury scale than intense rivalry. It was about winning at all costs, any which way you can, and it was definitely about rubbing it in.

As previously admitted I grew up an Ayr fan, mainly thanks to my father's and grandfather's affiliation with the club, but I'm not afraid to own up that I 'had a big team' – something that I know usually infuriates supporters of so many of the smaller Scottish clubs.

I never considered shying away from the accusatory question, "Ayr United? Ah, but what's your REAL team?" It was Rangers. I had spent so many great European nights with my father at Ibrox growing up that it couldn't be anything else.

As I mentioned earlier, my first proper experience of the Old Firm was at Ibrox on October 17, 1987, two years before I had bought the club. Graeme Souness had invited me along as his guest and I drove his wife Danielle from Edinburgh to Ibrox. I can still remember the emotions that day, like nothing I had ever, up to that point, experienced in football.

I spoke about nothing but the game for days afterwards. It was passionate and ferocious from first to last and even the aftermath would live long in the memory. It finished 2-2 but that really wasn't the story. Three players had been sent off and following a police inquiry, breach of the peace charges ensued. Numerous Scottish politicians were just itching to get involved. It was decades ago but incredibly, even now, no one seems to forget it or even wants to.

I can be a critical observer and one thing that did strike me after that game was the fact that Celtic fans were allocated almost a third of the main Ibrox stand, with a wall of police and security separating them from the Rangers fans. Celtic fans were also located in a section of the old Broomloan Road Stand AND the West Enclosure.

The second there was a contentious decision, I looked across and was shocked to see hordes of fans scrambling to get at each other. The stewards and police really struggled to keep order and it made me realise that action was needed.

It was madness to have opposing fans so close to each other, so one of my first decisions after taking over was to scrap the existing allocations. I consulted with our head of security Alistair Hood, I spoke to the police and I called two members of the Celtic board.

Everyone was in agreement and the police were probably the

biggest winners in that decision. In future, Celtic fans would have the Broomloan Road Stand and at Celtic Park, Rangers fans had a full away end. It made perfect sense and would set a template for all future games between the teams.

Kick-off times were also changed to minimise potential trouble. Remember, at this time, anything up to 100 arrests was not unusual during the build-up to, and following, an Old Firm game. Segregating the fans went a long way to reducing those numbers.

However, it almost backfired. Following a later Old Firm game at Ibrox, I was shocked to see how much damage had been caused by Celtic fans. Hundreds of seats had been ripped up and toilets vandalised.

I was angry and wrote to the Celtic director Chris Kelly saying that if it happened again, I would have no alternative but to ban their supporters from Ibrox. I don't think he believed me. His response was to write back claiming Rangers supporters had destroyed the toilets and lighting at Celtic Park. I sent Alistair Hood along on a fact-finding mission but of course, there was no seating at Celtic Park at this time and the toilets were extremely basic. Alistair could find little evidence of damage.

Inevitably, at the next Old Firm game at Ibrox, the same thing happened again. The damage was costing between £10,000 and £15,000 per game and that was enough for me.

I withdrew their ticket allocation completely. Celtic fans were furious. On their next visit, they had no supporters and the entire Celtic board refused to attend in protest, yet John Collins scored a goal and for a long time it looked like I would be getting plenty of egg on my face. However, Alexei Mikhailichenko scored an equaliser with 10 minutes to go. There was no one on the other side of the directors' box to politely smile at. I smiled anyway.

I had made my point and as far as I was concerned the matter was closed. I do accept, though, common sense sometimes just goes out of the window... on both sides.

There was and always will be so much at stake in Old Firm games. They were virtually league deciders. Nine times out of ten, certainly during my tenure, whoever won these games would win the league.

Also, technology was clearly beginning to change football. Once, on a match day, I went into the control room with Alistair Hood. It was just above the tunnel at Ibrox and I was amazed how closely fans could be monitored inside and outside the stadium. If someone stepped out of line or hurled something from Row D Seat 24, we could immediately identify the culprit and take action because 80 per cent of the crowd were now season ticket holders.

Around this time I was intrigued by the new Celtic owner Fergus McCann. I met him on numerous occasions and he was always pleasant to me. He was a canny businessman but he certainly did a solid job for his club by putting up the funds and getting them on an even keel.

As I said, he is one of the few men that has actually come into a football club and made some money before getting out again. So many of us are guilty of just leaving our brains at the front door and being tugged in so many different directions by all manner of obstacles, particularly fan pressure. I cannot imagine how much that has been ramped up since the onslaught of social media.

Fergus cleverly got in and out with his reputation not only intact but probably enhanced.

Dermot Desmond, who was to follow him, was different. Again, I met him regularly prior to games and we once had a private and lengthy meeting at my home seriously exploring the possibility of Rangers and Celtic joining the English Premier League.

It was organised by then Premier League chief Rick Parry and it involved five or six of the biggest clubs south of the border, Rangers and Celtic. Later, David Dein of Arsenal and Rick Parry, then chief executive of Liverpool, met myself and Dermot Desmond in my house. We all wanted to make it work.

The larger clubs in England were positive and saw the financial benefits but when the story eventually broke, it caused no end of grief north and south of the border.

The smaller Premier League clubs in England were threatened by it, despite both myself and Dermot offering to join their second tier before hopefully working our way up to the top league.

But so many Scottish clubs were terrified of missing out on the extra TV and gate money which the Old Firm generate. Ultimately, every team, owner and chairman has their own agenda and there were just too many obstacles. We wanted it to work but it was never going to happen and I seriously now doubt it ever will.

I have always believed Rangers and Celtic are much stronger together. They still have a collective bargaining power that matches anything from south of the border but Scottish football continually sells itself short.

———

Peter Lawwell was someone I knew previously. One of my companies GM Mining did business with Scottish Coal where Peter worked and I once invited him and his wife to Ibrox for a game. He was delighted to accept and back then was good company, but by the time he rose to become chief executive of Celtic he was on a completely different trajectory.

For nearly two decades he tried to build up a seat of power

and I honestly believe that by the end of his time at the club he was wielding far too much influence in Scottish football. At one point, after I sold Rangers, it seemed he was positively revelling in the demise of the club.

He held sway on committees through friends and always used the strength of his power base when he thought it was necessary.

Admittedly he was a well-paid employee, not an owner, and of course he had a job to do for his own club – and no one could argue he did it well for much of his tenure – but with very few influential or credible figures working to Rangers' benefit he became a pivotal figure in trying to grind them down and make them suffer.

To me, it seemed the mantra was always, 'Let's bury Rangers'.

During the first few years of my ownership I thought the TV deals we negotiated were decent, although nowhere near what was happening south of the border. We had a committee acting on behalf of SPL clubs which at the time included Rangers, Celtic, Aberdeen, St Johnstone and Partick Thistle.

But as the 90s wore on and the top flight of English football went global, the Scottish game seemed to become less and less important and the deals began to slide backwards. The TV lump sum was negligible compared to the figures being bandied about in England.

At a time when our smaller clubs needed a degree of certainty every year they never achieved it. That was solely down to the fact that there was little value for money in the TV contracts.

Nothing has changed and, more importantly, NO-ONE has changed, particularly the custodians at the top of the game in Scotland, who in any other business would have been more accountable and would never have survived as long as they have done. Those at the top of our game need ousting but who is going to change things? Who is going to be brave enough and smart enough to transform the system and our game?

———

The Rangers v Celtic mind games would always begin early. On Monday morning the newspapers would start building it up and there would be four or five days of interviews and analysis prior to a game.

This was one area where Walter Smith really stood out. Motivation. He would pore over the screed of stories and the endless quotes from players, managers and ex-players and he would even cut some of them out of the pages. He used others' words to fire up the players.

Hours before kick off, he would then paste some of the nastier articles on their locker or above the peg and he would tell them to their faces, "Just look what he is saying about you, son. Are you going to let him think that?" It worked time and time again, even although the players rarely needed extra motivation for the derby.

I think it has changed. Until recently so many of the players on both sides were fans before they became players. Proper Rangers and Celtic men. Now, most of them are hired guns. Of course they still give their all for the team and the manager but a historical understanding has gone.

My own ritual on the day of the game involved leaving Edinburgh at 10am, arriving at Ibrox around 11am and sitting quietly chatting with Graeme, Walter, Dick or Alex before sharing a sandwich.

At 2pm I made myself available to other Rangers directors to discuss issues that they might want to raise. And then I would meet directors from Celtic or any other club before kick-off.

Most clubs were courteous in their pre-match gatherings

but for some reason Steven Thomson of Dundee United rarely participated. Bizarrely he would always prefer to sit outside the stadium in his car then stroll into the directors' box seconds before kick-off. It was odd. Maybe I am doing him a disservice and he was just a big fan of BBC SportSound. On the other hand, Dundee United's Doug Smith, who had played with Walter Smith at Tannadice, was an absolute gentleman on his visits and I always looked forward to a catch-up with him.

I used to get pelters from Celtic fans which I have always accepted was just part of the game. Every time I stepped off the bus at Celtic Park, the hostile chants began but no matter how bad mine were, Graeme Souness always got it worse, Walter, very rarely.

The match that stands out for me was on May 2, 1999 and sadly dubbed The Old Firm shame game. We went to Celtic Park and won 3-0 to clinch the league but referee Hugh Dallas was wounded by a coin thrown from the crowd then later that evening he had a brick lobbed through the window of his home.

It was an evening kick-off to suit Sky Sports schedules and the atmosphere was ramped up right from the off. Celtic had to win to prevent us winning the league and it was just never on the cards. Our fans were ecstatic from the moment Neil McCann had scored the opening goal in 12 minutes and I can still remember heading back into town with the team and watching a double decker full of our fans almost tipping over in Bridgeton as they scrambled to one side of the bus to gleefully mock Celtic supporters.

Everyone connected with Scottish football would probably expect me to say that Celtic fans were the most difficult. They really weren't.

Dad's my boy: David, aged six, with his father Ian. at Hamilton Races *(right)*. Ian and David's mum *(below)* Roma at a dinner in Ayr and David wolfing down birthday cake at the Belleisle Hotel in Ayr

Try, try and try again: David *(back row, second left)* was an outstanding points scorer for Dalkeith Rugby Club

High rollers: David, with school pals Paul Clancy and Phil Sinclair en route for a wine trip and rally to France

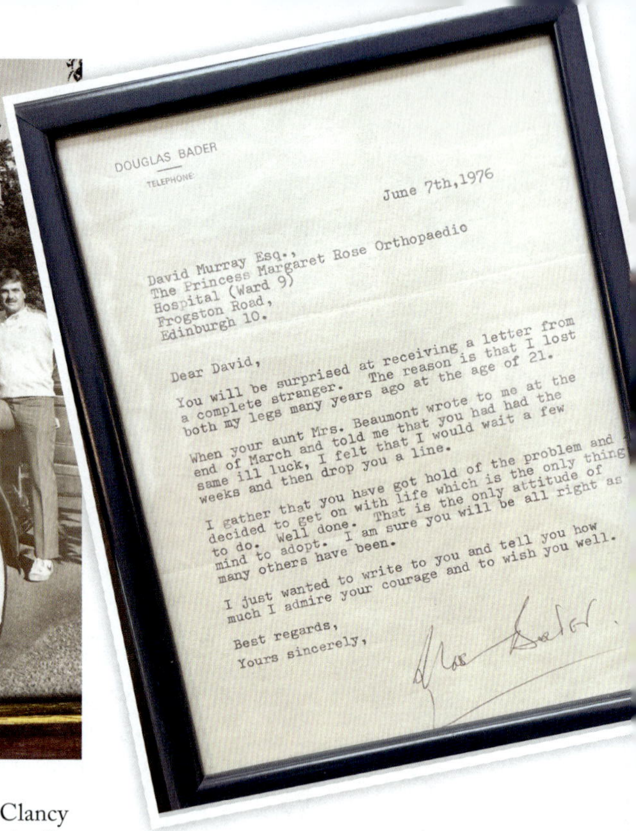

DOUGLAS BADER

TELEPHONE

June 7th, 1976

David Murray Esq.,
The Princess Margaret Rose Orthopaedic
Hospital (Ward 9)
Frogston Road,
Edinburgh 10.

Dear David,

You will be surprised at receiving a letter from a complete stranger. The reason is that I lost both my legs many years ago at the age of 21.

When your aunt Mrs. Beaumont wrote to me at the end of March and told me that you had had the same ill luck, I felt that I would wait a few weeks and then drop you a line.

I gather that you have got hold of the problem and decided to get on with life which is the only thing to do. Well done. That is the only attitude of mind to adopt. I am sure you will be all right as many others have been.

I just wanted to write to you and tell you how much I admire your courage and to wish you well.

Best regards,
Yours sincerely,

Life lines: The words from Douglas Bader that gave David inspiration after he lost his legs in a car crash

CRASH VICTIM'S PLEDGE TO HUNDREDS OF WELL-WISHERS

I will not let you down

IAN McLAUCHLAN

By Jim McGhee

David Murray, the 24-year-old East Lothian rugby player who had both his legs amputated after a car crash, lay in his hospital bed and made a promise to the hundreds of people who have wished him well.

"I will get there. I will not let them down," he said.

As he began several weeks of painful physiotherapy in the Princess Margaret Rose Hospital in Edinburgh before getting his artificial legs, he had a special word of thanks for the captain of the Scottish rugby team, Ian McLauchlan.

David, until his accident an enthusiastic member of Dalkeith Rugby Club, said: "Ian came in to see me last week and said he would be back with a surprise.

"He returned on Monday with Douglas Morgan, the former Scottish scrum-half, and tossed me a rugby ball. It was the one used in the Scotland - Ireland match in Dublin, and both teams had signed it. It lifted me quite a bit.

"I do not think I would have been as far ahead if I had not been for all the good wishes I have received. The surprise of the rugby ball was the climax. There was no reason for the guy to do that at all."

The accident, which ruined David's rugby career, happened almost two weeks ago as David, of 45 Charteris Road, Longniddry, was returning from a match against North Berwick.

He scored the winning points in his team's 15-9 victory and joked about last night's return clash.

In the Dalkeith Shield match last night, Dalkeith beat North Berwick by 18 points to nil.

The historic rugby ball he will treasure was taken home by his wife Louise (22) for safe keeping. In the meantime, David is concentrating his efforts on overcoming his cruel handicap and getting back to Louise and their two young children.

"They said physiotherapy would start next week. But I said it should start now. I am determined," added David.

Backing him up has been the invaluable support of many people.

To all of them, and all the others who sent cards and telegrams, including several rugby clubs, David said: "I would just like to thank everybody and say they need not worry. I will not let them down."

DAVID MURRAY . . . with a message to his well-wishers

I promise: David pledged to Scotland rugby skipper Ian McLauchlan and hundreds of well-wishers that he would bounce back from car crash trauma

So brave: David's late wife Louise pictured at his 40th birthday in Prestonfield House, Edinburgh

Maul together: The rugby ball signed by Scotland and Ireland players given to David one week after accident

Shake on it: In November, 1988 David is welcomed to Ibrox by Graeme Souness after buying Glasgow Rangers FC

Big plans: David announces proposals for the new club deck on the main stand which cost £25million

The close season: David and Sean Connery in the Ibrox Director's Box for a summer friendly

Nearly men: The Rangers team which lost the 2008 UEFA Cup Final to Zenit Saint Petersburg in Manchester

Mo-ment never to forget: On July 10, 1989 Rangers sign Maurice Johnston

Two of a kind: Ally McCoist and Paul Gascoigne celebrate a cup win

Gr-eight day: Archie Knox, Gazza and manager Walter Smith celebrate 8 in a row at Ibrox

Five across the back: Alex McLeish, Walter Smith, David, Graeme Souness and Dick Advocaat at the wedding of David's son Keith

Bond of friendship: David and Sean Connery enjoy a glass of wine in Sean's Gstaad apartment

Scare: In July, 2011, David recovering in Edinburgh Royal Infirmary, two days after an operation for an aortic aneurysm

An honour: Her Majesty The Queen presents David with his knighthood at Holyrood on July 4, 2007, for services to business and charity

Family first: David, Keith and David at a dinner in L'Enclume in Cumbria

The ground where most abuse was delivered was actually Pittodrie. I don't know if it was a hangover from the days where Fergie had turned an entire city against the West of Scotland but every time I went there, you could feel the wrath… and it was only a matter of feet away. There was no hiding place.

The visiting directors' seats were bang in the firing line and the Dons' fans proceeded to dish out some shocking insults from the first minute to the last. Stewart Milne was well aware of it but nothing changed in all the time I went there. Graeme did, as you might expect, little to calm the situation. Eventually I did raise it with Stewart only to be told in no uncertain terms that he suffered exactly the same treatment at Ibrox, which I know was not the case.

I think I eventually gave up after my fifth visit. That was the day that I had asked one of the directors' room serving staff if we could please get an extra sandwich due to the numbers in the room. He disappeared for five minutes and came back from the kitchen with the extra sandwich. I said thank you then the waitress asked me for £10 which, after looking slightly surprised I, of course, paid immediately.

When the Aberdeen directors came to Ibrox next time, I made my point by laying on the biggest spread we had ever provided. There was no extra charge.

The Aberdeen relationship – probably borne out of events on the field – was always tense. I vividly remember sitting in my car in South Street in St Andrews when two Dons fans leapt from the street on to the bonnet of my car and started booting the windscreen and screaming insults. All I could do was drive off – fortunately for them, quite slowly.

My relationship with the Rangers fans took a bit of a hammering at one point after I tried to curb some of the songs. I had no choice but to take action. The club's reputation was in tatters across not only Scotland but Europe as well and I was so tired of the constant bile and of the Billy Boys and F*** the Pope… and it seemed that fans were hellbent on pushing politicians and even UEFA into the fray. It was almost goading.

The First Minister at that time – Jack McConnell – had called a summit and following that I agreed that action would be taken.

I met with a cross-section of Rangers supporters groups and released the following statement:

'These supporters groups represented should be applauded for coming forward in recognition of the importance of this issue. I am delighted at the progress we made.

'Over the last two years the club has strived fervently under the banner of Pride Over Prejudice working with the authorities to impose indefinite and lifetime bans.

'I look forward in the coming weeks to implementing some of the actions that were discussed. It is absolutely clear to all concerned that all supporters now need to commit to silencing the minority.

'This meeting coincidently had coincided with UEFA's written grounds for the decision rendered by the Appeal Body in relation to Rangers' two Champions League matches against Villarreal.

'UEFA have issued the Club with certain directives in order to combat sectarianism. Firstly the Club has been ordered to announce 'measurable targets in order to reduce sectarian behaviour amongst its supporters'. Secondly 'to control their anti-sectarian activities by producing comprehensive statistics that are communicated to the public'.

'Finally to make a public address announcement at every official fixture, be it international or domestic, stating that any sectarian chanting and any form of 'Billy Boys' songs is strictly prohibited.'

David Edgar of the Rangers Supporters Trust, Mark Dingwall

of Follow Follow and Jim Templeton of the Rangers Supporters Assembly then jointly agreed the following statement:

"The message now could not be clearer – that the spotlight is upon the supporters and the club and it is their duty to work together to stamp out the minority who are damaging the reputations of all those connected with Rangers Football Club.

"Not only does this small minority tarnish the reputation of Rangers, but of Scottish football and our society in general and hopefully anyone who is interested in Scottish football will work with us in assisting to eradicate this behaviour."

My name was all over this and some of the earliest fan websites used it against me and began a campaign of Murray Out, all this whilst still winning the league that season The vitriol was nasty and made me question myself and my actions. Did I go too far in banning certain songs?

It was crystal clear that so many of the fanbase just did not want to change. Following Rangers every week was their life so that definitely became a bit of a turning point in my time with the club. But I did have to act. We were under the microscope from so many authorities and organisations. I'd been taking my boys to games for a long time and they knew all of the songs but deep down they realised that I had to try to bring the club into the 21st century.

I feel sorry for those men and women running football clubs now. The expectation from fans is wild, tens of thousands of them all seem to have business degrees and inside knowledge and they care more about the balance sheet. They make such ridiculous demands. In the old days all they truly cared about was the result.

Fans today are also not shy at expressing opinions and they have so many outlets at their disposal to vent their feelings. Of course they are perfectly entitled to do so but the vast majority of 'opinion' seems to be just cruel, and it is relentless. Over the past few years, I have had to change my Wikipedia page countless times when someone mocks my disability or accuses me of drink-driving at the time of my accident.

During my initial years of owning Rangers, the football debate would properly begin on the day leading up to a match, we would all analyse it, managers, players, media and fans, during and afterwards on a Saturday evening and then a bit more in-depth on a Sunday. You might debate it with work colleagues on a Monday but that was it more or less parked until the next weekend when the cycle would start again.

Now? Every single fan is a journalist, millions of them, all without a filter. It is a 24-hours-a-day social media onslaught and the threats and the language can be frightening. It is all-consuming and unhealthy.

Over the past decade I've spoken to so many football club owners who just want the sick keyboard fans to stop the drip, drip, drip of personal, poisonous bile. In most cases, not all, the owners have an attachment to the club or a love of football and they will not continue to put their families through the mill. Sadly I fear there will be no change until it is properly policed. I cannot understand why it isn't.

Football, and in particular, the rivalry with Celtic, was all consuming. I worked out, around the same time that I was banning the songs, that the club was taking up 80 per cent of my time and energy… and that would always be to the detriment of my business.

15

WALTER AND ME

THEY SIMPLY DON'T MAKE MEN LIKE WALTER SMITH anymore. I am not a sentimental sort but I treasure and keep a text that Walter sent me 10 days before his death on October 26, 2021. I don't need it as a reminder of his class, although it illustrates that – as every interaction with him did.

Rather than thinking of himself, Walter was apologising for not making it to my 70th birthday on the Royal Yacht Britannia in Leith. It read: "Chairman, a very happy birthday. I hope it goes as planned and both you and the family have a great day. Apologies again for missing out, Walter and Ethel."

At Walter's funeral, which I attended along with Graeme, there was a photo of him and Ethel, his wife, together as toddlers in their prams. That was how long they had known each other for, so I was very touched when Ethel recently told me that the great thing that we had as manager and chairman of Rangers was mutual respect.

I was at the club for 1,250 games and Walter was manager for 626 of them, just over 50 per cent. We were so tight together, there was almost a telepathy between us. You know how the other one thinks and the lines you don't cross. He had his area of responsibility and I had mine, although I was more involved in the football side than with Graeme, as I learnt more about agents and Rangers' traditions over the years.

Walter's qualities were crucial to the success we had under Graeme, and then even more so after Souness's departure. He was a catalyst, who could bring people together with his authority. Technically, he was very good. Walter could read a game and many a time I saw him turn matches with his substitutes and tactics.

I've seen him win a cup final despite being reduced to nine men after two red cards, the 2010 League Cup final against St Mirren. That was one of 21 trophies Walter delivered in his two spells in charge, a haul of silverware second only to the great Bill Struth in Rangers' history – Walter deserves to be regarded with the same reverence.

I'd spoken to Walter even before I agreed to let Graeme leave for Liverpool, to see how he felt about taking over. I think he then spoke to his family, which was the right thing to do, before opting to stay rather than join Graeme at Anfield. I was delighted.

It's easy to see it now, with the benefit of hindsight, as a smooth transition on our way to nine consecutive titles, but Aberdeen pushed us extremely hard that season and Walter had a battle on his hands to ensure we finished top. It was a tense, edgy time for both of us, but he was my first choice to take over and he had a contract right from the start, contrary to some reports that it was only confirmed after we won the league against Aberdeen on the final day.

We had to weather a serious wobble before that showdown when we lost 3-0 at Motherwell in our penultimate match. I was concerned after that, and Walter would have been, too. We had injury problems, and several players were patched up to play through the pain to get us over the line. John Brown, for example, needed an injection in his Achilles tendon to play against Aberdeen.

They say that everybody remembers where they were when John F. Kennedy was assassinated in 1963, but I imagine that most Rangers fans, excluding those inside Ibrox to witness it in person, can tell you where they were when Mark Hateley rose above Michael Watt to head the first of his two goals into the net. It was crucial for Rangers, for me as chairman, and for Walter, as he stepped out from behind Graeme to become Rangers' manager in his own right.

In my life and business, there are many major decisions I've had to make and that would be one of them. Your gut instinct tells you what the right thing to do is and it told me the man to turn to was Walter. I never regretted that. We were so fortunate to have him ready to take the reins.

Walter was a good man-manager but had a steeliness about him – you wouldn't want to cross him or get on the wrong end of him. He didn't change. He was always consistent, the same guy all the time. He kept all his old friends from football, guys like Dick Campbell and Doug Smith. They were pals he'd had for years.

I think that's how he got Archie Knox from Manchester United, because he and Walter were such good friends. Immediately after coming in, Walter identified Archie to be his assistant. The attraction of Rangers for Archie, of leaving Manchester United, was a great credit to the club and Walter.

They worked as a team and had a fantastic bond. Archie spoke his mind. He had been a successful manager himself and was a tough guy. He had a saying about players which I loved, 'don't sign him, chairman, his erse has dropped', which meant their legs had started to go and they weren't carrying their backside properly.

Walter was a good listener. I think I have only learnt that relatively recently, that you learn more by listening. It's a form of cold-reading someone isn't it? When you come into a meeting to discuss something, it's important to get the other person to show their hand first, so you know what you are dealing with.

He had a gravitas about him, too. He was always immaculately turned out. I find it amazing when you have 65-year-old managers wearing tracksuits and trainers. They think they are one of the boys, going on the trip to Tenerife. Walter had a maturity about him in all aspects of his life. He'd come up from a hard school – trained as an electrician – so he was well acquainted with things outside of the football bubble.

We'd go away for a few days together when we could and we spoke every day. I remember sitting on the beach one day in Jersey with Walter, just talking about life. We were good strategists.

We would have a forward planning meeting to ensure we stayed on top every season and Walter would lay his current team out in a 4-4-2 and where he thought we could improve it. Then we would figure out who we could afford, who would be leaving and who would be doing the deal. It sounds bloody basic in retrospect but that's the way we operated and it took us to nine-in-a-row.

We'd have lunch together before the games at Ibrox during that remarkable run. Walter, Archie and I. Tiny, the chef, made us fish and chips before every game. This continued for years until we had a bad couple of games and I said I thought we should change it. I was just back from France and said, "Do you fancy a salad niçoise?" So Tiny had to go and get tuna, olives and anchovies. Then, after the first time we had it, we said, "b****r this, let's go back to the fish and chips."

Home or away, the rule was that I was not allowed in the dressing room within an hour of the game. That came about after the 1992 Scottish Cup semi-final when we were playing Celtic at Hampden, I jokingly said to David Robertson pre-match, "Davie you're soft as f***, you never kick anybody, you need to get wired in." The game started and he was sent off within two minutes. Walter looked at me and said, "Never again!" Ally McCoist saved us in that match – he scored a goal, and we went through.

———

At Ibrox, I'd be in the manager's room, always available for any director who wanted a meeting with me about the running of the club. In the second half, if the game was going well, I'd go and stand in the tunnel and my car was waiting for me outside. If we lost, I'd stick around, which fortunately didn't happen too much. The win rate then was more than 65 per cent.

Some people might not have liked me because I wasn't party to the 'Rangers social set' in Glasgow. I'd do my business and go home but I loved the banter in the manager's office before and after games, there was a piss-take there – no matter who you were.

Walter built shrewdly on what he inherited from Graeme, despite the 'three-foreigner rule' in place at the time, which unfortunately included our English contingent. You don't just get success because you spend the most. Look at Manchester United since Sir Alex Ferguson left. Walter had the ability to look at individual signings, but also to put them together as a unit. His initial signings were Andy Goram from Hibs, a deal that Graeme began working on, and David Robertson from Aberdeen.

Both proved brilliant business and became part of a predominantly Scottish side that carried us to a domestic treble and so close to a European Cup final in 1992/93. We beat Leeds United, England's champions, home and away, in the first season of the Champions League, which Campbell Ogilivie, our secretary, had been so integral to creating.

I was younger then, not far off the age of some of the players, so you maybe relate with them in a different way than you would today. The banter was amazing, non-stop stuff, the bond was good, they socialised together, with Walter at the helm. We had no training ground, so we used to go to the West of Scotland cricket ground and at Jordanhill School in Glasgow to train and maybe some of the spirit came from that.

We had players playing for the jersey, mainly Scottish, which not many clubs have now, including Rangers. That Scottish core to the dressing-room was important but more and more, at all clubs, players are hired guns. You get people who have been with you for three weeks kissing the badge. The manager should be telling them to stop taking the p*** out of the fans. Rangers have completely lost their Scottish identity and need to get it back to be successful again because Celtic have it through players like Callum McGregor, their captain.

The win over Leeds was particularly sweet and enhanced the reputation of Scottish football in general. In theory, Leeds should have beaten us, but we had that grit and determination to overcome them. In the first game, Gary McAllister scored at the start and it was stunned silence at Ibrox but then big Dave McPherson looped one in and we win 2-1.

Winning away to Howard Wilkinson's side at Elland Road, other than beating Parma 2-0 at Ibrox when Dick Advocaat was manager, is as good a performance as Rangers produced when I was chairman. Yet we couldn't repeat that season's run again for some reason. There were early exits in the qualifiers to teams like Sparta Prague, Levski Sofia and Gothenburg, and heavy defeats to the likes of Juventus and Ajax, Europe's elite then, when we did make it through to the group stage.

In Graeme's final season before Walter took over, we lost out to an excellent Red Star Belgrade team, featuring Robert Prosinecki, Sinisa Mihaijlovic and Darko Pancev. I had a private jet and picked up the boys in Jersey.

When we got there, the police were waiting for us on the runway to take us through the crowds to the stadium. There's 80,000 inside hours before kick-off and five or six fires going on the terraces. It was an amazing atmosphere. These matches were political meetings just before the war in the Balkans started.

———

Forests have disappeared due to all the newspaper analysis of why we struggled to translate our success in Scotland into better European performances. On reflection, two reasons stand out for me. Firstly, Rangers' squad was better suited to domestic football – you could even include the wins over Leeds in that category – than continental competition. Secondly, the Scottish season should have started earlier in the summer to give all our clubs a chance to hit their stride before facing opponents who were often well into their seasons when we met them.

I don't think we had the tools for European football – we had the tools for domestic football. We could take on Leeds because that was effectively domestic football but look at the quality Marseille had in what was effectively a semi-final against us – Rudi Voller, Didier Deschamps, Jean-Pierre Papin. We had the grit and determination, but sometimes you need that extra bit of quality just to turn it for you and we maybe lacked that, collectively, despite later adding world-class players like Brian Laudrup and Paul Gascoigne to the squad.

Did we have the right players, tactically? Did we have the desire? Maybe those teams were hungrier because they saw their way out in life, to get a transfer and do better for their families. It was a combination of things, including bad luck at times.

It doesn't help Scottish football every year that we start the season too late. It sounds like an excuse, but it's factual. I don't think it prepares you properly for Europe. It's okay when there's a club straight into the Champions League, but teams who play in the qualifiers, go in cold.

If we started and finished the season a month earlier, because we are not going to be in many European finals at the end of the season, it would remove what is a huge disadvantage. Teams are playing a few friendlies, one league game and then a knockout in Europe. We could start in June, because that way you are up to pace. If you play a team from Sweden, they are 18 games into their season. It does have an effect. It's like a boxer who is ring-rusty before a big fight.

The wins over Leeds whetted many people's appetites for more games like that and led to talk of Rangers and Celtic joining England's Premier League, which would have transformed us financially. Like I mentioned earlier, momentum for this probably peaked around the millennium when David Dein of Arsenal and Rick Parry, then of Liverpool, met myself and Dermot Desmond in my house. Like Fergus McCann, I got on fine with Desmond and could talk openly to him, principal to principal.

They were supportive of it happening, but when they went and spoke to the other clubs it turned into a case of turkeys not voting for Christmas. We said we would go into the lower divisions initially and work our way up, but the initiative and interest just drifted away. Some of the top clubs wanted it, not all of them, but it was the same clubs rotating at the bottom who didn't.

It would have transformed things for us, without a shadow of a doubt. We would have had to make Ibrox an 80,000-seater stadium. A bit like Liverpool have done recently, by putting tiers on top of tiers to increase the size of Anfield.

Laudrup's agent was Vincenzo Morabito, and he was a good contact for us in Italy, although it was Archie Knox who did a lot of the legwork on that deal. We paid £2.5million, but I don't think there's any doubt we got value for money. And although any Rangers player is naturally under scrutiny, Laudrup told me that when a game went badly at Fiorentina, he and Stefan Effenberg, the German midfielder, had to be brought out of the stadium in the boot of a car!

One of my big disappointments was that Brian didn't stay at Rangers in 1998. I met him in the Channel Islands with his wife and I thought he was going to stay, but he had freedom of contract and went to Chelsea. That was his choice. We couldn't expect to get the benefit of freedom of contract, then when it went the other way to moan about it. Those are the rules of engagement and we'd done some big deals that way ourselves.

A good agent is one that gets you the deal you want. It's a concern when I see former players running out of money soon after they retire. That means their agents haven't done their job properly. We dealt with many agents over the years, and I still don't know where the money we paid to a couple of them went – I am not sure if the players got it all.

I hate to say this, but looking back it also depends how important you were down the pecking order, which players you were offered by them. There's no doubt that clubs like Juventus and Real Madrid were first in the pecking order back then and we were down the food chain a bit. You hoped that by working with people, you would move up that chain.

You had to be sharp in your game to sign coveted players in the face of fierce competition for their services and it often helped that we had that short chain of command compared to other clubs and to Rangers now. If you have numerous people who have put money into a club and they are wearing a blazer and a tie, they have all got a say and it can take too long to do a deal or to react in complicated negotiations.

———

I am not sure some supporters realised how difficult it was to keep doing these deals and delivering players like Laudrup and Gascoigne. I used to meet fans' groups and come out of the meetings and think, 'God, almighty' about their expectations of who we should be signing, but you had to respect that because they had spent £480 on a season ticket.

Another awkward deal was signing Duncan Ferguson from Dundee United for £4million, then a British record fee, in 1993. Jim McLean was not the easiest to deal with, but Duncan was determined to join us. He was delighted to sign for Rangers and started off quite well, but a relatively minor incident in a match against Raith Rovers at Ibrox eventually led to him going to jail due to previous convictions for assault.

He should have been banned for a few games. For it instead to be taken up by the Procurator Fiscal, when you look back now, is totally ridiculous. Plenty of similar incidents weren't dealt with so severely. Is that the microcosm of Scotland? It was like a kid-on head-butt in the wrestling, where they stamp their foot on the ground to make a noise, that he aimed at Jock McStay.

Another Italian agent we used was Andrea D'Amico, who represented Alessandro Del Piero among others and was excellent.

I met him when we were over at Juventus and took a beating there in the Champions League and he brought us Lorenzo Amoruso. Walter had gone to watch Fiorentina and Amoruso was playing against the original, Brazilian Ronaldo and came back and said we should try and get him. Manchester United were also after him. We had Amoruso and D'Amico waiting in the office for a fax to confirm that offer but, thankfully, it never arrived.

Amoruso was one of several Italians that Walter signed in his final season. He loved Italian football for its tactical sophistication and particularly Marcello Lippi, the Juventus coach, who looked like Paul Newman. We signed Sergio Porrini from Juventus, who was a 'steady Eddie' defender we possibly paid too much for at £4million. Amoruso missed most of the season through injury, though, and striker Marco Negri scored for fun to start with, but then got injured and was never the same player afterwards.

The pursuit of a 10th title in 1997/98 – to overtake the nine won consecutively by Jock Stein's Celtic and give our fans the bragging rights over their rival – also wore down some of our veterans, who missed more matches than they previously had. People don't realise, but it takes a mental and physical toll going for trophies and titles. There's a cumulative effect that can catch up with you.

European exits to Gothenburg in the Champions League qualifiers, then Strasbourg in the UEFA Cup didn't help, and I probably made a mistake by saying in advance that Walter would be leaving in the summer of 1998. I was trying to be honest.

I'd love to renegotiate some of the deals or correct mistakes I made, but I had to start planning ahead. I identified Dick Advocaat to take over and had to go to Eindhoven, to meet Harry van Raaij, PSV's chairman, to take his manager away.

He was even less happy a month later when I came back for

left-back Arthur Numan, a Dutch international. Between times, Numan had flown over to watch a Celtic game on TV, which could never happen today.

What was it that Walter said at the time? "David Murray must be the only person who sacks you in a nice way." We were very close and a big part of it was being straight with him and not negotiating with other managers behind his back. I couldn't meet him and say, "How have you been this week?", knowing I was talking to his successor. It wasn't my style.

It was difficult for Walter but I had to plan. We could have tried to keep it in-house but that wouldn't have lasted. Dick came to a game where we were playing Hearts and said, "I want to sign Neil McCann". Life goes on, Rangers carries on, it wasn't a disrespect to Walter to do that. I suppose I could have sold the club then but I admit I had the football bug at that stage, and it never crossed my mind to do so.

Walter had the last laugh anyway because I had to ask him to come back as manager at the start of 2007 after an underwhelming 35 games under Paul Le Guen. That second spell was a bigger success because he had fewer resources to work with.

The first era was a continuation of Graeme, then fine-tuning with Gascoignes and Laudrups, but we'd hit rock-bottom under Le Guen. I had a pre-Christmas party with 100 guests in November 2006. I asked Walter if he would come back at it, and I think I convinced him, even if Ethel wasn't so sure about the idea. If people want to criticise my tenure, fine, but in the final five years with Walter, we won eight more trophies together.

We were toiling when he left the Scotland job to take over, yet 18 months later, we were in a European final. Walter came in with a different mindset. He'd had a hard shift at Everton, then he'd been Scotland manager, so he came in totally focused on

A new era: David at the opening of his new Murray Group HQ in South Gyle, Edinburgh, 1990

Escape: Plane crash took two lives but F1 star David Coulthard walks off

Race ace Coulthard tells of escape from 140mph plane

amazing disaster

UK OK: David and Richard Branson at the Scotland launch of Margaret Thatcher's UK 2000 initiative in Norton House Hotel which Branson later bought from David

Eck of an appointment: David unveils Alex McLeish as manager of Rangers in December, 2001

Stay with me: David has kept special gifts including a one-off signed CD set from Rod Stewart who spent time at his house in New Zealand

Beginning of Le Guen-ned: French manager Paul Le Guen was unveiled as the new Rangers manager in March, 2006

Murray happy returns: David and his sons celebrate Keith's 21st at Hopetoun House

Laughs Anne smiles: David welcomed the Princess Royal to a SABAT awards lunch in a marquee on the pitch at Ibrox

Proud mother: David hugs his mother Roma during a celebration lunch in Edinburgh after receiving his knighthood

Still game: David and Graeme have remained close pals for almost 40 years and are pictured at David's Perthshire home in 2024

A big deal: Building in Glasgow built by David's Premier Property Group was sold to Strathclyde Pension Fund for £66m

On a plate: Highly-successful Murray Steel warehouse in Sheffield

Man of steel: David visiting the Murray steel profiling facility in Middlesboro, Teeside

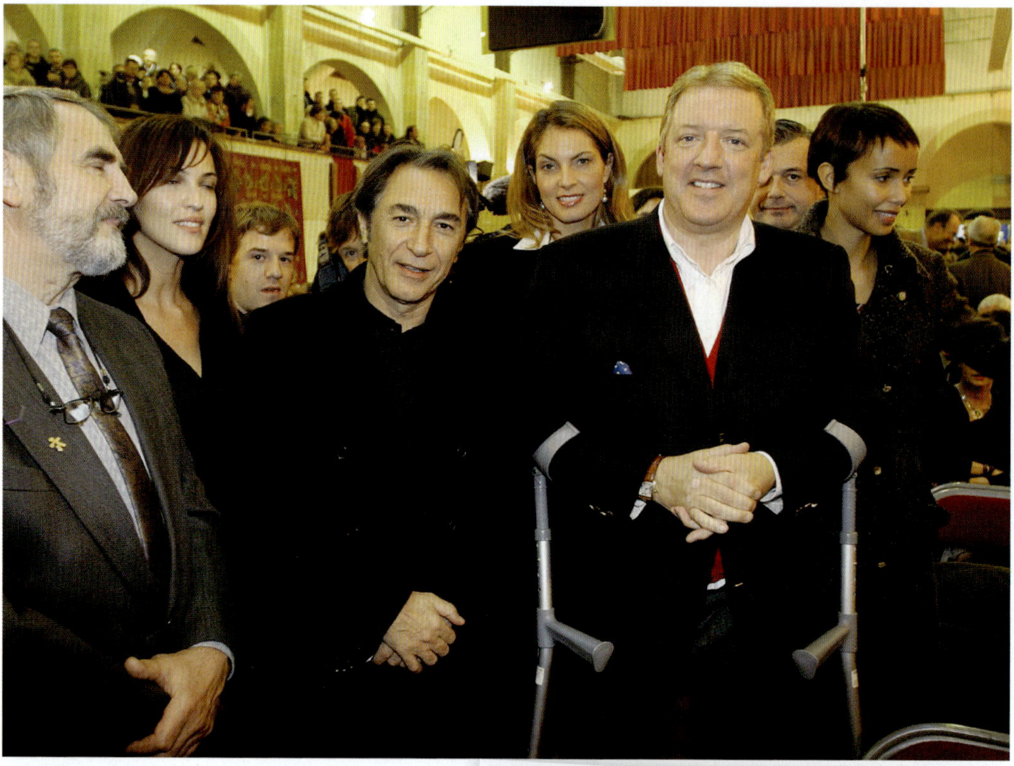

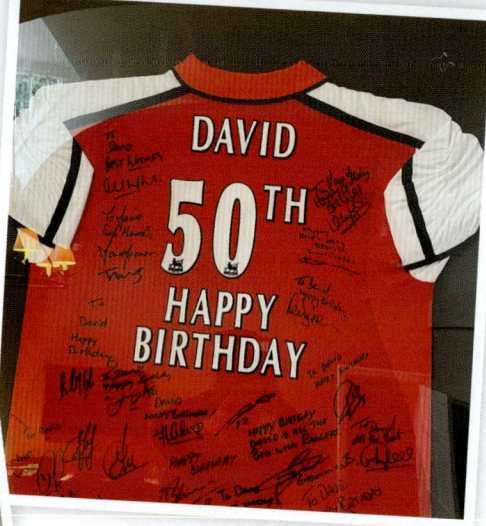

Winning bid: Buying the Presidents barrel at the Hospice de Beaune 2007 *(inset)* A 50th birthday gift from David Dein and the Arsenal team

HERIOT-WATT UNIVERSITY

We the undersigned Principal and Vice Chancellor and the Secretary of the University certify that

David Edward Murray

has by resolution of the Senate been awarded the honorary degree of Doctor of the University

In witness whereof this certificate is sealed with the Common Seal of the University on the 15th day of November 1986.

Principal and Vice Chancellor

Secretary of the University

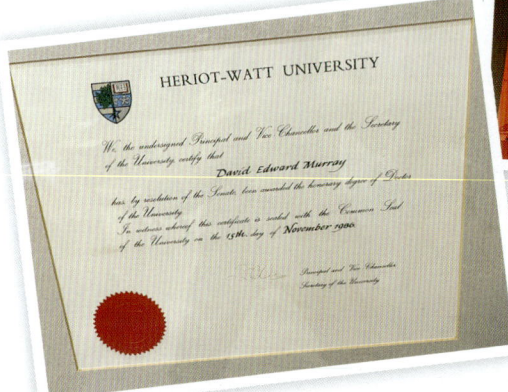

An honour: The honorary doctorate from Heriot-Watt University that he received at the age of 35

Next generation: Keith, Gill and their sons, Struan *(left)* and Fraser in December, 2024

Special moment: David was a proud man at granddaughter Charlotte's christening in Gullane, East Lothian in 2009

Just Capital, Murray: The family business has bright future in the hands of David and Keith

Man in the middle: David surrounded by his family at his son's 50th – partner Sarah *(front left)*, granddaughter Georgie *(back left)*, son David, granddaughter Charlotte and daughter-in-law Sarah

what he wanted to do. He knew how he wanted to make it all happen.

Le Guen had signed the Swede Karl Svensson, but he was too soft for Scotland and Walter knew the weakest link is the one that the opposition would ruthlessly exploit. He wanted men, which I don't think Rangers have now, men like David Weir and Christian Dailly, experienced players he trusted and who passed on good habits to the younger players in his squad.

I remember meeting Danny Wilson at a hotel prior to a Hibs game at Easter Road. The club had financial problems and the crunch was coming and he was playing alongside Davie Weir at centre-half at 17. We sat outside together, and he said, "I want to go."

His agent had set up the deal for him to go to Liverpool for quite a lot of money. I said, "It's your choice, you're a young man and it is a short career, but you could learn a lot more by staying, playing beside big Davie. I am easy either way and that's the truth." He lacked a bit of experience, and I think he went away too early.

The run to the 2008 UEFA Cup final in Manchester had the same resilience and grit about it as the 1992/93 team, yet it was perhaps more of a tribute to Walter's tactics as it was achieved with a less talented team. It was hard to believe it was happening as we passed test after test. In theory, the opposition had 11 better players, but we were a better unit.

I'll never forget Allan McGregor's save at Werder Bremen, then run by Steven Whittaker in Lisbon, the penalty by Nacho Novo to win the semi-final shootout at Fiorentina. It was a phenomenal thing. Walter covering over the cracks and creating a unit that pulled together with camaraderie.

The great move was bringing in Ally McCoist, Kenny McDowall

and Ian Durrant in with him. That was good for the banter with the boys. There is a time to be hard and soft, a time to be pals and not pals, Walter had that blend. They came as a package. Walter had been at Scotland with Tommy Burns and Alistair. He wanted youth with him and a bit of spirit, so he had Alistair, Kenny and Durranty. Kenny was the main coach, and Ian was a good part of that unit. His terrible injury curtailed his career, but he fought back well from it and was a Rangers man through and through.

Paul Jackson, the doctor, was already in the club when Walter returned. I met him for the first time at a youth cup final at Hamilton's ground one night when Charlie Adam and Chris Burke were playing and he was great for the club, and for me, personally, as a doctor.

Paul wouldn't panic, and he always walked on in his blazer and flannels, rather than in a tracksuit and boots. The doctor is there as a medical expert and co-ordinator, not pretending to be a player or coach. He has a practice with 5,000 patients, so he's seen it all. He's highly respected in medical circles and has several doctors in his family, although his father worked at the Ailsa Shipyard in Troon.

Unfortunately, the run to the UEFA Cup final was followed by losing a Champions League qualifier at Kaunas in Lithuania just as the economic crash caused the banks to fail and the steel and property markets to collapse. I could have coped with everything else, if the bank hadn't gone bust. I could have traded my way out of it gradually, but it was just too much to deal with at once.

I had £900million-worth of joint ventures with the bank, which were written down in value to a major extent. That was the only time that Walter and I came anywhere close to a falling out. He said the bank were running Rangers at that point, to which I replied that the banks were running most clubs in that case.

Walter always said he would leave when I did and he did so, signing off with yet another title, his 10th as manager, in May 2011. I thought I had the written guarantees from Craig Whyte, after passing the club to him, that would give Ally McCoist a fighting chance as Walter's successor. That wasn't the case and it soon became apparent that the bills weren't being paid, far less the manager being backed. Again, much more on that later.

Nobody will ever know how good a manager Alistair could have become for Rangers because it was going very well for him at one stage, but I have no doubt that when things are going bad off the park, they do affect things on the park. It filters through. He never stood a fighting chance. You knew that Nikica Jelavic, the Croatian striker, who was one of Walter's last signings was going to go – and off he went to Everton in 2012.

There was a murmuring on the board that was a distraction for the players and fans and it certainly wasn't kind to Alastair. I am still friendly with him today.

It's very hard to judge him as a manager because of those circumstances but thank God he was there because after the troubles he became the glue that would somehow hold it together under enormous pressure.

And I am so happy that he's gone on to carve out such a hugely successful media career. His knowledge of British and European football is good but when you couple that with his endless enthusiasm and his insider stories, you have the perfect co-commentator. He deserves it.

For some of the senior players, it was maybe like your father's gone and your brother is managing you after Walter and we all know how that feels now. Football misses him, his friends miss him and, most of all, his family miss him.

Alistair and I, or anyone else who worked with Walter, will

confirm he was a class act, a giant of Scottish football. He was the embodiment of what it means to represent Rangers with dignity and humility. I'll be keeping that text from him.

16

GAZZA

PAUL GASCOIGNE WAS CLEARLY AT HIS HAPPIEST ON A football pitch and it was a proper coup for Rangers that he brought his full repertoire of skills to Scotland during the peak years of his career. It's no secret that it was off the pitch that Paul had to deal with demons and I suppose, in that sense, he was the classic case of a flawed genius.

He was such an effervescent personality around practically everyone that he met – adored by players, fans and a media that just couldn't get enough. But beneath the swagger and the jokes, he was also an incredibly lonely man.

Paul needed constant company and he struggled to sleep or simply switch off from the attention. He was anxious and lived on his nerves constantly.

There were so many memorable moments, mainly good ones, from his time with the club. I vividly remember one night, he turned up at my home in Edinburgh and I invited him in. He actually challenged me to an arm-wrestling contest and his face was a picture when I took off my legs and got down on the floor to accept the challenge. Now over the years my shoulders have taken the strain that should have been on my legs so I have a strong upper body. The result was that in a nanosecond, I nearly took his arm off. He lay there stunned, then burst out laughing. No damage done, thank goodness, but it would have been a surreal sight for anyone who had walked in.

Another time, the night before a match against Hibs at Easter Road, I was due to attend a Rangers supporters club function in Musselburgh on a Friday night. I joked to Walter that I would take Paul, and, to my surprise, he backed the idea and said that it would stop him getting up to any mischief at the team hotel.

I picked Paul up and we went to the gig. I began chatting to a few people inside the function room but half an hour later a couple of worried fans grabbed me and warned me that our boy was standing at the bar sinking pints. It was just hours before a big game. When I got to him he said, "It's alright, chairman, I've only had two or three."

That was bad enough and I actually thought Walter might kill me, but he was fine with it and simply said, "Probably better that, than sitting here bored." Sure enough, Paul played so well the next day he was man-of-the-match.

If anyone knew how to manage Paul, Walter did. They struck up a friendship in 1994, when Walter was on holiday with his family in Florida. His sons Neil and Steven spotted Paul, Walter introduced himself and they just hit it off straight away. That was what sowed the seeds of us signing him from Lazio a year later.

Paul had become a global celebrity after starring in England's run to the semi-final of the 1990 World Cup and he signed for Lazio in 1992. The success of Channel Four's Football Italia television programme was due to following his adventures in Serie A. They marketed an entire series on him.

But by the end of the 1994/95 season, it was clear that Lazio were ready to let him go. Walter asked me and I said, "If we can get him for a reasonable price, let's go for it." Walter flew to Rome, knocked on Paul's front door and established that he was indeed prepared to play for Rangers, but we heard through the football grapevine that Bill Fotherby, who was the managing director of Leeds United, was doing similar groundwork.

Eventually the deal came down to three clubs: Rangers, Aston Villa and Chelsea. Sergio Cragnotti, who owned Lazio, and the Cirio tomatoes group, and Dino Zoff, the legendary Italian goalkeeper who had become Lazio's coach and then sporting director, set up a series of meetings at The Ritz Hotel in London with Ken Bates of Chelsea, Doug Ellis of Aston Villa and us.

I was scheduled to go in first, but tactically I didn't want that, so I made an apology to say I'd been held up when in fact I hadn't been. I really wanted the last kick of the ball to negotiate the deal. I went into the room and immediately said, "Mr Zoff, nice to meet you. You are famous for only losing five goals in one game in your life." and he replied, "Ah, ze Hibs." Napoli had lost 5-0 at Hibs in November 1967 and I was at that game as a 16-year-old. We did the deal from there.

It was a huge coup for us. We paid £4.3million for him and the negotiations with his agents went on and on. There was a certain amount of risk because Paul had a bad injury at Tottenham and then another serious one at Lazio where he had only played 47 games over three seasons, but Walter was a great fan of his and they became close during his time at Rangers.

Even when Paul was going through a troubled patch, Walter insisted that he come to his house on Christmas Day for lunch with his family.

What a circus it was when we signed him. There has never

been a crowd at Ibrox for a signing like there was that day. We still had the financial power to compete with the big English clubs at that time, although that era was coming to an end. We had successfully signed Brian Laudrup the summer before from Fiorentina, which was down to Archie Knox, and rejuvenated his career at Rangers and we almost reached the Champions League final a few years before.

When Paul was involved in controversy, we always stood by him and sometimes took severe criticism for that. He was the biggest story in town and I am sure he put extra figures on to other clubs' gates and definitely on to newspaper sales. He loved playing pranks on his teammates but behind all that he was an incredibly generous person.

When Rino Gattuso joined Rangers in 1997, Paul told him that everybody was entitled to a half a dozen suits made by the club's tailor. So Gattuso gets all these suits made then gets the shock of his life when a bill drops for more than two grand when he had been told it would be free. Paul had been at the wind-up, however. He then picked up the tab himself.

He was close to Alan McLaren, who we signed from Hearts, and I went to Alan's house to say goodbye to Paul when it was time to sell him in March 1998. It was a touching moment. Paul went into his bag and gave me an expensive cigar and a beautiful bottle of Bordeaux wine.

He went to Middlesbrough the next day. He has said I told him not to go, but that's not true. What happened the next day was he said he wanted to come back, and I said, "Paul, it's too late. We've sold you and you can't come back."

I found out that Bryan Robson, Middlesbrough's manager, trained him hard in the morning to make sure he was fit before they did the paperwork, which shouldn't have happened. Imagine if he'd got injured. Middlesbrough paid £3.4million, so we had him for three years for his wages plus £900,000.

Paul often wondered if he could have helped Rangers to 10-in-a-row, but, after Walter went he wasn't sure how he would have got on with Dick Advocaat. He jokingly said, "Advocaat? I didn't know whether I'd play for him or drink him."

17

IT'S AN HONOUR

WHEN I WAS 16 AND STILL AT SCHOOL, I WENT ON AN adventure that ended rather badly. One of my school pals, Roger Sutherland, had saved up a bit of cash and bought a battered old Commer van with a faded McKinlay's Whisky livery peeling off the sides.

We rounded up two other friends and just took off but this was no trip to North Berwick. Roger just kept going down the A1 and by next morning, we were in central London.

We hadn't told a soul. We parked up in a side street somewhere around Marylebone and went off looking for work. Within two hours, we all had jobs. Two of us were lugging meat around the Regent's Park Zoo for animal feeding time and the other two were hauling crates in a fruit market.

It was pennies in the pocket more than pounds, no questions asked, but it all came to a crashing halt a week later. We were sleeping in the van when there was a loud thump on the back door.

It was two policemen and they asked, "Are you David Murray?

I replied, "Yes". And they told me, "Your mother wants you home." I began to argue back and he lowered his voice and said, "Right now, son."

It was fair enough. We returned to Edinburgh that day and when I finally showed up at Broughton High School, the deputy headmaster Ecky Thorburn hauled me aside and growled at me, "Murray. In life, we all get two certificates – one when you are born and one when you die. I don't see you getting too many in between."

Another doubter-in-chief of my prospects had been my Aunt Bess who owned an off-licence in Ayr and a pub in Drongan. She had paid my last Fettes school-term fees of £600 before I had to make the switch to Broughton High in 1966 and she told me quite abruptly, "You'll never be as good as your faither."

On December 31, 2006 it was my aunt's fateful observations that I remembered as the New Year's honours list was announced. I was to receive a knighthood. James Dyson was also knighted and Rod Stewart was to receive an MBE.

Her Majesty the Queen bestowed the knighthood on me at Holyrood Palace in July 2007. As I went forward she quietly asked me, "How are the team performing?" I replied, "A bit like my last school report card… could do better."

It's one of a handful of moments during my life in which I was genuinely moved. Meeting Her Majesty and becoming a knight of the realm for services to business and to charity meant everything to me. My family was so proud. In particular I was thrilled for my mother, who had held us together through such difficult times when we were younger.

Following the ceremony I had a brief state-of-the-nation chat with Sir Malcolm Rifkind then headed to Cosmo in Edinburgh's North Castle Street for dinner with my family and friends and senior colleagues. Sean Connery even flew in from the Bahamas to celebrate with us. It was a day I will never forget.

My first award for business 26 years earlier also meant a great deal to me. I had come through the crash and its aftermath and had built up a good business, so much so that I had been nominated for the SABAT Award for Young Entrepreneur of the Year.

It was a prestigious award and I was actually surprised how nervous I was. It made me realise how far I had come in life and in business after my accident. Louise, who was so proud of me that day, was with me in the marquee at Prestonfield House when I collected it and I was in good company. Thomas Tait, a paper manufacturer, was the inaugural recipient 12 months earlier and then Brian Soutar got it the year after me. I remain a close friend of Brian to this day.

The next award I received was in July 1986. It was an honorary doctorate from Heriot-Watt University. As I sat there in the Church of Scotland building on The Mound, wearing my gown, I saw another graduate face that I recognised. It was a bloke called Bernie Heggarty who had been a fellow cross-country runner at Broughton High. I asked him about his life and he told me that he was a professional student and had just completed his third degree.

This was an alien concept to me. I wanted to build my business as quickly as possible and I realised that in my era very few of the entrepreneurs I know went to university. Some, like me, judged success not in academic achievement but in pound notes and fear of failure.

I rarely read books and I clearly remember Sean, who was self-educated and became hugely knowledgeable about all manner of subjects, talking about Fettes College. He said in his book: "Tony

Blair was here, David Murray was here and Sean Connery was also here. The only difference was that I was delivering the milk."

In December 2008, I was awarded an Honorary Doctorate from the University of Edinburgh in McEwan Hall. In my speech I recalled the school prediction from Ecky which by now seemed a distant memory.

Despite my knighthood being the greatest of honours I rarely use the title Sir before my name, at least in written correspondence.

Honours

1984 – Young Businessman of The Year
1986 – Honorary doctorate, Heriot-Watt University
2006 – Chevalier du Tastevin
2006 – Queen's Award for Voluntary Service
2007 – Knighthood, New Year's Honours List
2008 – Honorary doctorate, Edinburgh University

18

WINES IN A LIFETIME

"WINE HAS BEEN A PART OF CIVILISED LIFE FOR SOME 7,000 years. It is the only beverage that feeds the body, soul and spirit of man and at the same time stimulates the mind," wrote respected American wine maker Robert Mondavi.

It probably wasn't how I might have phrased it in 1979 as I began my proper education into the wine business... in Dundee city centre of all places.

Through my late teens and early 20s, I would perhaps have a glass at Christmas or on a special occasion. I was certainly not even close to having any deeper understanding of what was good and what was bad. And then after my car crash, I abstained from alcohol altogether for at least two years. Eventually, when I felt able to have a drink again, it was wine. Always wine.

I never liked beer or lager and the smell of gin or whisky was abhorrent to me because it only reminded me of my father's heavy drinking. I have never once drunk a spirit in my life.

One of our customers was a company called Kestrel Marine in Dundee. They made onshore structures for oil and gas platforms.

Their buyer was a man called Graham 'just call me Haggie' Haggart. These lunches traditionally ran over time, and I was buying, so I asked Haggie to choose the wine. He selected Chateauneuf Du Pape and seconds after it arrived, he sniffed it, inhaled some of the fumes, took a sip, sloshed it around his glass and exercised his jowls as if he was testing Listerine for the first time. I asked him if he was okay and he quickly explained his routine.

He was a member of the Dundee Wine Group and had been for years. He was massively interested in wines and the industry. He was also highly knowledgeable and we began doing business with his company.

For my 30th birthday, Haggie arranged the gift of an antique wine cradle which he purchased from the world-renowned wine expert Hugh Johnson. I was hooked.

Haggie then left Kestrel to work on the Hugh Johnson Wine Collection in London, which I had launched with Hugh and it sold all manner of accessories, decanters, glasses and corkscrews. We remained in contact and my knowledge of the business was constantly expanding.

Around this time I went to New Zealand on business and on the spur of the moment I bought a stunning house called Waimanu in Herne Bay, Auckland.

I immediately asked Haggie if he would like to go to New Zealand and run the house. He agreed and over the next few years he helped maintain and run it. It was a stunning property and many people rented it, including Rod Stewart and his then wife Rachel Hunter, the opera star Dame Kiri Te Kanawa, the actor Anthony Quinn and Paul McCartney. Rod in particular was a huge fan of the place and as a thank you for one of his extended stays, he sent me a framed picture containing a selection of his discs.

One day, Haggie answered the external buzzer at Waimanu and after a brief exchange, he opened the gates. Seconds later the gentleman appeared at the front door at Waimanu and came right to the point. He said, "I hope you don't mind the intrusion. I represent someone who would like to buy your home and he is prepared to pay $5million for it."

Haggie invited him in and immediately called me. The gentleman explained that he represented the Sultan of Brunei who was coming to Auckland for a Commonwealth Heads of Government Conference and he and his entourage would require a suitable property.

I didn't even hesitate. The house was duly sold, however, what I hadn't counted on was that Haggie was to become part of the package. He ended up going to Brunei to work for the Sultan.

By this time, I knew quite a bit about wine and at an auction in Christies, I began collecting it. When lot 21 came up – two cases of 1970 Chateau Latour, I successfully bid £900 for each one. The auctioneer was then obliged to ask me if I would like the other 12 lots and I said yes, much to the dismay of one gentleman who had his heart set on two cases. On the way out of the door, I agreed to sell him two cases but for £1,100 each. He was happy to pay it, which I suppose is not surprising – the wine is currently valued at £6,000 a case.

I began spending more time in France. I remained in contact with Haggie and met with Hugh Johnson who was a walking, talking encyclopaedia of wine.

I had also reinvested some of the Waimanu sale in the property in Juan-les-Pins on the Cote d'Azur and I had decided that I was going to get fully involved in the wine business. My younger son Keith would go on to play a huge role in this. Haggie agreed to come back from the far east, where he was now working, to help me and we immediately set about trying to identify a chateau and vineyard where we could make wine.

It did take a long time and we probably racked up thousands of miles but finally in 2005, we identified a Provence chateau called Routas, just over 100km north-west of Cannes. It bordered a famous estate called Chateau Miraval, later to be bought by Brad Pitt and Angelina Jolie but once also a music studio where albums were recorded by AC/DC, Sting, Sade and The Cure. It was pristine and successfully producing excellent wine.

Our chateau was in pretty poor condition and a major renovation project was required. But its location was something else. It was a 90-minute drive from my home in Juan-les-Pins. When it became clear that we were interested the owner welcomed Keith, Haggie and me to the estate and made us the most incredible bowl of pasta with top-quality truffle, clearly in a bid to seal the deal.

Of course, it worked but I vividly remember taking a couple of close friends to visit soon afterwards and after 10 minutes of the guided tour, which included countless musty and empty, dark rooms with loose floorboards and doors that were hanging off, one of them asked, "What the hell have you done?" I told them to ask me again later.

It was just the beginning of a project which has taken our family 19 years to bring to fruition. There are now 110 acres of vines, all producing and 90 per cent of what we make there is rosé.

The previous owners had focused entirely on red wine but Keith knew that rosé was about to take off globally in a big way. A

Provence wine called Whispering Angel was becoming a massive success story which just confirmed his theory. We settled on three varieties of grape – grenache, cinsault and syrah – and we have tweaked the percentages of each every year.

We now export to Thailand and Canada but the vast majority of our wine goes to the United States.

Our 290-hectare estate has wheat fields and olive trees and black truffles and porcini mushrooms can be foraged in some of the surrounding forests. In summer, red poppies and yellow sunflowers dot the land. It really is quite stunning – a place where everyone who has ever been there says they feel at peace.

The terrain is punctuated by this incredible geological anomaly, the 270 metres deep Infernet Hole (Devil's Hole) thought to have been created by a meteor. I wish I could get closer to explore it. The hole is a favourite refuge of local wild boar which are sometimes a little too fond of the Routas grapes. More recently, wolves have also been reintroduced into the area.

Chateau Routas requires constant investment. For example, a new harvest machine costs €90,000. As of 2025, 95 per cent of the vines have been replanted and the expert team of seven people are producing 280,000 bottles annually.

We were all totally thrilled, particularly Keith when, in 2018, internationally-renowned wine expert James Suckling voted Chateau Routas rosé best value for money and best of show.

In the early days, Keith had correctly identified the United States as the perfect market for our ambitions. He and his wife Jill bought a house in New York and began exploring the city and identifying distributors before venturing further afield across America. They knocked on doors – lots of them – and their persistence paid off. Today, Routas wine is available in 35 states.

The system of selling wine there goes back to the days of

prohibition and is a challenging one. It involves importers, distributors and retailers but once you have navigated it, there are huge gains to be made. Boston-based MS Walker, which was founded in 1933, is our biggest customer in the United States.

In 2022, Keith appointed a new winemaker – Fabrice Grossmann, a renowned rosé specialist following the retirement of Jean Louis Bavay, who had been at Routas for three decades. He is overseeing the installation of new equipment and techniques and we are all excited about the next decade.

Keith has also recently launched a special edition rosé in partnership with former Rangers star Brian Laudrup.

The wine business is precarious to say the least, primarily due to weather. In 2017 we had a disastrous year when just one night of heavy frost cost us dearly. We lost 60 per cent of our harvest. It was a devastating blow and it can happen at any point.

It's alarming to think that you can have a warm January and February, with the buds and flowers appearing, then in one single night in April so much damage can be caused. It is indeed an expensive form of farming.

During moments like these we have no choice but to call our customers and simply explain what has happened. Naturally they will be disappointed but practically all of them understand. Keith also has every weather app and is on the phone every day.

Back home in Scotland in 2007 we had bought a company called Wine Importers, a major distributor of numerous brands. And in 2011 we also took control of one of the country's oldest wine merchants Cockburns Of Leith – founded in 1796. In 2022, we opened a shop in Frederick Street, Edinburgh.

Cockburns' customers in the past have included Charles Dickens and Sir Walter Scott.

In 2006 we purchased Domaine Jeusiame in Burgundy, before

finally selling it in 2020. It was a complex and difficult business to manage. Burgundy wines are without doubt among the finest in the world but during our 14 years there we only had seven or eight full harvests and every year seemed to bring another niggly issue. We were all a little sad but relieved when it was time to hand over to the new owners.

I had taken Sean Connery with me when we originally bought the place and the father of the previous owner was so thrilled. He said we should open a bottle of 1929 Santenay Gravieres to celebrate. "It was the year I was born," he said. Sean piped up, "1929? That was a special year for me too. It was the year I was conceived."

I would love to remember this moment by saying that the wine was one of the finest I have every tasted. Sadly it wasn't.

My favourite wine is Musigny by Comte De Vogue. I open a bottle every Christmas Day. Sean told me that he couldn't see past Rioja which he had developed a taste for while living in Spain. He also loved our Routas wine and just being around the vines. Keith cannot see past Puligny Montrachet… and practically any other wine from Burgundy. They are special.

In the town of Beaune, I was made a Chevalier Tastevin – a prestigious honour for people from all walks of life who have contributed to the success of the Burgundy region where at that time we bought Jeusiame, we were the only British family who owned a vineyard in Burgundy.

I continued collecting for a long time. I once bought a case of six bottles of 2002 La Tache which I would dearly love to drink, however, it would be a gamble. It cost me £900 a bottle but is now worth £5,000 a bottle. If I have one bottle, the other five immediately lose value by not being part of a case.

There is great pleasure in sharing wine. In 2007, I bought what is called the President's Barrel at the famous Hospice de Beaune charity auction. Most of my close friends have been receiving bottles ever since.

When I go out for dinner, I'll always look at the wine list before the menu and I'm now confident enough to recommend a bottle to friends or colleagues.

It is rare that I have been truly disappointed by a bottle of wine, however, as I initially explored selling Rangers, a Russian buyer called Vladimir Antonov had expressed an interest. He arrived for a preliminary meeting and obviously knew about my love of wine.

He handed me a bottle of 2005 Richebourg DRC (Domaine Romanee Conte) which is without doubt one of the finest wines on the planet. I tucked it away and five years later opened it on a special occasion.

As I do with all good wines, I opened it two hours before drinking, just to allow the air in. That was the moment I realised that something didn't add up. The label was perfect, the colour of glass correct, everything about it looked right, however, the aroma was utterly rancid and one sip confirmed it… this Russian's wine gift was a fake.

I found out later that Mr Antonov was actually a banking fraudster who, in 2019, was arrested in London and after a trial sent to a penal colony.

19

THE MEDIA

I ACTUALLY HAVE FOND MEMORIES OF MY FIRST experiences with the media in Scotland.

In later years, the relationship was to sour slightly as certain writers and commentators queued up and were, it seemed, encouraged to take a verbal swing at me on a daily basis.

At one point, particularly around the time I sold Glasgow Rangers in such difficult circumstances, I would be waking up every morning thinking, 'I wonder what's coming today.'

Newspapers were always a big part of Scottish life. In the early 1960s, every Saturday night, my dad would send me to Ayr railway station between 5pm and 6pm where I would pick up a copy of the *Evening Citizen*, also known as the Green because of the coloured paper it was printed on.

It contained the afternoon football scores, but usually only up to half-time, and I couldn't really see the point of that, yet there was always a clamour for the bundle when it arrived. Around the same time as I was running home, in the town centre, fans were streaming out of Somerset Park and gathering around TV screens at the local DER shop where the teleprinter would be churning out the final scores. Saturday evenings were always exciting for a 10-year-old boy hooked on sport.

Throughout my teenage years, the *Daily Express* was the dominant newspaper in Scotland. My family bought it religiously every day but by the time I was making my way in business, the *Express* had moved to Manchester and had lost most of its Scottish readership. In my offices I always insisted on a *Scotsman*, the then-*Glasgow Herald*, the *Financial Times* and one of the tabloids, usually the *Daily Record*. Nowadays, with the printed products seemingly in permanent decline and shedding their news teams, I'll only purchase the FT on a Saturday and then the *Sunday Times*.

A tabloid editor once told me the two things that really sold his newspaper were the Old Firm and crime. If the two were ever combined, and it happened occasionally, the news stands would virtually sell out.

In 1990, I was approached by Charles Fraser, a prominent Scottish businessman, former chair of Lothian and Borders Enterprise and director of Scottish Media Group, and also by Jack Irvine, a recent editor of *The Sun* in Scotland. They asked me if I would be willing to back a new tabloid Sunday newspaper.

Now I have never seen myself as a press baron. While Rupert Murdoch and Robert Maxwell were going head to head in the tabloid wars with the *Sun* and the *Mirror*, owning a newspaper, for me, was just like any other business opportunity.

I was told there was a gap in the market so I agreed to back them, but quickly realised this investment was a massive mistake.

We assembled what was considered to be a renowned and hungry team of news and sports journalists, writers, advertising executives and columnists. We gave starts to some exciting new talent and a launch team was put in place in one of the empty office suites at Ibrox while we searched for a viable home, which eventually we found on the top floor of a building in St Vincent Street in Glasgow.

We agreed a deal with *The Herald* to print it and on March 10, 1991, the first edition hit the streets.

It was a sobering moment. Right from the off, everything seemed stacked against the *Sunday Scot*. The set-up costs were exorbitant, the technology I had been told was inconsistent, there was no 'dummy edition' to iron out any flaws, the first edition was riddled with errors and the first splash story really was a non-event.

But probably the most important factor was that I had not realised that half of Scotland would just never buy it in the first place, simply because of my association with Rangers. Looking back, that now seems rather obvious but we were desperate to give it a real push for the first month.

The first edition – backed by a TV campaign – sold 120,000, which nowadays would actually make it Scotland's biggest selling newspaper but back then it was a major disappointment. I knew by the end of September that it was never going to work.

It was to last just 18 weeks and during that time I lost £6million, however, before winding it up I paid every bill, every creditor and every member of staff. It was one of those deals you just put down to experience. It wasn't my first and it won't be my last.

Our managing director Jim McDonald had actually supported me all the way on the project and as a multi-faceted group, we were constantly looking for investment opportunities around this time.

I suppose it's a lot like running a football club. The chairman or owner leads by putting up the money and putting the experts in place that he thinks will bring success. On this occasion, we made a mistake and we moved on.

It's curious to look at the CVs of some of the very senior media people who were attached to the *Sunday Scot* and strangely there isn't one mention of the newspaper anywhere. One can draw one's own conclusion from such glaring omissions.

At least I can hold my head high. I delivered my part of the bargain on the way into the venture and I paid the bill, in full, on the way out too.

━━

As owner and chairman of Rangers I was constantly establishing relationships but Walter Smith and I had an agreement which never changed throughout the entire time we worked together. He handled all football matters, I was in charge of all business dealings. Media strayed into both camps.

The Scottish media were always trying their utmost to wheedle out snippets from Walter's playing side or from my business dealings but Walter and I never broke ranks.

I tried to make myself available to every journalist. I maybe didn't see eye to eye with them but I was the chairman of Rangers and it was my responsibility to speak to everyone… everyone that is apart from the late Glenn Gibbons. He was the one senior journalist who never spoke to me and to this day I still don't know why. It almost seemed like a badge of honour to him.

Of course there would always be differences of opinion – but as long as it was reported honestly and I had been given the chance to respond accurately and fairly, then I would not have a problem.

One of these difficult moments was when the late Scottish *Sun* journalist Rodger Baillie – who I had always enjoyed a cordial relationship with – called to tell me, "I have it on good authority that you are selling Ibrox to raise £40million." I replied, "That is categorically untrue, Rodger. It is a complete and utter fabrication and if you do write that it could have consequences. If a word of that appears, I promise I will never speak to you again."

It appeared as the back page in the next day's *Sun* and I was disappointed for Rodger because the decision had clearly been taken out of his hands.

The Scottish media were certainly friendly during my final five years. We won eight trophies, turned over £250million with a net spend of £10million and got to a UEFA Cup Final.

But then I made the mistake of selling the club to Craig Whyte – something that I bitterly regret and something that I will discuss in far greater detail later. We had even made a profit of £1million that year.

I firmly believe that if the Bank of Scotland had not gone bust, the football club would have had a chance of grinding it out but the steel and property markets had collapsed and to cap it all, Rangers lost to Kaunas in a European qualifier.

What I believe is called a media frenzy rapidly followed. Journalists who I previously thought were allies or that spoke to me regularly just waded in and turned on me. It was remarkable. It suddenly seemed that every editor, writer and columnist suddenly had a vested interest in the fortunes of Rangers.

In the 14 years since, I have certainly been on a different path and the journalists who called so frequently just stopped… until the day Walter Smith passed away. Suddenly my mobile went into overdrive and in the space of just an hour, I took a dozen different calls, most of them which began with the words 'Long time no speak'. I felt like I had stepped back in time.

I generally had good relationships with editors and understood the value of nurturing those one-on-ones.

Of course there have been moments I regret. After the writer and broadcaster Gerry McNee had been banned from our club, I spent a lot of time and effort smoothing things over and then invited him back in, only for him to write the most vicious article. He was actually predictable… one week the target would be Rangers, the next Celtic.

And it wasn't just the football journalists. The business teams could be even more brutal than the sportswriters. One of the senior editors at *The Herald* delivered what can only be described as a hatchet job after Murray Group had endured a difficult year. I learned later that his wife had lost her job that day and he was an angry man. His 'opinion' piece was a disgrace and I wrote a furious letter to their editor.

I had been in Jersey and invited the journalists Jim Traynor and Graham Spiers down to do interviews. During their trip I had taken them to the fabulous Italian La Capannina restaurant in St Helier but when Jim wrote the article on his return to Glasgow he decided to embellish it by describing the 'succulent lamb' on the menu. It's more than 25 years since he wrote that yet people still talk about it.

It's been a while since I've heard about it so just to remind anyone who's interested or who wants to bring it up again, the dish was called Costolette di Agnello Grigliate – grilled lamb pieces – and, believe me, they were indeed succulent.

Jim Traynor often had a go at me but he would always pick up a phone first and ask me questions.

I didn't always agree with what he wrote but I believed he was balanced in his reporting.

Aside from the brilliant Hugh McIlvanney, I had a great deal of respect for Jeff Randall, formerly a BBC business journalist and business editor of the *Sunday Times*. That was even before

THE MEDIA

I discovered he was a huge Rangers fan whose dad took him to Highbury to watch the annual Arsenal v Rangers friendly when he was a boy. We became close and he once joined me on a European trip to Copenhagen.

When I owned Rangers I never shied away from the press. We had a dedicated media department whose remit was to deal with the day to day issues and interviews and if things were going well on the pitch, I rarely heard anything from Scottish journalists. But if we had a bad result or there was any hint of a crisis at the club then that would always be my responsibility.

I always made it my business to front up and take the flak. I still do.

20

ME AND DICK
(AND PAUL)

WHY DID DICK ADVOCAAT SUCCEED AS RANGERS'
first foreign manager and why did Paul Le Guen later fail in the
role? The simple answer to that question is that Dick embraced
both the job and life in Scotland, while Paul did not.

In fairness, Dick also had a bigger budget to buy with, and he
bought better players with it. In both cases, I hoped their contacts
on the continent, after managing successfully in the Netherlands
and France, would bring better players to Rangers than a Scottish
manager could.

Not all Dick's signings worked out, but the team he built around
players such as Arthur Numan, Giovanni van Bronckhorst and
Barry Ferguson played fast, fluent football in the Dutch style
and he won five trophies out of six in his first two seasons after
succeeding Walter in 1998.

Paul's signings (and they were his signings) were
underwhelming by comparison – Karl Svensson, Libor Sionko

and Filip Sebo. The only success who survived to play for Walter's teams was Sasa Papac. Paul lasted half a season after taking over from Alex McLeish in 2006 before returning to France to manage Paris Saint-Germain.

Critics came out of the woodwork after that, to tell me where I'd gone wrong, but nobody was saying that when we announced that Le Guen was coming the previous March. He was regarded as a coup, not only for Rangers but for Scottish football, after winning four consecutive titles at Lyon and turning down the chance to take over at Benfica and Lazio before accepting our offer.

One thing I feel strongly about, and took pride in when I was running Rangers, was that we stood by our managers – and I will explain why that didn't happen with Le Guen, who was the exception to that rule.

What clubs do today if things don't go well is change their manager and hope they get a bounce. For example, when I was asked for my opinion by current members of the board, I advised Rangers to stick with Van Bronckhorst in 2022 rather than bringing in Michael Beale, so I am not being smart after the event. I felt there were too many sycophants influencing the board – pals of pals. A successful club needs one or two owners running it to work properly rather than too many small shareholders doing so with a wide variety of opinions.

The problem in the modern-day is that boards listen to social media and the fans too much and can't take a shouting at when they need to. I've had a few of those but I would stick by a manager in the bad times because it's a criticism of you as well, so you must pull together whenever possible and have a chat about it. I rarely had a cross word with my managers, I just said, 'I'll speak to you about it tomorrow'.

ME AND DICK (AND PAUL)

You must always remember that you are also criticising yourself when you sack a manager. Everyone now is about short-termism, but to have success, you must stick by people. You either believe in the person or you don't. If you are sacking the managers, there's an argument you could sack yourself, too.

I took quite a lot of pressure off my managers because I would stand up for them. It's not because of ego, but I wasn't frightened to go to a press conference, and I tended to do them when the proverbial hit the fan. I never went to many of the celebrations. If there was a big party for winning something, I was away home, but, if we lost a big game, I'd do an interview.

As chairman of a football club, it's very easy not to take responsibility and hide from the media and not let the fans know what is going on. If you do that, the club will drift. An owner, a chairman or managing director should inform their customers – they are paying the wages after all – but he also needs to see the bigger picture.

I remember meeting supporters' groups and they would put pressure on me to buy players, saying, 'we have to do this or that' in our meetings. Everyone is an expert. They don't look at the broader picture of a balance sheet, funding, running out contracts, freedom of contract, depreciation, auditing accounts and running the business as a going concern. It's a complicated thing and you are not always going to get it right. There seems to be less scrutiny of how the club is being run at AGMs now.

With Dick's appointment, we were able to put a plan in place, and a lot of that was down to Walter. He was disappointed, but he was honest and knew what we had to do. Walter wasn't interested solely in himself – he was also acting in the best interests of Rangers at that time.

I had to take a tough decision, as I'd done with Graeme before,

187

that we needed to make a change and Dick brought more than his famous brown brogues. He had a presence and discipline about him, and his team played good football. We had some great games under him at home and abroad.

My memory is that nobody stood out at the time as a Scottish successor to Walter. I felt in Scotland there was a stereotype. They had been to Largs to do their coaching courses, and they all knew each other.

That's not a criticism because it's down to each individual club, but I tried to break that and look at it as a European situation and I don't deny that bringing in players using the contacts that Dick had influenced my thinking, too.

We were fortunate to get him because he was in demand and doing very well at PSV Eindhoven. As I mentioned earlier, I flew over and had to deal with Harry van Raaij, their chairman. Walter and I had already agreed he would go at the end of the season, which in hindsight some people say is wrong, but all I was trying to do was be totally honest. I told Walter what I was doing, so Dick would come and watch games from the stand and gain an understanding of Scottish football.

I connected him with John Greig because I knew he needed a liaison guy, so Greigy got to know him right away and could tell him what to expect going up to Pittodrie on a Wednesday night, for example. They became close friends.

Dick started to identify players on these trips to Scotland, so we were able to do a lot of preparation in advance. He saw us play Hearts and said right away he'd like to have Neil McCann as a fast, direct winger in the Dutch style. Arthur Numan was signed after flying over to Scotland to watch an Old Firm game at my house, and other players were, too.

Dick said who he did and didn't want. He identified Barry

Ferguson, who was already getting first-team minutes under Walter, as a playmaker and Barry shone in some big European games for us.

Derek, Barry's older brother, was a good player for Rangers, too, but I had to tell him to behave himself off the park. I asked his mother and father through to see me at my office in Edinburgh. I always feel if you want a serious chat with someone, it's good to get them out of their place of work. I used to say that to Walter if someone was to get a bollocking.

They go into the manager's room, come out and think, 'I got away with that one', but I prefer saying, "Let's go for lunch or come to meet me and have a chat about it". It's fairer and has a better impact in terms of them understanding the direction of travel – rather than going straight back onto the training field and thinking you got away with it.

The Fergusons are a nice family, but Derek didn't listen to the advice, unfortunately. Wallace Mercer at Hearts bought him off us for £750,000.

Dick brought a foreign discipline in, some of the players found it hard, but he made Barry a better player. He was going into big Champions League games and holding his own. He liked the boys to be smart in blazers, brown shoes and ties. He'd had a decent playing career, then played for Chicago Sting in the USA and loved it there.

As a coach, he was good enough for Rinus Michels, the great Ajax and Netherlands coach, and good enough for PSV.

I got Dick on the way up. He came to us in 1998 when he was 51, but with quite a bit of experience already behind him. He'd been the Dutch manager at the 1994 World Cup, when they reached the last eight before losing to Brazil.

Dick was a football encyclopaedia and stressed that the game should be played on the ground, not in the air. British football was often about dominant big centre-halves who head the ball, but he'd point to players like Franco Baresi, who was 5ft 9ins at the back for AC Milan and say, 'look, you don't need to be 6ft 4ins'.

PSV played exciting football and, crucially, Dick bought into what we were doing while using his Dutch connections to sign players like Numan and Van Bronckhorst, whose agent, Siggi Lenz, I recall, had survived a plane crash in Surinam in which 176 of 187 passengers died.

Stefan Klos, the German goalkeeper, I signed myself because I knew the agent. There were rumours about him getting silly money, which were absolute rubbish. It took about three meetings to get him for £700,000 as he came towards the end of his contract at Borussia Dortmund and that proved fantastic value for Rangers in the seasons that followed.

His first signings were Lionel Charbonnier and Rod Wallace on the same day. Wallace for free, Charbonnier for £1million. Wallace was a bargain and scored freely in his first season, while the French goalkeeper was an interesting individual. He was into horse racing and art and started well before a serious injury led to us signing Klos.

Dick had a crazy first game against Shelbourne Rovers in the UEFA Cup, where we were losing 3-0 after signing all these players. My son David was in a pub in Tranmere, where the game was being played, and said, "Dad, this is a riot going on here," but we recovered to win 5-3.

Tugay, the Turkey midfielder, was another great signing, and I thought we let him go a wee bit too early. It was through Graeme Souness we got him, his Galatasaray connections, and I am sure that helped Graeme take him down the road to Blackburn

Rovers, too. Dick was a fine technician and tactician. He used Tugay as a sweeper in Monaco in the Champions League and he did very well that night as we won 1-0. Everything was Dutch. Dutch assistant, Dutch doctor.

We had a Dutch identity, despite players like Ferguson and McCann, and I admit that led me to push for the signing of Colin Hendry, to add another Scotland international to the squad. That was a joint decision by us but it didn't work out.

Dick insisted on a new training ground, too. He said we had to bring players through. It cost £14million to build, and we got a grant from the Scottish Sports Council for £1million. It was Dick's idea to call it Murray Park. People think it was my ego, but it wasn't. I thought it would be a legacy to leave behind, but unfortunately, the way it turned out, that didn't happen.

The people who came in after me wanted to change everything, but they didn't change it for the better. They had bigger plans than I had, but let's see their track record. Graeme Souness always said to me, 'show me your medals'. Well, on that score, we won 35 trophies in my time as chairman/owner – 1.6 per season.

Dick and I agreed we'd look at some other facilities, so we went on a plane to Middlesbrough first and had a good look round theirs.

Having been in the property business, I realised we had to buy floors, chairs and lights that had endurance. Then we went to Liverpool's new place, the academy run by Steve Heighway, their former winger, and it was impressive. We also saw their training ground at Melwood, where Ron Yeats, the former Scotland international who recently passed away, showed us around. We did all that in just one day.

Building it put us in debt, but it produced players like Alan Hutton, Chris Burke and Charlie Adam, who all became assets of the club. I am disappointed that Rangers don't seem to be getting the players through today like that.

We sold Hutton for £9million to Tottenham and their chairman was Daniel Levy, who had been on the board at Rangers to represent ENIC and is a shrewd businessman. ENIC probably wouldn't have run Rangers the way I did, but I was under different pressures. They were looking at it from an investment point of view because they were trying to build a global football brand, putting £40million into Rangers and receiving a return on it.

When you looked at Dick's CV, he had worked under Michels, and I was an admirer of Dutch football – the style of it. You go back to Johan Cruyff at the 1974 World Cup or later to Ruud Gullit at the 1988 European Championship and so many players of a Surinamese background in the squad.

Scotland still doesn't exploit this area as well as other football nations do. Our rugby and cricket teams have successfully incorporated players from New Zealand and South Africa for example in recent years, so why do we not do it more in our supposed national sport?

When I met Dick, he told me his principles and I liked them. We had to have the training ground and we had to have a clear system that reflected how he wanted to play football. It was pleasant to watch, and it brought some remarkable results in Europe. You go to Bayer Leverkusen and win over there, the Parma victory, with the likes of Gianluigi Buffon, Fabio Cannavaro and Lilian Thuram in the opposition squad, that got us into the Champions League, then beating PSV home and away in the group stage of that competition.

I went to Eindhoven, and they were a classy club who looked after us. I left just before the end and heard the roar as Jorg Albertz scored our late winner, then we destroyed them at Ibrox when Derek McInnes did a fine marking job on Luc Nilis, their Belgian striker, and cut off the supply to Ruud van Nistelrooy, who Manchester United later signed for £18.5million.

We couldn't compete with that fee or for Jaap Stam, who United paid PSV £10.6million for just before Dick joined us. It was around then that the gap in television income for Scottish clubs compared to their English counterparts really started to tell in the transfer market and on our revenues.

The Dutch players we signed were in the £3-5million bracket but still excellent value. Numan and Van Bronckhorst, who we later sold to Arsenal for a £3million profit, set the standard and were later joined by the likes of Michael Mols and Fernando Ricksen. Dick tried a few strikers, but the two he liked most were Mols and Shota Arveladze.

The night Mols got injured against Bayern Munich in Germany in November 1999, we were on the verge of reaching the knockout stage of the Champions League. That knee injury had the same impact for us as when Henrik Larsson broke his leg against Lyon a fortnight earlier for Celtic. Mols was magnificent at that time. How many players had to buy a ticket to come back in again when they tried to get close to him? He had the tightest turn of any player I have seen. Those serious injuries affected both clubs and the players.

Fernando is sadly no longer with us, after a typically courageous battle against Motor Neurone Disease, but he was a character. Dick liked Fernando so much as a player, he later took him to St Petersburg with him, too. I loved him as a person. I went to the training ground one day and he thought it was funny to rock my car to set off the alarm and I joked, "Any damage and that will be off your wages."

Dick always had the ability to change a game. It wasn't just the success; it was the style with which he achieved it. I was trying to change our approach into one better suited to European football and it worked to an extent.

The fans all turned up dressed in orange for a Scottish Cup final. While some of that was down to a lingering sectarian element among the support that the club had to grow out of to progress, I acknowledge that for other fans it was a genuine way of saying they were proud to be playing attacking football from the Dutch school, full of good passing and movement.

With Graeme and Walter, there was the Scots connection with the jokes and the patter we would share, but Dick had a good sense of humour, too. We had some lovely days at Gleneagles with my family and spent Christmas Day together, too. It was a different relationship to that which I had with Graeme or Walter because Dick had come to a foreign country, but we were still in the trenches together with that telepathic understanding – he knew what I was going to say, and I knew what he'd say.

The Dutch are direct people, experts on everything, and there was no messing about with Dick. It was black and white. He fell out with a few players. He and Lorenzo Amoruso had a fraught relationship, and he didn't fancy Colin Hendry, so they didn't get on. Paul Ritchie didn't work out either after we signed him for free from Hearts, and I am sure he was disappointed about that, but he got paid, quickly moved on to Manchester City, has done alright for himself and is a decent young man.

Dick rarely changed his mind but at one point he told me to sell Neil McCann and Jorg Albertz to Gordon Strachan at Coventry City, then changed his mind, leaving me to break the news to a furious Strachan, who didn't hold back in telling me how angry he was.

Some people blame the Advocaat era for the financial problems that subsequently affected Rangers, but his net spend was £36million. When signings didn't work out, we sold them on. There was a churn to our squad, and we sold players like Van Bronckhorst on for a profit. I'd argue that the increased value of the squad was far more than £36million.

It's easy to look back with hindsight and be critical, but I was living in the moment, Saturday to Saturday, and I had one plan – to win. You have supporters breathing down your neck, you have your personal pride, and you are the chairman of Glasgow Rangers, so I knew what I wanted to do. Yes, we probably overspent at times. When the bank was no longer there due to the financial crash of 2008, which nobody knew would happen, most struggled to cope with that situation.

Signing Tore Andre Flo for £12million from Chelsea, a Scottish record at that time, was the one you could criticise most if you were being objective, but I was quick enough to move him to Sunderland for £9million. Bob Murray, their chairman, later wrote in his book that I did a number on him.

So we lost £3million but he did score 38 goals in 72 games.

There's no doubt, though, that we ran out of steam in Dick's third season. Martin O'Neill arrived at Celtic and they beat us 6-2 at Celtic Park, then we beat them 5-1 at Ibrox with Flo scoring on his debut. Celtic were leading in the league, though, and I had to ask Dick to step back.

There's an argument in any football club under any manager where they have a shelf life if they are giving the same message all the time and there's no doubt that the same players responded to Alex McLeish, winning both cups and then a Treble after he took over in 2001.

When I made that decision, I brought Alex to my house and had Dick in the meeting with me, so there's no question of stabbing anyone in the back.

We ran into Dick again in the 2008 UEFA Cup final during his time at Zenit St Petersburg and that was a strange situation. They had just bought a midfielder called Anatoliy Tymoshchuk for €15million, and I am not sure we had spent that much on our whole team for that game. Carlos Cuellar, outstanding in our run to the final, cost £2.5million from Osasuna, and we then sold him to Aston Villa for £7million.

Dick always promises his wife that he's giving up football, but he never does and he's now coach of the Curacao national team. It's not a coincidence that he managed Rangers for more games than any of his other jobs and has said it was the happiest spell of his long career.

He could have returned as an interim manager in 2017 after Pedro Caixinha was sacked. Rangers were playing Hearts at Murrayfield, and I got a call from somebody on the board at Rangers, asking me to check if Dick was available. He was but the board decided against it.

While Dick took to Scotland well, I don't think Paul Le Guen's family settled here. Dick involved himself with Scottish culture more. He was happy, whereas Le Guen was a fish out of water. Dick was bullish and confident, while Paul was more reserved, like a schoolteacher. He was quite bland was Paul, very matter of fact, Dick was more passionate.

I don't think the fans understand the need for a manager to be close to his chairman, but it's important. I tried to build the same bond with Paul, but the chemistry just wasn't there.

I invited his family to my house one day and had to rush back from a lunch with Gordon Brown, then Prime Minister, Alistair Darling, his Chancellor, and Mervyn King, the Governor of the Bank of England at Gordon's house in Inverkeithing. There was one picture up in Gordon's house – of Jim Baxter playing keepieuppie at Wembley against England in 1967. Along with Gordon and Sir Alex Ferguson, I later donated money for a statue of Jim in his home village of Hill O'Beath in Fife.

Le Guen didn't have the CV of Dick. He'd only been at two clubs. What is quite hard to judge is: Is it the club or the manager? At Lyon, he had Juninho Pernambucano, the Brazilian playmaker, who was a free-kick specialist and maybe carried the team. Paul was from a wee village in the north of France where his mother was the mayor. He was not a bad footballer, who had won the Cup Winners' Cup with PSG and had 17 caps for France.

When you looked at it on paper, I thought he was the right man for the job. We have all got degrees in hindsight, but Le Guen was flavour of the month and we tracked him down and arranged to meet him. Martin Bain, the chief executive, also spoke to Ralf Rangnick, who had done well at Schalke and did well with Austria in the Euros last summer, but we identified that Le Guen was the guy and arranged to meet him.

It was pouring with rain, and we went by private plane to this small airport at Dinard in northern France. There was no minibus to pick us up, so they sent a fire engine and I had to hold on to the back of it with my crutches to go into a terminal to meet Le Guen and Yves Colleu, his right-hand man. We sold them the idea to come to Rangers, told them what the budget was, and it was a big coup for us because his CV at the time was right up there.

I was working on the philosophy again that he would have the connections to bring players, which we had been quite successful with before.

By March 2006, he had agreed to replace McLeish. He signed a three-year contract. It was reported that he was the first Catholic to manage Rangers. I didn't even ask that or care. Dick could have been a Catholic for all I knew.

Paul had a poor start, won only two of his first 10 games and was knocked out the League Cup by St Johnstone, but things accelerated after he dropped Barry Ferguson, the captain, at Christmas. I was in Paris for New Year and Andy McInnes, the former *Daily Express* journalist, phoned me and said, "You have a problem – Ferguson and (Kris) Boyd are refusing to play", so I said to my guests, "I've got to go back".

The biggest problem was a lack of mutual respect between Paul and the players. That was the bottom line. He wasn't improving players, wasn't motivating them. After a short period of time, it was a movie he didn't want to be in. He was quite distant, and he had his own disciplined views. I knew it was coming, but I didn't know how it was going to come and, basically, he gave me the opportunity, which I went for.

The late Philippe Flavier was one of my contacts in France, a very good French agent. I'd seen a story in a French newspaper linking Le Guen to Paris Saint-Germain, so I asked Philippe if there was any truth to it. He said Le Guen had met PSG – that was all I wanted to know.

I jumped on the plane and flew back, and asked Le Guen to meet me at the Norton House Hotel near Edinburgh Airport. I sat him down and said, "I believe it's not going too well". I had already found out, too, from the person looking after the family, that they weren't happy. You need all the cards before you play your hand.

"I am sorry to say this, but I believe you have been in negotiations with PSG," I continued. "And if that's true I need to report it to UEFA." His face went red before I added, "I think the best thing is you just go". He said, "When?" and I said, "Now. Sign that, here's one I made earlier."

I didn't pay any notice payments to him or his staff and, sure enough, they all went to PSG and he then went on to manage other teams. It was a short period, the track record was there but results weren't great, and a decision had to be made.

Inadvertently, he made it easier for me, but it was wrong for him and us. The chemistry wasn't right. I wouldn't phone him on a Saturday night and talk about football, like I would with Dick, Walter and Alex. They could phone me in the middle of the night if they wanted to. That relationship wasn't there. We only spoke on matchdays. Did we get it wrong? In hindsight, yes, but not one person criticised us for bringing him in.

Walter was quite nervous as the endgame with Le Guen played out in 2007, and we had to pay compensation to the SFA, I think it was £100,000 to get him. I know people wanted him to stay with Scotland but I had to do what was right for Rangers. It was a huge call.

We met, the deal was done, he improved things immediately and within 18 months we were in a UEFA Cup final. I am still not sure what my Plan B would have been if I couldn't have persuaded him to come back.

21

CHARITY: IT'S PERSONAL

IT'S AN AWKWARD QUESTION THAT PEOPLE occasionally ask, "So, just how tall are you?" and then they quickly correct it to, "Err….I actually meant how tall WERE you?"

I am, I WAS, 6ft 2ins tall, I have size nine-and-a-half feet, an inside leg measurement of 33 inches…at least that's what I could claim up until I had my accident. My legs were amputated about nine inches above the knees and I have since had limited mobility thanks to cleverly-constructed mechanical legs attached to a frame and a hardy pair of lightweight metal crutches. They are not state-of-the-art but they are what keeps me standing tall.

Prior to the crash I could also boast a 34-inch waist (I wish I could still claim that) and I was more than handy at most of the sports I loved – rugby, cricket and football, probably in that order. I think I still hold a points-scoring record at Dalkeith Rugby Club. I know an old picture is on a wall in the clubhouse. But all this changed overnight.

In the wake of the crash, I suddenly had to come to terms with the fact that my sporting career was over.

The Princess Margaret Rose Hospital and the amazing work that happened there after my accident was really a huge part of my inspiration for setting up The Murray Foundation in 1996. I met so many people, NHS staff and volunteers there who helped me and everyone else and who were endlessly kind.

The other inspiration came from that letter from Douglas Bader. Across a number of years I had met so many amputees and it seemed the right thing to do. Give something back. Our goal was clear: the relief of distress of any person who has suffered the loss of a limb or part of a limb as the result of a traumatic incident. In February 2017, the foundation's core purpose changed slightly to include other charities.

One of those I have been a major supporter of is the Erskine Hospital in Renfrewshire. At my 70th birthday party on the Royal Yacht Britannia in 2021, I asked for no presents and requested that people instead donate to Erskine.

When we launched the foundation we were immediately inundated with requests for help and further information. We had counsellors at most major hospital receptions and just tried to meet as many people as possible.

Over the years, I have actually made many personal visits to people if I thought it might make even the smallest difference to their lives.

On one occasion, I took a call from someone at the foundation who said they had received word from a woman in South Lanarkshire whose son had just lost his leg in a farming accident. He had it caught in a baler. He was in his late teens and he was a huge Rangers fan and his mum wondered if I might write to him or have any advice that might cheer him up. They were both in a dreadful state and it seemed he just wanted to give up on life, which can be a common reaction.

I'd heard enough. I got into my car, called a close friend of mine and asked if he wanted to come along. I picked him up and we set off via the M8 and M74 and 90 minutes later, rang the front doorbell. I don't know who was more surprised – the mum or her son. She ushered us into the living room, where he was sitting on a sofa, and went to put the kettle on. I sat down beside him and joked, "Just the one leg, was it? What's the problem?"

He cracked a smile and we spoke for the next two hours. He was terrified but by the time I left, we and he had a plan for his recovery. I told him that even on one leg, he could do whatever he wanted, and could achieve twice what I could do on none. And I made him swear he would keep me and the team at the foundation updated and tell me how his life was unfolding. I spent the final 10 minutes telling him stories about his favourite Rangers players and swearing him to secrecy.

The visit had gone exactly as planned, unlike the journey home. Just 10 minutes after leaving the family's house I got a puncture in the middle of nowhere and it was well after midnight by the time we made it back to Edinburgh.

But it was worth it. The boy who wanted to give up showed courage and he found some positivity and he went on to be a success. He didn't stay on that couch for long. He took all of the medical advice he was given, went on to do a course at college, got a job, bought his first house and I continue to follow his career. We have stayed in touch and very recently I sponsored him as he took part in a celebrity boxing match. That's what real fight is all about.

I also made contact with a Norwegian man called Nils whom I read about after he was run over by a taxi in the city's Rose Street and became a double amputee. He had come to Scotland and built up a successful business. I invited him back to our family home for tea and we spoke candidly about his future.

———

In September 2006 I was so proud to accept the Queen's award for voluntary services at a ceremony in Glasgow City Chambers.

The foundation work didn't stop there. We set up a hotline that people could telephone which I sometimes manned and we leafleted hospitals in Inverness and Aberdeen explaining our work. We set up working groups helping prosthetists in many Scottish hospitals and we held an annual lunch where we raised funds for assisting younger people who had lost limbs.

There are currently nearly 11,000 amputees in Scotland. Many of them are because of road accidents just like mine but the majority are also due to lost legs caused by smoking, diabetic complications or poor circulation. With those there was a stigma attached. At one time, I rented the swimming pool at Dunfermline College in Edinburgh so people could have special amputee-only days behind closed doors and feel comfortable about it.

But in 2025, it is an altogether different world we live in – almost certainly because of the sheer inspiration of the Paralympics or the Invictus Games and the constant media coverage. I also cannot praise enough the incredible efforts of some amazing and driven athletes such as David Weir, Sarah Storey, Tanni Grey-Thomson, Ellie Simmonds and remarkable people such as Olivia Giles.

Olivia had both her feet and hands amputated after rapidly developing meningococcal septicaemia. She was close friends with someone who worked in my office and I remember being asked to meet her for a bite of lunch at Astley Ainslie Hospital in Edinburgh during her recovery. I took Sean Connery with me and Olivia was so shocked to see him walk through the door. I thought his appearance might help her at such a difficult time.

What Olivia has achieved since then, including setting up her own charity, has touched so many lives.

One of the few sports that didn't require massive physical effort on my part was snooker. While I still couldn't get round the table very easily, I had half a clue about how to build a decent break.

A group of us had been out for dinner one night at Gleneagles and I invited two or three of them back for a nightcap at Dunbarney.

One of them was Scotland's world snooker champion at the time, Stephen Hendry. I have a three-quarters sized table in the house and of course I challenged him to a quick frame. It would have been rude not to. As is customary with most professionals, he generously gave me a start of 30 points. Now, we were probably slightly the worse for wear, however, I beat him by 31 points. He was not a happy world champion. After a sharp exit home, the next morning, he returned to my house with a brand new set of Crystalite balls and his own cue demanding a rematch. There was no way. I told him that I had played the world champion once and I would never do it again.

My obsession – there is no other word for it – with sport never really let up and I'm sure it never will. Our country had so few good facilities to develop talent so when the Dunfermline College site came up for sale I wrote to the Labour sports minister at the time Sam Galbraith and offered to put a substantial amount of money into what I thought could be a fantastic Scottish Institute of Sport. The site was perfect, the facilities were all there, the halls of residence were still perfectly adequate. The whole campus certainly required more than a lick of paint but there was a fantastic infrastructure.

I wrote to Sam, a respected neurosurgeon and a man who I had met on numerous occasions, with a sound proposal and with one swoosh of his pen, the matter was closed. His reply said 'no' and within weeks, the Scottish Government at the time said that the land would be sold off for housing. What a wasted opportunity.

It saddens me that so many of our young sports stars – our Andy Murrays, our athletes, our golfers, have to head to Europe and the States to fulfil their potential.

I've now been on my crutches for 49 years, far more than half my life. In the beginning I frequently questioned whether or not I would make it, be able to cope, have any kind of meaningful existence.

Well, I've far exceeded my expectations. It was my family and friends, the doctors, the nurses and the physios that I met, other amputees and finally the words of Douglas Bader that put it all into perspective:

"I gather that you have got hold of the problem and decided to get on with life, which is the only thing to do."

22

ME AND ALEX
AND THE
RANGERS FAMILY

WITHOUT A SHADOW OF DOUBT, ALEX MCLEISH HAD A more difficult job than his predecessors because Rangers were downsizing financially during his time as manager from 2001 to 2006.

Yet against that he came from Hibs to a bigger job at a bigger club and was successful, so it did his CV no harm. He went on to win the League Cup against Arsene Wenger's Arsenal with Birmingham City, manage Scotland (twice), Aston Villa, Nottingham Forest and Genk. He wasn't stuck for work afterwards because people respected what he did at Rangers.

If Dick ran out of steam against Martin O'Neill, then Alex took an experienced group of players who appeared to be waning and gave them a new lease of life.

He won the first five trophies he realistically could have against the man many argue is Celtic's second greatest manager behind Jock Stein. The league had already gone by the time Alex took over from Dick in 2001/02, but he won both domestic cups and then followed that with the Treble, including winning the league on the final day in the same season that O'Neill's team reached the UEFA Cup final in Seville before losing it to Jose Mourinho's Porto.

Sometimes you sense that players need to hear a different voice and that was my hunch when I asked Dick to become director of football and help me select his successor in 2001. If it's the same person delivering the same message it eventually dilutes the importance of it.

I looked around to see if there was a suitable Scottish candidate, and there's no doubt that Alex was doing well at Hibs playing entertaining football with good signings such as Franck Sauzee and Russell Latapy and bringing through young players like Kenny Miller, who we had already signed. Dick and I talked about it before settling on Alex. Dick had managed against him and thought he was tactically aware, clever in how he used the players at his disposal.

We then had a meeting with Alex, Dick and Blair Morgan, Alex's agent, at my house before I had to phone Rod Petrie, Hibs' chief executive. Having done other business outside of football with him, I knew those negotiations would not be straightforward, but eventually we got the deal done.

Part of the attraction was my memory of Alex as a player. He was a brave footballer and had played nearly 700 competitive games for Aberdeen. Although Dick didn't believe football was played in the air, Alex was dominant with his head, but he could play on the deck as well and scored a famous goal against Rangers in the 1982 Scottish Cup final with a curling shot.

He'd been a top international and was dedicated to one club. I liked the cut of his jib.

Although people outside of Scotland are usually aware of the rivalry between Rangers and Celtic, they sometimes don't appreciate the animosity between Rangers and Aberdeen. Pittodrie was possibly a more hostile place for Rangers to go to than Celtic Park and much of that emanated from the period when Sir Alex Ferguson was manager at Aberdeen and was determined to beat the club he'd previously played for.

People sometimes forget that there was a brief overlap when Ferguson was still Aberdeen manager before moving on to Manchester United in November 1986 and Graeme Souness becoming manager of Rangers in May that year. If you want to get a flavour of the intensity of matches between the clubs at that time, find the footage of the classic game where Graeme hit a shot with his left foot, it hit the post, dragged along the line and Jim Leighton tried to pull it out and then ran to the halfway line to complain to the referee that it hadn't crossed the line.

You could see the venom, the effort, in every Aberdeen player and I respected that.

I've only met Alex Ferguson a few times. He'd come to the games occasionally because he was a Rangers man, often with his brother, Martin. He was a determined individual whose father worked in the shipyards, so he started from humble beginnings.

You must respect what he achieved. Whatever way you want to look at Alex Ferguson, he was a winner. I don't know him very well, but Walter spoke highly of him. The town probably wasn't big enough for the two of them, when he and Graeme were briefly in Scotland together as managers, but there was a respect there.

Ferguson was Alex McLeish's mentor at Aberdeen and an

important guide for him, so he had done a great training with a great manager, and it stood him good stead to go to Motherwell and Hibs and become a manager in his own right. At Easter Road, he had assembled a very good group of players, and he was managing them well.

At Rangers, Alex proved he could win crucial big games and handle the pressure of those occasions, ensuring his players rose to them. He started with a League Cup semi-final win over Celtic when Bert Konterman scored the winner with a rocket of a shot in extra-time and then went on to win the Scottish Cup final 3-2 with a late goal from Peter Lovenkrands, who refused to be intimidated by Celtic's Bobo Balde. Lovenkrands was a Dick signing for £1.5m who became a great servant for Rangers and scored several important goals for us.

The standard of player on both sides was much higher than it is today and many see that game and the season that followed when Rangers won the title and the Treble on the final day, and Celtic beat Blackburn and Liverpool on their way to the final in Seville, as a zenith that Scottish football hasn't repeated since – and doesn't look likely to as the financial gap with England continues to grow. From then on, it was getting harder to attract the top players to Scotland.

In terms of Rangers and Celtic, it was probably as strong as both clubs had been at the same time since the five-year period from Celtic winning the European Cup in 1967 to Rangers winning the Cup Winners' Cup in 1972. In 1967, Rangers also reached the semi-final of the European Cup Winners' Cup before losing to Bayern Munich and Celtic reached another European Cup final in 1970.

It's good for Scottish football when both Rangers and Celtic are strong. It was like two gladiators fighting in that fantastic final in 2002 and it could have gone either way. We had Claudio Caniggia, Ronald de Boer, Shota Arveladaze, Neil McCann, Peter Lovenkrands and Barry Ferguson, who had become the kingpin in midfield for us and scored a great goal from a free-kick. Celtic were probably more physical than us with John Hartson, Chris Sutton, Balde and Johan Mjallby.

I always remember talking to Graeme and Walter when I started as Rangers' chairman and they would stress the importance of a strong spine to the team – goalkeeper, two centre-halves, two in midfield, and two strikers. Walter would always say, 'wingers get you the sack' but Alex used them well, the likes of Lovenkrands and McCann.

He went toe-to-toe with O'Neill and we won the league on the final day of the following season. Sutton said it was a fix. That was good theatre for the media and probably explains why he's now a pundit rather than a manager. I always say it's easy to stand on the side and criticise if you are not in the game.

Not many of that team cost a lot of money in fees, but eventually we couldn't compete on wages because of the TV money Sky were pumping into the English clubs. I was looking at Bournemouth's balance sheet recently, £120million turnover and £104million of that was TV money. There's not a business there without the TV money.

That's why the same teams are going up and down between the Championship and the Premier League. Norwich go up and don't spend money, they take the benefit of it and go back down ready to come back up again. For many clubs, 90 per cent of their income is TV money, and, without being disrespectful, they are making up the numbers rather than challenging the top six.

I remember sitting in my office with Fergus McCann of Celtic, Geoff Brown of St Johnstone and Stewart Milne of Aberdeen, and we were trying to organise TV deals and we thought we were doing well when we were getting £18million here and there. But the bottom team in the Premier League gets as much as the whole of Scottish football does.

In 2002/03, the standard was still high, but we were slowly getting left behind. Celtic as well. They couldn't keep signing the Suttons and Hartsons and so on either. We couldn't compete with Championship clubs, never mind Premier League ones.

Hartson and De Boer came for a medical on the same day at Rangers and our doctor was concerned about Hartson's knee. De Boer, who also had a dodgy knee, we signed. You were trying to get players and rekindle them. There are no better examples of that than Brian Laudrup and Paul Gascoigne. Their careers weren't going that well in Italy and we rekindled them at Rangers.

After the Treble of 2003, Alex won another pressure match to take us back into the Champions League later that summer. That was crucial. The pressure was on financially because we needed the extra money of the Champions League to keep the wolves from the door. If we had any plans to do anything, we needed to win that game. I am honest enough to admit that.

Shota Arveladze's goal four minutes from time saw us win 2-1 Copenhagen, where Sean Connery was among my guests. Shota was a gentleman. He's near enough aristocracy in Georgia.

Alex had brought Henning Berg in as a back-up defender, and I remember there was this very fast South African winger, Sibusiso Zuma for Copenhagen who could run 100 metres in a shade over 10 seconds, but Henning was calm and explained to me it was all about reading the game and making sure you knew where the ball was going to be before he did.

Sean came into the dressing room with me beforehand, and like I mentioned earlier, Ronald de Boer told him his last film,

The League of Extraordinary Gentlemen, wasn't very good. That was rude of Ronald, but I put it down to pre-match nerves on his part.

Barry Ferguson, the captain, wanted to discuss bonuses beforehand, which I felt was a discussion for after the game, and we were in the process of selling him to Blackburn Rovers for £7.5million because it was getting tough for us financially.

———

We downsized in this period, but Alex had matured as a manager and we kept winning, which Rangers haven't managed to do in recent years. At Hibs, he was experienced at a certain level, but with us he became a battle-hardened European manager. He got the most out of the players that he inherited from Dick. Bear in mind, that compared to Hibs, he was man-managing more experienced and valuable assets. We had players in the autumn of their careers, but Alex was getting every last drop out of them.

We had to be smart to raise funds and Jean-Alain Boumsong was arguably the best business I've done in the transfer market. We signed him on a Bosman from Auxerre in the summer of 2004, then sold him to Newcastle United for £8million six months later. There was an investigation into that deal, but it cleared everyone involved and nothing went on there. I was just lucky to get him through my contacts in France.

We only sold him because the money was right. He was a good player, but he let himself down in a couple of games and the chance to turn a quick profit on him was too good to turn down. Boumsong came from Auxerre, where I had good relationships with people. Their chairman was Jean-Claude Hamel, who fought in the Algerian war in the 1950s and 60s during which over one million people died, and later received the Legion d'Honneur, France's highest merit, and they were backed by a guy called

Gerard Bourgoin, known as the 'King of Chicken' in France because of his poultry business.

Guy Roux was their manager for 44 years from 1961 to 2005 and built the best youth academy in Europe. I met him. Like me, he was also a member of the Confrérie des Chevaliers du Tastevin, for supporters of the wine industry. He was a wee man but he enjoyed his wine and was respected for the players he produced over four decades.

The funds raised by the Boumsong deal helped Alex refresh the squad and he again won the league on the final day of the season in 2005 against O'Neill's Celtic, an even more dramatic climax known now as Helicopter Sunday because the helicopter with the league trophy had to change course from Motherwell, where Celtic lost two late goals, to Edinburgh, where we beat Hibs.

With these final-day wins, the overriding emotion as chairman is relief. I am pleased for the fans, that they can celebrate in their community because that's important for them. If you drive round certain towns in Scotland, it's top of the agenda, certainly in some older, industrial communities that have maybe seen better days and have no steel industry, shipbuilding or coal-mining that was the basis of their income to sustain them now. It means everything to them.

I never lost my admiration for the fans who travelled from far afield to watch both clubs either. A Rangers supporters' bus from Wick, from the very north of Scotland or those who come from Ireland or England to support their respective teams. What dedication every week.

You didn't need to explain Scottish football to Alex or the importance of winning against Celtic. His father was a Rangers supporter but died young, so he had to grow up fast. That tough side to him could come out when things weren't going well.

For example, I remember a tense meeting in 2004, during the period when I stepped down as chairman, and John McClelland took the role. John had a go at Alex and said it wasn't going too well. I'd already told Alex, 'don't worry, I am sticking with you', but I had to give John his place. John said, "You might have to consider your position" and Alex just growled back, "I f****** might have to". It was tough at that time and, if you push Alex, you will get a reaction like that from him.

I tried to defend Alex, but I am not sure that would happen today. Instead, they would fire you and get a new manager in. That doesn't always work, there must be a plan of who that new manager will be and why he's a better bet than the existing one.

The chairman must take some of the responsibility for picking a manager while the critics don't know what is going on behind closed doors. They don't know that certain players are not pulling their weight or personal problems people are having. I knew the whole picture and I had to see it through.

A lot of people wanted him out, including some of the board. We had board meetings three or four times a year and they were all minuted, so everyone knew what was going on. Dave King could phone and had a half-hour slot to ask questions. I'd also be available at least 20 of our home games every season for a less formal chat.

The deal was I'd be there at lunchtime and I was in the manager's room until kick-off. If anybody wanted to see me or ask any questions about the running of the club, they knew where to find me, That's the way I did it.

Ninety per cent of your fans want to support the club through good and bad. You get five or six per cent who like to shout, that small minority that take it to extremes. They put stuff on websites and sometimes they should be ashamed of themselves. Some of them were protesting outside because that's what they do, and the police warned me my security was under threat while it was going on.

Today, clubs listen to this stuff too much. Social media is bigger today than it was, but why read it? Personally, I think it's a weak person in a football position who allows the people online to affect their judgement. If that's the case, should the people that are writing about you be in the job? No, you are in the job for a reason, and you must make the decisions. If not, then resign.

Alex came to my office in Charlotte Square and there were about 30 media outside the door, maybe expecting me to sack him, but I was determined to stand by him, I just said, "You go out the back and I'll deal with the press". I just saw that as part of my job.

Fire Alex, then what? We did well in Europe in his final season, we made it to the last 16 of the Champions League and when Lovenkrands scored away to Villarreal we only missed out on the quarter-final on away goals, but the league had gone. By that stage, I had started looking for a new manager, but I'd told Alex that, I didn't stab him in the back, I said, "Let's face it together".

—

Not winning the league last season was a lost opportunity for Rangers, and I see Celtic progressing as a club and dominating Scottish football unless something fundamental happens to change that.

There's a race at the top between Rangers and Celtic, then a race to be third between Aberdeen and Hearts and that's all about firepower, about money.

Rangers have built up a lot of loans and going forward you can't continue to get directors to cover losses. You need new money to make things happen and I don't know how you are going to do that. I wouldn't have had the money, even at my peak, to do that.

There's a lot of shares now, but they are not worth a lot. The stadium needs a revamp. You see pictures of toilets with no seats and the corporate areas are tired – the same rooms that I did up 20-odd years ago.

Celtic have done well with their transfers and are in a better financial position now, there's no denying that. Rangers are at a huge disadvantage and it's not just about money. There's a lot of things that could have been handled better since I left and some things that I could have done better, but we were still winning trophies when I was there because I had good management with me.

I couldn't have done it without them and the backroom staff. Alex had Andy Watson as his assistant and Jan Wouters carried on after Dick stepped down and had huge experience in World Cups for the Netherlands and was a tough guy, a good guy. Ian McGuinness came from Ayr and his family knew my family, but it was Alex who brought him in as doctor, and he then went to Birmingham City and Aston Villa with him. Ian remains a good friend and is now doctor to the Qatari national team and at the Aspire Academy out there.

I found a great picture of the four managers – Alex, Dick, Graeme and Walter – standing on that lawn together with me at my son's wedding, but even better than that I also have one of the four wives having a glass of champagne together. Name me another club in the world that could do that? If you're not in it together, what's the point?

23

FINANCIAL MELTDOWN

IN HINDSIGHT, ONE OF MY BIGGEST PROBLEMS WAS that we were obviously borrowing far too much money, which had become regularly available.

The Bank of Scotland was offering us money hand over fist, and we took it, using it for more and more ways to build and expand our business. At one time I think they had given us £960million.

All of the borrowing – everything – was matched up with income, so it all seemed secure. Then the unthinkable happened – there was a global economic crisis in 2008 which led to the bank collapsing.

People might reasonably expect that you have to go cap in hand to a bank to ask to borrow money and you have to have lots of figures and evidence to prove that the new venture is worth it and will be an unparalleled success.

In the years leading up to 2008, for me and a few other business leaders in Scotland, it was far from that. Peter Cummings, the director of the Bank of Scotland who led the support of all the entrepreneurial activity, had me for dinner twice a year to discuss the relationship between the Murray Group and the bank.

At one of those dinners, he offered me more and I said, "Peter, I actually think we've got enough at the moment."

The start of a huge increase in borrowing from the bank and the transforming of my business came in a conversation at a dinner at the Bank of Scotland's head office on The Mound in Edinburgh, in September 2001 when Halifax merged with the Bank of Scotland to form HBOS PLC. Eventually, following massive financial turbulence in the global banking market, HBOS was acquired by Lloyds TSB.

I did not know it then but it was to be the start of a roller coaster ride for our business and for me personally. The dinner was one held on behalf of my company as one of the bank's major corporate customers.

It was an event that I always enjoyed, to be honest, because you were made to feel so welcome which, in hindsight, was not a surprise. They have a special menu with your name embossed on it, no expense was spared on the food and wine and they made you believe you were their No1 client; the bank certainly knew how to entertain.

George Mitchell, who was an executive director of the bank and who headed up its Corporate Division, told me at the dinner that the Bank of Scotland was being taken over by Halifax Building Society in a move that would create the merged Halifax/Bank of Scotland or HBOS.

As a result, George told me that because of the increased financial firepower of the bigger group my business's loan facility would be rising by £200million to £300million.

In many ways, although that got me on to higher borrowing

and gave me the financial clout to do a lot more with the business, in hindsight, I don't think it was good for me nor for the Bank of Scotland. I'm not saying there was any wrongdoing or negligence on anyone's part, but money was just so easy and we accepted it.

I was one of a handful of entrepreneurs that Bank of Scotland backed. The others included Tom Hunter, Jim McColl, Brian Souter and his sister Ann Gloag.

In 2008 it had been clear that the country was heading into major trouble and one of the biggest effects on all of us from the gathering economic storm was property revaluations.

The group was taking what they call "impairments" of £150million a time each couple of years. It is a technical word but one that covers a lot of financial pain.

I wasn't exactly happy with the situation but it was painfully clear that the bank had a far bigger problem than me. HBOS's total write-down was about £10billion.

The year before we went down, the bank gave me £150million in equity, the loss that year was only £8.5million on a turnover of £648million but there was £150million property write-down.

By this time the bank was providing the money as part of a 60-40 joint venture – they were effectively a banker-shareholder. Now, if you were looking rationally from the outside you would say that if they owned 40 per cent of something and they are approving everything not just as a banker, but as a shareholder, then when the properties were bought, you might say they were complicit in all the decisions.

Yet I had to take their 40 per cent of the write-downs on my balance sheet. In eight of the 10 years up to the crash we had made an operating profit. But in truth the bank was making access to money far too easy for us.

They lent us up to £900million into a joint venture called

Murray BS. When the crash came it created a domino effect. When the property market crashed, the steel market dropped by 45 per cent and it had a huge effect on our business which had been selling 550,000 tonnes of steel a year.

Financial blows for the group were coming thick and fast.

Rangers lost to FBK Kaunas in August, meaning that there was no repeat of the heroics of the previous year when we had reached the final of the UEFA Cup in Manchester.

A dreadful night in Lithuania meant we lost the match and we didn't progress in the Champions League, which would have earned us about £25million or £30million. Rangers was ring-fenced from the rest of the business. It was a standalone financial facility which meant I had made sure that the cash problems hitting the rest of the group didn't directly hit the club. The fact that I did that has, of course, long been forgotten.

The property market collapsed, the metals business slumped and it was clear that the group was in major trouble. Our property portfolio had been valued at £760million – the bank wrote it down by £300million. But worst of all the bank went bust.

It didn't matter how clever or brave I was, I might have been able to handle two of these blows and, over and above that, I really wasn't feeling well.

When it came to the crunch, there was one key Murray Group board meeting. Sitting around the table with me were investment banker Angus Grossart, financial director Donald Wilson, operations director Ian Tudhope and my son David.

Andy Cummings of Lloyds Bank, the executive who had taken over our loan book, said he would come up to Scotland for crisis talks. I had told him, "No, I'll come to London." At the board meeting we discussed who should go with me and I said I would take Andy Godfrey, the group auditor and head of accountancy firm Grant Thornton. I thought it would be better if I took my auditor who could give them chapter and verse on the numbers.

As it turned out he had a separate private meeting with the bank – he did a lot of work for them – and they asked him if they could trust me. He said, "Absolutely. Yes."

A key piece of advice I received at this time was from Ian Cuthbertson of Dundas & Wilson, who was a renowned corporate and company lawyer and had done a lot of turnarounds.

He sat me down and said, "There's a lot of money at stake here and I deal with the banks in situations like this all the time. The best advice I can give you when you go into this is this: act like an arsehole and they'll treat you like an arsehole."

Those words stuck with me and we did everything by the book, did the best we could starting with going down to London and talking everything through with the bank.

When we all finally sat down around a table I said, "Let's work this out together."

I was honourable, told the truth, never lied and did everything to the letter. There was definitely a bit of what I might call shadow boxing and there was a metaphorical punch thrown here and there but we did a workout and every single supplier that was owed money got paid.

I have no doubt that if I had gone down and started mumping and moaning, they could have turned around and liquidated everything and nobody would have got paid, which would have been a mess for a lot of people.

Everyone received 90 per cent of their pension and every creditor was paid. That result came about probably because I didn't 'act like an arsehole'.

I stayed with the business working with Donald Muir, who the bank had put in to do the turnaround. I had to deal with him and the bank. Normally what happens in these situations is they get rid of the head honcho in the business and the turnaround guy comes in and runs it.

I believe part of the reason I was kept on was because Rangers was part of the group. Had it been a straight property and metals business it could have been different but the fact that I had Rangers gave me a bit of leverage – the bank wouldn't want to be seen to be acting against one of Scotland's greatest institutions.

Normally the founder would simply be out but the diversity of the business was a handful for one turnaround guy to handle because where on earth does he start?

If people had looked at the sheer breadth of what we did, how diverse our activities were, they might have thought us crazy but that, along with the strength of the Rangers brand, really helped us get through.

All of that plus the fact was I knew where all of the bodies were buried – not literally – and I could be a real asset to them in trying to iron out any difficulties. So, I made the agreement with the bank that I would stay on for a couple of years to help sort it out and realise as much of the value from the business as possible.

Unfortunately, as it turned out they ruined the steel business because they downsized it too much to get cash in – a business that was selling more than 550,000 tonnes of steel a year at one time.

They squeezed cash and reduced stock, closed depots and sold bits of the business to competitors just to get their money back. I must admit even to this day that one hurt a bit, to be honest, but since then, fortunately, we have been able to do a bit of a Lazarus and come back. Since then, I have taken parts of the steel business and helped the team build them up and again they are performing very well.

In the workout there was a bit of selling things at stupid prices. They didn't wait but they had to obey the liquidity framework they were under. I think they threw away into three figures of millions simply by not waiting longer and working it out.

Peter Cummings and I have talked about this a few times and his view was that if the bank hadn't gone bust we could have traded our way out of it. But as it was, we had to sell off assets cheaply. One example was an office block at 141 Bothwell Street in Glasgow city centre, which we had to sell to Strathclyde Pension Fund for £72million. It was sold two years later for £90million.

Another example was big four accountancy firm PWC's head office at London Plumtree Court which we bought for £100million on an eight per cent yield. I borrowed the money at five per cent, so we were making three per cent on £100million which is about £3million a year.

This was an example of where I got hurt when the bank went bust and Lloyds came in. They wrote down the value to £47million. And I was having to take the whole hit on my profit and loss account in what was a 60-40 partnership. Three years later, by working together, the site was eventually sold to Goldman Sachs for a figure in excess of £90million.

As part of the property portfolio, we had three shopping centres: one in Hartlepool, one in Mansfield and one in Wishaw in Lanarkshire. We bought them for £150million and had to sell them for £90million. Boots Pension Fund bought them and made a good return on them.

As part of my deal to work with the bank I had said to them, "If you pay me a salary, I'll help you work it out but I want to buy certain assets from the business."

At the time data cabling company Brand-Rex and the bus building business Alexander's hadn't started doing well. I wanted to take them to build them, while from Murray Estates I wanted some of the property development sites, none of which had planning permission at the time. All of the assets had to be independently valued.

The idea was that we would take these assets and would develop them as Murray Capital, led by my son David who had set up an office at the other side of Charlotte Square in Edinburgh from where our previous office was – and where I was still working.

He then started the work of building Murray Capital. When we got them, Alexander's wasn't making a lot of money, neither was Brand-Rex but then we, collectively with the management teams turned those around because we were traders and knew what would make them tick. That's how we got those out – we paid for them and got them back. We got what we wanted; we really couldn't have done any more.

It was a tough time but you've got to dig deep. The only comfort for me was that I had some personal assets and could go again. We owned some property and had some pension money so I could have started to rebuild that way. But by being able to get those assets out it was a smoother transition to rebuilding the business. David made a fresh break across the Square to another office.

By about 2013 I had finally assisted in tidying up the old Murray Group for the bank. Then I went to join David at Murray Capital.

24

THE SALE OF
GLASGOW RANGERS

MORE THAN A DECADE AFTER THE EVENT, THE question I still frequently get asked is: 'Do you regret selling Rangers' and the answer is always: 'No…my time was up.' 23 years was too long. We had enjoyed the greatest success in the club's entire history but it was clearly time for change. Do I regret the sale to Craig Whyte? Absolutely.

This has never been on record but a deal had been agreed six years earlier and I walked out on a room full of lawyers and accountants in a suite at a London hotel when only my final signature was required to complete the transaction. One simple signature. I look back now and think: 'Did I really do that?'

But ask me if I regret the manner in which the club finally changed hands in 2011 or dealing with the man I ultimately sold it to and then sitting right inside the lion's cage for the subsequent circus: Of course I do. I apologise. It was a huge error of judgement in the middle of a financial crisis.

I am always quick to share my thoughts and experiences with people – most of them lifelong fans – looking to invest their all in Scottish football clubs. I tell them that no matter how well they do or how much they love their club, they will ultimately lose money. I ask them how badly do they care?

They will face non-stop scrutiny of their private lives and their finances and, more than likely, endless social media abuse when the team begins to struggle. A couple of decent results from a cup run might bring some respite but any underlying problems will inevitably resurface again. If you're happy to lose money and put your family through that hell then go for it. So many still do and good luck to them.

The Murray Group had spent millions on Rangers through the 1990s but it really had taken its toll on my core businesses. I suddenly found myself with limited time for the people who had helped build something special. On one hand I had a team in Edinburgh doing their best to keep our metals businesses viable and at the other end of the M8 I had this giant of a football club demanding constant attention. I was completely torn and this was probably the point at which I had first considered selling the club.

The team, under Alex McLeish, was under-performing. John McLelland had taken over many of my Chairman's duties, a move which was meant to alleviate some of the strain. John was a good man but I am always a believer that if you are the front man, you have no hiding place. I was still the leader. I rarely missed a home game. I worked with the chief executive and the staff on a daily basis. I was taking dozens of calls every day. I dealt with the media at all times. Rangers was 90 percent of my life and the Murray group was 10 percent. That wasn't right.

In March 2005, I was hosting a dinner during a MIPIM international property conference at the Belle Rives Hotel in

Juan-les-Pins. During the event I was introduced to someone telling me that a gentleman called Jack Petchey, later to become Sir Jack and who recently passed away, was seriously interested in buying Rangers. He asked me: "Is that something you might consider?"

"Maybe," I replied. Standing with me, Ian Tudhope, Managing Director of our Premier Property Group, exchanged cards and numbers with him. I was certainly intrigued. This was the first time I had seriously considered selling the football club and given my doubts about running two major businesses, it led me to explore further. Much further.

Jack's credentials were impeccable. He had grown a car hire and car sales business into a billion-pound plus property and timeshare empire from London and the south of England. Importantly, certainly as far as I was concerned, he was also a football fan. He had been a director of West Ham United during the 1970s then bought Watford FC from Elton John in 1987 before selling it back to him seven years later. He knew all about the history of Rangers Football Club and I just thought he was a good fit.

Once back home our business teams began round after round of financial and legal negotiations in London and Edinburgh.

At one point, it transpired that his property advisors had been loosely examining whether or not they could reconstruct the Copland Road stand and replace it with flats and ancillary developments around Ibrox stadium. Privately we were told he would never get permission and the issue never came up again in the last round of talks.

There was a bit of financial analysis and negotiation that followed but eventually I was convinced. This was it. Papers were drawn up. We had agreed a deal. Jack Petchey would become the new owner of Rangers and the price was £40million.

Wondering what the media, but more importantly the fans, would make of it all, and when we might break the news, I flew to London. At the Dorchester Hotel on Park Lane, we booked two meeting suites and waded into the final submissions. I had Ian Tudhope, Donald Wilson and Martin Bain with me plus our team of lawyers, while Jack had brought his sizeable legal team with him.

We sat on one side of the table and they sat at the other and at various intervals, going through the paperwork line by line, we took short breaks.

Eventually we reached the crunch point where it was entirely down to me. The tension in the room was something else. So many hours of graft had gone into this one moment. A new chapter in the history of Rangers FC.

With a layer of paperwork on the desk I was handed a fine black Mont Blanc pen to make the final signature – something I do so many times every day – but I hesitated. Something stopped me. I looked up, then back at the document and I gripped the pen once again, put the ball-point to the document then paused for a second time. I endeavoured to renegotiate an additional sum and then realised that I just couldn't sign it.

I looked up then told everyone in the room: "I can't do this. The deal's off." I picked up my crutches and surrounded by open mouths, sighs and despairing groans all around the table, I walked out. I then remembered: It was my room. I walked along the corridor, even wondering at one point if I was going to change my mind.

I'm not sure why I couldn't sign off the deal. Perhaps it was just the fact that I was letting go of something that I cared so deeply about and putting the club first. The guys told me there had been a fair bit of anger around the negotiating table after I had left.

Many hours and long nights had gone into preparing the

documents but the deal really was off, and for good. Jack and I never spoke again and a little bit of me still wonders what might have happened in the following years if he had taken over. On the journey back to Scotland I reflected on the fact that I had done the best thing for the club but not for me, personally, as it proved later on.

As I outlined in the previous chapter, there was obviously the defeat to Kaunas, which meant Rangers missed out on European football. I don't think anyone realised at the time just what a significant loss that was. Financially it hurt more than any other result in my time at the club. But the biggest impact on Rangers and on Murray International and on hundreds of businesses and families across the country was the eventual collapse of the Bank of Scotland. It was a disaster.

After months of speculation and negotiations Lloyds finally acquired HBOS but instantly the game had changed. Relationships and agreements that we had built up over decades just vanished overnight. As I explained earlier, we had new bankers and it seemed that their sole aim was to pile pressure on us to settle any outstanding loans promptly.

Of course I understand restructuring is required following the collapse of any financial institution but there was no working through a process. They wanted instant results and were relentless. Rangers were in the fight of their lives and I could do little to halt it.

When the club did eventually change hands six years after I had come so close to letting it go, I never imagined for a second that the story and its aftermath would reverberate right across the sporting world.

A number of major factors contributed to the eventual sale but there was one in particular, very personal, that I have never disclosed.

In August 2009 came a moment that I will never forget. I was driving back from Edinburgh to my home in Perthshire for a meeting with Keith Miller of Miller Construction when I thought I was going to black out. I pulled over on the M90, quite close to Dunfermline and realised that something was far wrong.

I called the Rangers doctor Paul Jackson and managed to get to the Accident and Emergency unit of Queen Margaret Hospital in Dunfermline. I thought I was having a heart attack. The doctors took me into the room and wired me up, ran some tests and to my enormous relief they said my heart was fine.

But rather than plough on to Perthshire, I drove back to my house in Edinburgh where Doctor Jackson met me. He did further tests and confirmed that I was indeed okay, however, I went to Murrayfield Hospital the following day to have a CT scan and a colonoscopy. Later that evening, I took a phone call from the hospital.

They had taken away a polyp to check if it was cancerous which thankfully it wasn't. But what the doctor – Ian Penman – told me next was a complete shock. He said I had an aortic aneurysm.

They would monitor it carefully and get scans every three months to ensure there was no growth but I was told there was a strong possibility that I would require an operation at some point without the correct monitoring, I was advised, medically, that it was life-threatening.

Within hours I met Alistair Johnston at my house in Edinburgh after he had flown in from America and appraised him of my situation. Taking all factors into consideration, I immediately asked him to become Chairman of Rangers. He, of course, agreed and I then told him that my diagnosis must remain private.

The final operation confirmation would eventually come in May, 2011....an eventful month that I would never forget. The aneurysm had reached a width of 5.5cm and surgery was required. The hardest part was the pre-med which essentially was a day of tests to ensure I was still fit and healthy enough to handle a seven-hour major operation. If not, there was a secondary route with an insert through the thigh which I was told had a 'mixed success rate'. Fortunately I was able to have the full procedure.

Outside my close family and circle of friends no-one knew because I didn't want it to be seen as a deflection of what was happening with the sale of Rangers.

It was an intense period in my life. In three months, I had married my wife Kae, Rangers had won the league and I was selling the club to Craig Whyte.

On July 28, 2011, I finally had the seven-hour operation which was carried out by Rod Chalmers, a renowned vascular surgeon, with whom I had built up a relationship over the two years of having numerous scans.

I was in hospital for 10 days and with 27 stitches from one side of my stomach to the other I knew it would be difficult because I had to get walking again. But I was determined to get myself up again in time to attend my grandson Struan's christening at Gleneagles and my 60th birthday party at Prestonfield House.

Those were my priorities. There is a picture of me in my hospital bed days after the operation and one look at it would tell anyone that I was no longer in a fit state to lead the club. I really had stayed too long and it was etched all over my face.

I know the former Scotland manager Craig Brown – now sadly no longer with us – went through exactly the same thing years later and I spoke to him about his close call. He was lucky to survive at that time and so was I.

During that recovery I realised that so many parts of my life would never be the same again but one thing stood out – that the sale of Rangers Football Club to Craig Whyte had been a total debacle.

The following is from the sworn testimony that I gave to police investigating Craig Whyte. He was arrested in 2015 and charged with taking over the club by fraud. He was subsequently cleared in 2017 following a trial at the High Court in Glasgow:

'In 2009 due to market conditions the money group undertook a process of financial reconstruction called Project Charlotte. Lloyds Bank no longer wanted to be involved not only with Rangers Football Club but in the football industry as a whole.

'As a result of this it was very important to me at this time that I gave my overall group 100% of my attention without the distraction of being involved with Rangers on a daily, sometimes hourly, basis as it entered this difficult financial period.

'I resigned as club chairman on the 26th of August, 2009, and during my last year as chairman, and following my resignation, the remaining directors were John McClelland who is the vice chairman and represented the club at UEFA level, Martin Bain who was the chief executive and who ran the club on a daily basis, Donald McIntyre who was the financial director, Dave King, Alastair Johnson and John Greig who were non-executive directors.

'Following my resignation Alistair Johnson was appointed chairman and appointed to the board at this time were Mike McGill and Donald Muir as non-executive directors. With regard to Lloyds on the banking arrangements with Rangers this was a stand-alone facility which was ring fenced with no recourse by the group or the club in either direction. This facility had no cross guarantees, meaning that it was a banking facility between Lloyds and Rangers Football Club.

'All board members were made fully aware of the funding of Rangers Football Club by Halifax Bank of Scotland (HBOS), and latterly Lloyds.

'With regard to the club's debt, in October, 2009, the level of debt was £33million and at the time of the sale to Craig Whyte on the 6th of May, 2011 the debt had been reduced to £22million.

'The deal for Craig Whyte to purchase Rangers was structured in such a way that Craig Whyte purchased the debt and obtained an Assignation of the Bank's floating charge security. In effect this meant Rangers Football Club was indebted to Craig Whyte to the value of £18million. Under the Share Purchase Agreement (SPA) Craig Whyte had no right to charge interest or demand repayment and as a result effectively stood in the Bank's shoes. He was also under an obligation to convert the debt into equity in the future.

'Due to the economic climate the Murray Group was in a difficult financial situation and it was decided to put in place a group of corporate advisers to assist in the sale of the club. PriceWaterhouseCoopers, Seymour Pierce and Vantis were appointed to assist in the sale of the club. A 'teaser' prospectus was prepared for distribution to interested parties. These interested parties were then required to enter a nondisclosure and confidentiality agreement and then information was released to them thereafter.

'Before my resignation from Rangers Football Club I saw my role in the club as Executive Chairman, chairing the board meetings and assisting Martin Bain and others on a daily basis in running the club as smoothly as possible. The detail of the sale to Craig White is contained within the Share Purchase Agreement and the Project Charlotte 'CD Bible' of documents.

'With regard to the role played by Lloyds Bank at the club, I can say that historically the club had been a long-term customer of Bank of Scotland. When Bank of Scotland entered into financial difficulties it was acquired by Lloyds Bank. When Lloyds Bank saw the level of debt within the Murray Group and the funds invested by the group in the club they recognised the need to restructure the group.

'Lloyds also had the debt facility to the club and were concerned about how the debt would be paid back as they no longer wanted to be funders in the football industry. After negotiations it was decided to enter the process of promoting the sale of the club as soon as practically possible.

'These discussions led to Mike McGill and Donald Muir being appointed as directors of the club. Their role was to act as representatives of the Murray Group at the request of Murray Group and the Bank and also to manage the relationship between the Bank and the club. After 12 months this relationship passed directly to the executive directors of the club and the Bank. I am aware that Mike McGill, who is also the group finance director of Murray Group has provided a comprehensive statement to the police including all relevant available documentation relating to the sale of the club.

'I can confirm the legal advisers to the Murray Group during the sale process were the solicitors Dundas and Wilson.

'In order to protect the interests of the minority shareholders of Rangers Football Club an independent committee of directors was appointed. The role of the independent committee of directors was to give an opinion on the mandatory offer and to recommend, or not, the offer given to the shareholders. The independent committee of directors comprised Alistair Johnson, Martin Bain, Donald McIntyre, John McClelland and John Greig.

'Through the sale process, a variety of individuals approached our advisors regarding the potential of acquiring the club. Throughout the period of negotiation not one of these parties was able to provide the credibility and proof of funds so that matters could be taken forward.

'In October, 2010 Murray International was contacted by Gary

Withey of Collyer Bristow advising that he had a potential buyer for the club AND had proof of funds to back up this offer.

'Craig Whyte was subsequently identified to me as the potential buyer. I then met Whyte for the first time, having never spoken or met with him previously, on 18th October 2010 at my home in the south of France. I was chaperoned by Robert Spelman of Dundas and Wilson who also notified the Panel on Takeovers and Mergers of the meeting.

'Following this meeting and having agreed principles, the progression of detailed negotiations with Craig Whyte in the main was handled by Mike McGill and Donald Muir. I was informed throughout October, November and December, 2010 the deal seemed to be heading in the right direction with heads of terms being negotiated and we received acceptable evidence of proof of funds.

'As previously stated the deal continued to make progress through detailed negotiations with Mike McGill and Donald Muir. The final figure of £1 was reached after negotiations which included Craig Whyte agreeing to settle the small tax case as part of his acquisition price.

'This was all included in the Share Purchase Agreement (SPA) between Murray MHL Limited, Wavetower Limited and Liberty Capital Limited which was signed by all parties on May 6, 2011. The SPA included undertakings that £5million would be available for the playing squad, £1.7million available for health and safety needs for the Ibrox Stadium and £2.8million for a tax liability.

'I can say that the small tax case was a figure of £2.8million which was part of a previous tax avoidance scheme for three footballers between 1999 and 2001. This was not similar to the large tax case as this was a Discounted Option Scheme around March, 2011 and after a series of negotiations the club accepted liability and came to an agreement with HMRC for £2.8 million.

'*With regard to the large tax case much has been said and written about Employee Benefit Trusts (EBTs). Rangers agreed contracts of employment with its players and staff. The EBT scheme involve the contribution of funds into an offshore discretionary trust managed by independent trustees.*

'*The trustees could and did make loans to individuals carrying interest and scheduled re-payment dates. There was no contractual or beneficial entitlement to the funds on the part of any individual and the monies paid to the EBTs were not remuneration in terms of any rules applying to the Club.*

'*Since 2001, when the EBT scheme was introduced to the Group and subsequently managed by the previous Chief Executive Donald Wilson, the amounts contributed were disclosed in the audited financial statements of the Club. As the law stands, it is the right of every taxpayer to minimise his or her tax liability. It is my opinion and that of the Group that tax avoidance is a right. It is tax evasion which is a crime.*

'*In December, 2010 as a result of legislation changes introduced by HMRC, EBTs were rendered tax inefficient. Thereafter the club made no further contributions to EBTs.*

'*As previously stated in the media by me, for the avoidance of doubt, many thousands of employees in many areas of business and commerce, have benefited from EBTs. The club sought only to provide financial security for players and staff within the rules of football and the law.*'

My testimony then explained how Craig Whyte's solicitors, Collyer Bristow, confirmed that the funds for the purchase were in his account in April 2011, before continuing:

'*On the morning of Friday, May 6, 2011 at 10 Charlotte Square,*

Edinburgh one copy of the SPA was signed by myself. The other two copies were signed the previous evening but held undelivered. In attendance were myself, Mike McGill of Murray International Holdings, David Horne of Murray International Holdings, David Davison of Dundas and Wilson, Robert Spelman of Dundas and Wilson, Craig Whyte, Gary Withey, David Greer and Phil Betts. This is the only time that I met Gary Withey.

'Given the above, it is my opinion that Craig Whyte had legal control of the club on the evening of Friday, May 6 2011 when the sale was completed. The deal was signed earlier but only completed after banking hours on this date. This meant that the buyers were unable to transfer funds… I believe the funds materialised around midday [on Monday morning].

'After the acquisition of the club by Craig Whyte/Wavetower on August 25, 2011 we sought confirmation that the purchaser was compliant with the obligations set out in the SPA and asked for details of the £9.5million in the Client Account. We received a draft response from Collyer Bristow on October 11, 2011 advising that the SPA obligations had been complied with.

'The letter from Collyer Bristow was entirely unsatisfactory as it was unsigned. On January 3, 2012 we did eventually receive a signed letter confirming the SPA obligations had been complied with and £1.7million would be invested in the infrastructure of the Club and that £7.8million was still being retained.

'We continued to seek clarification and confirmation regarding the obligations within the SPA. To this end there were numerous letters between Collyer Bristow and Mike McGill. In addition, two meetings took place between Craig Whyte and myself – one in Edinburgh and one in Monaco in November, 2011. The purpose of these meetings was to see in what direction Craig Whyte was taking the club, with emphasis on the need for clarity on the working capital facility.

[…] 'Throughout the negotiations with Craig Whyte we were provided with assurances given not only by Craig Whyte but Collyer Bristow confirming the funds required for completion of the deal. …

'Approximately three weeks prior to the completion of the deal by Craig Whyte I received a 'private and confidential' document from Martin Bain. At this time Martin Bain was expressing his concerns on the suitability of Craig Whyte to acquire the club. I reviewed this document and concluded that the report was for another subject matter which occurred 12 months earlier and there was nothing of a substantial nature preventing us from completing the deal or suggesting we should not.

'By virtue of Craig Whyte's association with Gary Withey and Collyer Bristow, together with the other advisors Cairn Financial and MCR, lent a certain degree of credibility to the Craig Whyte offer…

'I have had no previous dealings with Craig Whyte prior to my meeting with them at my home in the south of France to discuss his acquisition of the club.

'As far as Ticketus is concerned the first I knew about this arrangement was when Martin Bain asked me to do a precognition in relation to his defence in an action against Craig Whyte. This arrangement was brought to my attention at the end of December, 2011. Prior to this I was not aware of any involvement of Ticketus in Craig Whyte's acquisition of the Club.

'Over the course of several years the Club had utilise the services of Ticketus but this was only in small amounts. In relation to Craig Whyte's acquisition I personally never had any contact with any individual at Ticketus or participated in any arrangements. In relation to Craig Whyte, the first time I became aware of his previous disqualification was when it was exposed in a BBC documentary in October, 2011.

'Quite categorically if I had been made aware of how he quite intended to fund the deal we would not have allowed matters to progress. In addition if we had been made aware at the time of the conclusion of the deal with Craig Whyte that he had previously been disqualified and linked to the Ticketus situation we would not have proceeded.

'In relation to the conclusion of the deal with Craig Whyte, the final decision to proceed with the sale lay with the board of Murray International. At that time, taking all factors into consideration, having been involved with and seen many other supposed interested parties, in our opinion with the facts available to us it was the only offer on the table.

'Following the club being placed into administration, in the media, I used the word 'duped' in relation to Craig Whyte and the deal. I used this word for a variety of reasons, these being: It was not Craig Whyte's money being used to fund the deal, it was that of Ticketus and as previously stated if we had been aware of the fact the deal would not have been completed.

'Looking back to May 6, 2011 funds do not appear to have been in the client account at Collyer Bristow …. The working capital of £5million also does not appear to have been there. Craig Whyte failed to disclose his disqualification as a director of which we were totally unaware. The terms of the Shareholders circular were not delivered and various written and verbal confirmations given after completion were untrue.

'There is no doubt in my mind that the acquisition by Craig Whyte and what followed has definitely had a negative effect on my business image.

'In addition other members of the Board and staff have undoubtedly suffered significantly as a result of the tragic events. Needless to say the impact on the Club and its supporters continues and will do so for some time.

'In relation to HMRC, throughout the small tax case and EBT investigation, there have been many meetings with HMRC but I have not attended any of them. As regards the small tax case it was originally an internal matter handled by the Club. The final settlement with HMRC was assisted by Murray International Holdings and our Counsel.

'With regard to Craig Whyte's management of the club post acquisition. I am not aware of any Board meetings which took place subsequent to the acquisition. I am not aware of a continuation of governance that took place prior to the acquisition and only second hand information has been made available to me that regular board meetings were not taking place.

'I can confirm that this is a true and accurate record of events.'

Looking back, I had made a huge mistake. As it happened, Rangers went into administration in 2012 after failing to pay a multimillion pound HMRC tax and VAT bill. Administrators described their 'widespread' concern at the Ticketus arrangement, where the club were paid money upfront for season tickets sold for multiple seasons to help cashflow. I deeply regretted and still regret selling the club to Whyte. And I freely admit that if the information had been available to me at the time I would not have gone through with it. My decision was taken in good faith. There is only so much information out there. After someone has been disqualified for seven years it is not that easy to carry out checks. I also believe it is down to the individual to make us aware of that.

But I was in a situation where we had been endeavouring to sell the club for four years. We had received proof of funds. We had a legal document confirming he was going to spend money on players, eventually, once he had paid back the loan.

He met the criteria that were in his offer document. What we wanted to do was get debt out of the club. The phrase 'debt-ridden club' was being used a lot. Whyte made a statement that the club was never in better financial state when he took it over.

I thought: 'I hope to God I have done the right thing. I've passed it on. This is a guy saying he is going to spend money on players, on health and safety and do Ibrox up.' That was a legal offer document which you were entitled to feel would be honoured.

I know others had doubts. Paul Murray was keen to buy the club and I had nothing but respect for him. He is a Rangers fan and wanted what was best for the club. But at that time he was not able to make a satisfactory offer. He wanted debt left in and the tax case put to one side.

There have always been suggestions that I was under ferocious pressure from the bank to do the deal but that was not the case at all. The bank wanted their money back, of course, and I had made it clear that I wanted out of Rangers. At that time we were going into recession and people were not exactly queueing up to buy football clubs.

Lloyds had investments in more than 20 clubs but wanted out of the football industry. I wanted out but if we had known about the Ticketus issue we would never have done the deal. If I could turn back the clock, I would.

Whyte seemed quite affable and plausible. I remember someone asking at the time: 'Does this pass the sniff test?' and yes it did. He was Scottish, supposedly a Rangers supporter, he had the money and of course there was a Stock Exchange document there. If you can't believe that, then what the hell can you believe?

A journalist asked me at the time if our due diligence should have been more thorough. Well, it's easy to look back and say: 'Yes, of course it should' but anyone typing Whyte's name into Google back in 2011 would have found one article by Terry Houston in *The Herald* from years before. Nothing else.

It all seemed very strange and there was even a rumour that everything about him had been removed from the internet, but I've no idea how true that was.

What Craig Whyte had that other potential bids did not was the backing of a reputable legal firm. The fact he was clearing money into their clients' account and the fact that they confirmed they had sufficient funds to complete the transaction that was being negotiated goes a long way to being positive confirmation.

So many aspects of the Craig Whyte trial still rankle with me today. For starters, I believe it should have taken place in Edinburgh or another city or town.

For the avoidance of doubt, I have had it recently confirmed that prior to the trial, potential jurors were spoken to and the nature of the charges and the anticipated length of the trial were explained to them.

It was stated that anyone with knowledge of the case, with shares, bonds or a season ticket at Ibrox referred to at the time of the indictment, should and could not be a juror.

After the initial discussions Lady Stacey addressed jurors asking them if there was any good reason why they could not sit impartially in the case.

She asked if they knew anything about the case or anyone expected to be a witness in it and also asked if any shareholders, bond holders or season ticket holders at the time featured in the indictment?

Now Donald Findlay was a prominent season ticket holder, shareholder and club director. I understand that as a defence counsel, he wasn't subject to the same strict criteria as those on the jury. But I wish he had been, and it still doesn't sit well with me to this day.

Of course what has happened since has dominoed into a series of court cases which has so far cost the Scottish taxpayer more than £60million – a figure that continues to rise. These include Craig Whye dropping a £500,000 malicious prosecution claim against the Crown Office in 2023. That came after David Grier, a business consultant who was arrested during the probe into Craig Whyte's takeover of Rangers, lost a damages claim against the Lord Advocate. Other cases include administrators David Whitehouse and Paul Clark being awarded damages for malicious prosecutions after they were arrested before all charges were dropped.

It has now been 14 years since I relinquished control of the club and there is no doubt that my legacy was tarnished. The first 15 or 16 years of my tenure were outstanding from both a sporting point of view and a business perspective but the final few years were tricky and took a lot out of me. When we were in that tight period I ploughed a lot of money into the club.

I worked out that our company had put just short of £80million into Rangers during my time at the club. Others, including Dave King and Joe Lewis, invested seriously as well and of course we enjoyed a lot of success. But ultimately, when the crash came, I took the fall. No one else. I was captain of the ship.

It was undoubtedly a low point in the club's history and even now, more than a decade later, I still feel responsible. It's still difficult to believe that it got as far as it did but I will never try to hide. Thankfully for the fans, Rangers have survived and across the past few years have remained competitive, even reaching another European final.

I hope, in hindsight, Rangers fans will understand that there were a number of key factors going on in business and my life that they were simply not aware of at the time.

I was caught in the perfect storm of a bank collapsing, a

shocking result in Europe against Kaunas that cost us millions, a club essentially in financial difficulty and a medical condition that I couldn't announce publicly but put my life sharply into focus.

Also, over many years it has frequently been brought to my attention via websites and forums that I personally, or the Murray Group, had never really invested in Glasgow Rangers.

It seems incredible that fans could actually believe that, given how successful the team was, but lots of them did and still do, it seems.

So for the avoidance of doubt I offer a breakdown of the near £80million that I or my business has invested in the club. This information is available in both Rangers and the Murray Group accounts.

£6million – The cost of acquisition
£4million - Overdraft at time of purchase
£9.8million - First Rights Issue
£50million - Second Rights Issue
£7.8million – The ENIC acquisition

The total cost comes to £77.6 million – which would be £140 million today – but that does not include interest or professional fees.

We received six Directors Box tickets but all stadium advertising throughout my time there was paid in full by the Murray Group, as was the Chairman's Club.

In 23 years no flights or hotel rooms were paid by the club, except on the night of the UEFA Cup Final in Manchester.

25

THE AFTERMATH
AND EBTs

GIVEN THE LEVEL OF RAW EMOTION AT THE TIME OF Rangers' administration I chose to keep my counsel because there was enough noise being made in the media and endless manipulation of the facts.

So I now take this opportunity to dispel all of the myths surrounding the administration of the club. Let me be absolutely clear – it was not placed into administration in February 2012 as a result of the use of an Employee Benefit Trust (EBT) as a method of remuneration.

It was a direct result of the club, under the stewardship of Craig Whyte, failing to pay VAT and PAYE/NIC, on a systematic basis from the date of his acquisition of the club. Dave King and Paul Murray met HMRC three months before administration, but hindsight shows that whatever was discussed wasn't enough to reverse the direction of travel, which certainly wasn't positive. Soon, the club ran out of money and couldn't trade any more.

Despite having a petition to appoint administrators that ranked in priority to Craig Whyte's petition as Director, HMRC chose to allow Whyte to appoint MCR (which later became Duff & Phelps) as administrators.

The outcome of that is well documented in that the joint liquidators successfully sued David Whitehouse and Paul Clark, the joint administrators, for professional negligence. Around £5million was paid to the liquidation estate in respect of this action.

It is worth noting that as the administration and then liquidation progressed, the first tier tax tribunal found in Rangers' favour in 2012 and the upper tier tribunal again in Rangers favour in 2014.

It was clear from the outset that HMRC were going to pursue EBT schemes with some vigour.

This did not concern me in the sense we had always disclosed EBT liabilities in the accounts which were annually audited by Grant Thornton and were relying on robust legal advice in implementing the schemes. I also felt at that time HMRC would take a proportionate approach to the matter, because at the time Rangers were one of many organisations utilising tax-efficient remuneration vehicles.

A meeting was organised in London with the head of HMRC when a financial settlement was offered but immediately rejected.

Very quickly the demeanour at HMRC changed and the correspondence became aggressive and borderline inflammatory. If I could turn the clock back I may well have influenced our approach because those handling matters at Rangers at times got sucked into 'tit for tat' exchanges of correspondence when calmer heads on both sides may have found a common ground.

It also became apparent or at the very least felt that the Rangers

EBT had become the scheme HMRC wanted to pursue above all others, while huge public resource seemed to be allocated to work on this case alone.

And, most alarmingly, private information was being leaked on a regular basis to the media and in particular to a journalist at the BBC.

Assessments began to land with increasing frequency rather than any effort to at least look to agree the quantum in question.

The quantum that flowed through the EBT trusts was circa £47million, on a simple application on tax at 40 per cent and national insurance contributions at 10 per cent. The rates fluctuated between 2000 and 2008 so a detailed calculation would adjust these percentages slightly.

This suggested a tax liability of £23.5million may be due.

However, HMRC chose to:

* Gross up the EBT payments by the tax and national insurance and then calculate the tax liability. The base liability then became circa £37million,

* Interest of circa £10.4million was applied,

*A penalty of £23.9million was applied. This was virtually the maximum HMRC could apply under their rules, claiming that the schemes were illegal and we knew we were operating them illegally.

I was so pleased to see the liquidators appeal this £23.9million penalty with HMRC and then it was completely withdrawn, with full agreement that no illegality existed around the scheme.

However, at the time HMRC had very quickly taken this liability of £23.9million and amended it to a ludicrous figure in excess of £70million, as it turned out, without foundation.

Whilst our team at the club could possibly have managed the interaction better, there is no doubt in my mind that HMRC personnel, who were allowed to remain totally anonymous throughout the whole fiasco, became fixated by the case and matters became very personal.

In a modern world where most disputes can be resolved by negotiation and a commercial settlement, it was clear HMRC saw Rangers as the 'test case' and wanted a court ruling in their favour at all costs.

Why Rangers became the test case is only something HMRC can answer. Following the many years of wrangling and court cases, and whilst I do not know the exact split of the figures, I note HMRC have agreed a global settlement figure with the liquidators of £56million.

When you deduct the Craig Whyte liabilities of £10.2million, the small tax case of circa £5million then the final EBT claim (which includes inheritance tax) is £40million.

Had this been agreed at that time who knows what may have happened, given the various payment agreements HMRC are prepared to grant to other parties?

I will say this: When Rangers went into administration, the squad was worth far, far in excess of any debt.

This of course led on, after administration, to the arrival of Charles Green, Paul Whitehouse and Paul Clark, the nominated administrators who ultimately sued the Crown Office receiving circa £31million in compensation for wrongful prosecution.

And the full bill for payouts related to what is now called the Rangers FC malicious prosecution scandal could soar to unimaginable levels, according to a latest report.

Scotland's Crown Office has allocated £60.5million in unplanned costs for cases brought against the Lord Advocate by people connected to the acquisition and administration of the club.

THE AFTERMATH AND EBTS

In late 2022, Scottish Conservative justice spokesman Russell Findlay described the debacle as 'shocking' and said, "This toxic episode saw innocent men targeted. It has contaminated Scottish justice yet absolutely no one has been held to account."

26

BUSINESS TODAY

AS I APPROACHED MY 70s IT WOULD HAVE BEEN EASY to sit back and perhaps call it day, maybe even ease up a little. Not for me, thank you.

Today I am back involved in our steel businesses. I am helping to run the metals side of what is now the Murray Capital Group, which is selling around 100,000 tonnes of steel a year.

This came about because my son David, now managing director of the group, came to me in 2019 and said the metals business was in need of financial support of £4million because the sector was going through a difficult period.

The steel business hadn't been making money for several years and it needed investment to keep going. He asked me if I thought it would survive. I said to him, "Let's get on the road, then get round a table with the team and take a look at it."

The Hillfoot Steel and Murray Plate businesses were not doing well at all, so I added, "First and most importantly, we'll go down to Sheffield together, have a look around and speak to the troops."

We did exactly that and after weighing everything up I told

him we could collectively turn it around, making it much more profitable. He asked how, and I told him by having 'house accounts' – regular business from major blue-chip companies – and investing in urgently-needed profiling machinery with the latest technology. I got heavily involved in the buying process. Certain supply routes had been closed to the business which I reopened by talking to the suppliers and giving my word the business had a future.

Then I contacted British Steel and asked why they were not supplying very much. The senior executive I spoke to said very curtly, "Your business is going down."

I pointed out that their business had been bust about three times. I asked them to trust me and gave him my word that we would continue and pay our debts. They gave us £1 million worth of credit there and then. The account was built up and built up and now they are one of our main steel beam suppliers.

We now have more house accounts – customers that give us orders every week or every month. But we were lucky with price increases and timing. We got the opportunity to buy a big load of stock and I said, "Buy it!" I just knew it was right.

We had a lot of steel supply coming out of Ukraine until the Azovstal steel plant in Mariupol was blown up, so we've since opened up a lot of other avenues for supply.

Our metals business is performing well now because we deliver, we perform as historically well as we had done previously. The days of supplying full steel plate are limited – customers now want it cut to size, just in time, ready to weld and fabricate.

Because if not, then they've then got to go through a buying procedure, a delivery procedure and have the necessary plant and machinery and labour on site. With what we do, we can fit it into their manufacturing process quicker.

Murray Plates does steel plate, beams, plate processing, plasma cutting and drilling. What we are saying to a company is that if they want to make steel of a particular profile, they will have to buy the plate, they won't have the cutting equipment and what do they do with the waste? We can save a lot of time and money for people.

I can still, and do, work out the weight of a steel plate in my head. Say this is three metres by a metre so it's three square metres and for every millimetre it's eight kilos per square metre. So, if it's 20 millimetres, it's 160 kilos per square metre.

This is three so this steel plate would weigh 480 kilos. I do all of the figures in my head – I have always done that, since I was young and starting out.

Now, as I write, steel prices have started to go down, and we've got to keep moving the steel we have because cheaper stuff is coming in. Some people would say, 'I can't sell it for a profit so I'll keep it.' No, move it. It's dead stock… and dead money.

But the metals business is of course only part of the story. We have become an investment business now. We have the metals and the property company in Murray Capital which we managed to acquire from the bank in the time of trouble when I stayed behind to sort out what was left. We have the wine business and we have investments in a range of companies.

We took away Brand-Rex, which David and Craig McDermid developed and then sold to Leviton in 2018. Of our property investments, the Garden District in Edinburgh is the biggest one. We have planning permission for 1,200 houses there and it has been bought by Places For People. It is arguably the best developable site in Scotland sitting as it does on the outskirts of Edinburgh with all the added infrastructure amenities.

You have got Marks & Spencer, you've got the tram, the railway station and Edinburgh Airport nearby. That is an added bonus for the development.

We're selling the land on to house builders. The site involved massive excavation work. The infrastructure work on the site – putting the drains and the roads and the sewers in will cost £70million. But when you do a deal like that you've got a Section 75 notice under which you've got to build a local school and all of the other conditions that go with that.

It is a hugely attractive site with everything going for it. With all of the other developments being built out of Edinburgh towards the airport, there are no shops. Our development will be less than a thousand yards from the Gyle shopping centre.

I bought that site in 1988 and it's just coming to fruition now, all this time later, and we managed to hold on to it when the previous group went after the financial crash. We have invested heavily and only this year have we received a financial return.

Of all the properties we bought back from the bank, we have so far only had two receipts. We haven't got the £12million back that we paid for Murray Estates then and we have invested a further £30million into that business.

But much of the focus of the Murray Capital Group now is on investments. Trading, where I began my career, is short term.

But if David wants to invest £500,000 in an insurance broker, he can take a longer-term view on that. We have a wide spread of investments. The pattern is similar to what I did but there are more investments with slightly less equity – and less risk – in each one.

So we are now taking a long-term view. Where I started with a trading business is short-term, cyclical. But the growth of the group is a long-term game and investments are as well. With Rangers it was a completely different world. After suffering two defeats in a row you could find yourself completely under serious scrutiny.

Now, we have a mix of short-term and long-term, of sectors and of emotions. It can still be a bit of a roller coaster ride but not the one that I was on for so long.

My son David doesn't want to be in trading companies. David sees himself as an investor and day to day I'm dealing with the metals businesses and helping in the property business where and when required. And Keith is looking after our wine investments.

David is the managing director and a better manager of money than me, much better.

He's had better training than me if I'm being truly honest. As I mentioned, he went to Merchiston Academy in Edinburgh and then Heriot-Watt University. He worked for the football association in Thailand, then worked for sports business IMG in America, he went to Harvard for a while, then worked in the Bank of Scotland corporate department for two years, went to the London School of Economics and came into the business at 28.

He's got a completely different mindset from me. David doesn't believe in employing lots of people. Instead he wants to invest – 10 per cent, 20 per cent, 30 per cent – in a business, whereas I have been an owner-occupier. That's the difference.

He is far more strategic than me, I was and am totally opportunistic. When we were driving around recently I said to him, "Look at the farmland along the road there. We might get an option on it." He replied, "Dad, no. We've got enough."

David is a younger version of me but more controlled. I wouldn't have minded employing 4,000 people; David would have six people managing a portfolio. I was first and foremost a trader, but David is an investor, and he likes to churn investments. I am very proud of him. Both of my boys. I know that I am a difficult act to follow and to take on the mantle of running the overall business.

My son Keith has taken a different route. He is happy running Cockburn's of Leith, the oldest wine merchants in Scotland. We've also got Wine Importers in Livingston and, of course, Chateau Routas, our vineyard in France which has 600 acres and dozens of wild boar. This is consistent with him always having had a passionate interest in food and drink.

What is great is that the three of us are not crossing over each other. There is no conflict of interest between us, whereas if you get jockeying for position in a family business it can be deeply unsettling.

It is a family business, and we are all concerned with legacy. David has a view that when the kids reach the age of 16, they should come to the occasional board meeting. So, Keith's son Fraser and David's daughter Charlotte have recently attended their first board meetings. And in the next few years Georgie, David's other daughter, and Struan, Keith's youngest, will also get an insight into our group's workings and investments which may lead to them working in the business or whatever career path they choose in the future.

27

A POLITICAL FOOTBALL

THROUGHOUT MY BUSINESS CAREER I'VE NEVER gravitated towards politicians. Not one. I've met many, from all sides of the political spectrum and in every corner of the United Kingdom and most of them were well-meaning, full of promises and certainly never lacking in confidence.

They all seemed happy to use you where and when it suited them and I perfectly understood that. I know they have a difficult job, particularly now, when the scrutiny seems to be incessant. But as I get older, I seem to get more and more disappointed in our leaders, our MPs and MSPs. They lack experience, they appear to have so little in common with the business community and collectively they cannot seem to halt Scotland's inevitable slide into decline, driven there by some recent and shameful business, health and education statistics.

The late Donald Dewar once asked me to go around schools throughout Scotland. The Labour government was launching a plan to bring real business into the classroom and I was approached to help front it up.

Gordon Brown announced the scheme at the House For An Art Lover in Glasgow and I must admit I was a bit surprised to see a story about it in the *Daily Record* before we had even kicked off the initiative. Leaking is clearly nothing new.

I went to Govan High School on a Friday afternoon and the thrust of the scheme was fairly simple. We had set up a school shop which would run as a business. Young people would learn about balance sheets and profit and loss. It began as a swap shop involving personal items such as trainers and CDs. It was actually a success and the plan was to roll it out at other secondaries in the city then expand it depending on how successful it was.

Sadly, that was the last I ever heard about it. It just ground to a halt almost immediately. What a shame. It might actually have succeeded.

I spoke to so many politicians over the years suggesting that retired company directors could go into schools on Friday afternoons and explain how businesses worked using the world of sport and fashion as examples and using their individual balance sheets.

Tony Blair was one of the first politicians I encountered but he hadn't quite arrived at that point. It was at Fettes College in Edinburgh. I was in the year above but I knew his name. He was in the same year as Bill Gammell who would go on to become one of Scotland's leading businessmen.

I met Blair again at various events years later and because Scotland is a small country I got to know Gordon Brown, Alex Salmond and Nicola Sturgeon quite well.

Remarkably one politician I did come to know a bit better than others was Margaret Thatcher. In the mid 1980s, I had acquired a metal testing facility called Head Wrightson at a barren site in Thornaby, which was close to Middlesbrough.

While watching television with Louise one night, up popped an image which stunned me. It was Mrs Thatcher on what was famously later dubbed 'A Walk In The Wilderness'. The 'wilderness' was my bit of land and she was announcing that the site would be the start of a massive regeneration project bringing thousands of jobs and future prosperity.

The area was horrendously deprived and I also had a steel business in Darlington, County Durham at the time.

After the prime minister's appearance, I worked closely with Teesside Development Corporation chief executive officer Duncan Hall. We built a headquarters called Dunedin House, which was designed by my architect friend Gareth Hutchison and based exactly on offices we had earlier built in Edinburgh's South Gyle.

The opening of this office was performed by Chris Patten, later to be the last Governor of Hong Kong, and during the project I also had meetings with Michael Portillo.

The Government threw everything at it. In its 11-year history more than 11,000 jobs were created through government and private financial initiatives.

From this initial contact with Mrs Thatcher I was asked to lead the Scottish part of the UK 2000 initiative with Richard Branson leading in England. We jointly held a press conference at Norton House Hotel and agreed to work on various job creation schemes throughout the country.

Weeks after that meeting, Richard made contact and bought Norton House from me personally.

I came into contact with Mrs Thatcher on numerous occasions – once during a business meeting at Edinburgh Castle with others from the Scottish business community and then again in March 1990 when she visited Ibrox where I introduced her to the board and she was given a tour of the stadium. I don't think she was a football fan but she was certainly interested in the club's history.

The last contact I ever had was when Graeme Souness and I decided to fly to New Zealand with a stopover in Singapore. On the first leg of the journey we were sat beside Laurence Graff, the globally-renowned London jeweller who had two bodyguards with him and was delivering the world's most expensive diamond to the Sultan of Brunei. Also close by was Mark Thatcher.

He said, "I've just spoken to my mother and she was asking after you."

My only other link to Mrs Thatcher was an unfortunate one. In September 1984 I had flown to Brighton with my two school friends Phil Sinclair and Paul Clancy to attend an international basketball tournament. Our team Murray International Metals were one of the best teams in Europe at the time. We booked into the Grand Hotel on Brighton seafront.

Several weeks later, on October 12 at 2.54am, a long-delay time bomb planted in the hotel by the provisional IRA exploded during the Conservative Party Conference. Five people were killed, including an MP, and 31 injured. Mrs Thatcher narrowly escaped the explosion, walking unruffled out of the wreckage and going on to give a defiant speech. In a chilling statement the IRA later boasted, "Today we were unlucky but remember we only have to be lucky once."

Several weeks after the bombing I had gone to another basketball tournament in Dublin and on the Sunday, prior to my return, Special Branch went to my home in Edinburgh and asked my wife if I was available to speak to them.

She told the police I was in Dublin with my friend Paul Clancy.

When I arrived off the plane on Sunday night I was met at the airport by two plain-clothes officers who asked me to attend Drylaw police station. It wasn't an arrest as such but they wanted me there the following day at 2pm to answer questions.

I was there on the dot the next day, still wondering what the hell I was supposed to have done, but it quickly became clear. The officers confirmed that in the aftermath of the terror attack they had questioned staff at the Grand Hotel and asked them if they had spotted anything untoward in the previous weeks.

One of the porters told them he had come into contact with a gentleman with crutches, stiff legs and a thick Irish accent. No guessing who that might have been, although they clearly couldn't tell the difference between Scots and Irish.

The two officers asked about my movements in Brighton and it was obvious from their line of questioning that the bomb had exploded in or close to the room where I had been staying. They had clearly taken my name from the register.

However, what had made them doubly suspicious was that there was no mention of Paul Clancy on the hotel register. I was able to answer that quickly. All of our rooms had been booked under my name.

It was clear from early on in the conversation that there was nothing to see here but it was still a deeply uncomfortable two hours of my life.

28

WHAT COULD
HAVE BEEN

IN OCTOBER 2015 I BECAME AWARE THAT TATA WAS planning to close its Scottish steel plate division in the face of unsustainable running costs and increasing foreign competition.

This would have meant that the Dalzell steel plant in Motherwell and Clydebridge in Cambuslang were to go. Tata confirmed publicly on October 20 that the plants were to be mothballed with the loss of 270 jobs – unless a buyer could be found.

If this came to pass it would mean another major body blow to the once-mighty Scottish steel industry. I started immediately working on a plan to buy the facilities, with the support of the Scottish Government, and to give the plants, and most importantly, the workforce and the country's steel industry a future.

News of my plan emerged publicly in Scottish newspapers in November. The *Scotsman* reported the moves under the headline 'David Murray in talks to save the Scottish steel industry'.

A week later a *Daily Record* story headlined 'Union welcomes news of former Rangers owner David Murray's interest in under-threat Cambuslang steel plant.' The story quoted David Fearon, the Clydebridge representative of the steelworkers' union Community, as saying, "We will work with anybody credible who is serious about saving jobs and creating a sustainable future for Scottish steel-making."

What has never been revealed before now is the detail of my plan to provide the plants with a profitable future, including giving the workforce a 20 per cent share of the business.

Instead of backing my plan the Scottish Government decided to support Sanjeev Gupta's Liberty Steel. I really do not know why. At the time of going to print, Mr Gupta's business empire is being investigated by the Serious Fraud Office for suspected fraudulent dealing and money laundering; charges they deny. In 2021, the company's main lender, Greensill Capital, went bust, revealing that Greensill had lent £400million to companies owned or linked to Gupta using the coronavirus large business interruption loan scheme (CLBILS), which benefited from an 80 per cent government guarantee. In April 2021, the Serious Fraud Office began their investigation into Gupta's metals empire and links to Greenhill Capital, saying it suspected fraud, fraudulent trading and money laundering related to the financing of Greensill. Also at the end of 2024, it emerged that Gupta was being prosecuted by Companies House for failing to file accounts for more than 70 companies listed in Britain. He has pleaded not guilty.

Back in 2015, my business was one of Dalzell's biggest customers. I was buying 2,000 tonnes per month – a significant slice of their monthly output. Slabs of steel are made at other plants both home and abroad and sent to Dalzell by train. Dalzell heats the steel slab and rolls it into plate.

Dalzell was one of only two producers of steel plate in the United Kingdom. They could make 3m-wide plate steel, the other firm – Spartan in the north of England – could only make 2m-wide steel plate and is Ukrainian-owned. Clearly, going forward it will have to source its slab elsewhere.

In October 2015, I decided to float the idea to the Scottish Government. I went to John Swinney who was then Deputy First Minister and who I knew personally. He privately confirmed to me that he was aware of the imminent closure and put me in contact with Fergus Ewing MSP, then Minister for Business, Energy and Tourism.

On October 8 I had a meeting at my offices in Charlotte Square with Fergus Ewing and his advisers, including officials from the economic development agency Scottish Enterprise to discuss my plan.

A fortnight later, on October 22, I had a meeting with the then First Minister Nicola Sturgeon, her advisers and Rhona Allison, a director of Scottish Enterprise, at Bute House in Charlotte Square, Edinburgh, the First Minister's official residence and yards from my office.

My initial calculations envisaged an annual loss of around £8million, assuming the production of 100,000 tonnes of plate steel a year and prices remaining stable. Prices had halved over the previous three years. I took them through all of the facts and figures as I saw them. Nicola Sturgeon told me, "This is great, David – it all looks fine." At that time, with more work, I was fully expecting the deal to go ahead. Then following that meeting I had further discussions with both Fergus Ewing and John Swinney.

Tata was obviously crucial in putting any deal together so on November 3, I went to London to see them. I had a meeting with Andrew Checketts, Tata's Head of Acquisitions and Mergers.

He was very helpful, putting me in touch with senior executives of the business to give guidance on future market direction, world availability of slab steel and prices which would be key in ensuring continuity of production.

Throughout this period my businesses continued to buy large quantities of steel plate to support the mills. A proportion of this had been rolled at Tata's Scunthorpe plant. I was obviously well aware that if Scunthorpe closed, as part of the changes at Tata, that would provide new opportunities for Dalzell, although it had a limited thickness range.

Throughout this time, I was keeping a close eye on what was happening in the market, and I was aware that the end users of the steel were becoming increasingly concerned about continuity of steel supply and that some were already beginning to place orders elsewhere. I knew we had to act fast because the damage to the Dalzell plant was only likely to continue to grow.

On November 13 I then had a most informative discussion with John Caouki, the Director of Global Trading at Tata International. He sent me a detailed analysis of buying 200,000 tonnes of slab steel a year, coming in shipments of 20,000 or 30,000 tonnes. The current price quoted was $270 a tonne and we talked through the various supply options, based on quality and price. He advised that opting for a Brazilian supplier was the best option for our needs.

That same day I had a discussion with Anthony Ferrand, Director of Raw Materials at Tata, who was a regular visitor to China and he confirmed the view that the Brazilian supply route would be the best.

The detailed plan I formed was to set up a new business giving Tata a 25 per cent share of it, with them agreeing to lease all the plant, machinery and premises for five years with an option for us to buy them at the end of that time. Under the plan, the workforce would need to make sacrifices on wage reductions or additional hours to make the whole thing work and in return they would receive a 20 per cent stake in the business.

My company Murray Metals would have an equity stake of 30 per cent and would bring to the table a commitment to buy 40,000 tonnes of plate steel a year at an agreed commercial price.

Scottish Enterprise or other government agencies would have an equity stake of 20 per cent and would provide £10million in financial support a year for five years if required. Ultimately it would not have been the case because of a huge increase in prices and profitability.

As I said at the time, "Without this financial input the plan does not work. This, in my opinion, is the price we pay if we wish to retain a steel business in Scotland, particularly with the increase in steel requirements for wind turbines."

Another key part of the plan was that the business would appoint an independent chairman who would ensure that the interests of all the shareholders were properly represented.

Throughout this time, I was keeping Fergus Ewing completely informed of how my discussions with the various parties were progressing. I was utterly convinced that there was a basis of a solid, workable plan that would keep Scotland's steel industry in business and would provide profits and jobs which would obviously benefit the economy significantly.

I was also well aware that the SNP would be making their own political calculations. I was convinced that they would see saving Dalzell and Clydebridge as a massive political coup that would help them kill support for Labour, their arch-rivals in Lanarkshire.

I was going to give the workforce 20 per cent because I needed to keep them onside to make the deal work and to give them job security. A big steel plate mill is like a big washing mangle and I needed it to keep turning and to keep rolling plate to supply mine, and other businesses, and to achieve economies of scale.

My team and I had it all organised in our minds and it all looked like it was going ahead. Then there was a bolt out of the blue.

On December 9 I received a letter from Fergus Ewing thanking me for the proposal we had made. He wrote: "At our first meeting I was struck by your enormous commitment to the steel industry in Scotland – and that impression has been confirmed in our subsequent conversations. I am very grateful for your proposal and the structure of it is of interest to us.

"As explained, in confidence, we are hopeful that an offer will be forthcoming which will be agreed. If that takes place, then I hope it will secure the future for the industry in Scotland for the foreseeable future which will be a tremendous outcome.

"But of course that will only happen with a huge commitment from us all, public and private sector. We are ready to do our bit in full to ensure the success so far as within our power.

"I will keep in close touch and have greatly appreciated your advice on the sector and will continue to value it as time goes on."

It was abundantly clear they were going to go with another offer. I was disappointed to say the least and they didn't say who the other offer was from.

They had a deal there with me and they walked away from it. As it transpired, they didn't go with a leading Scottish industrialist; they went with a businessman from outside of Scotland. How do they justify the decision they made?

At the time I couldn't think why they didn't do it. They didn't ever give me a reason. They just said they had given it to somebody else. Was it politics at play? The only thing I had done politically was say 'Save the Union' at a Labour Party dinner. Not a surprise, really. Were they just taking revenge on somebody they regarded as a Unionist after the defeat in their 2014 independence referendum? Surely it was something else entirely.

I needed a guarantee of £10million to keep the enterprise going but they gave Sanjeev Gupta's company £7million loan to pay for it and, at the time of going to print, it remains unpaid. With my offer, the public purse, Scottish Enterprise and the workforce were all going to get a share.

Nobody has ever done that in that way. That would have saved the Scottish steel industry, given it a sustainable future and would have paid the money back over time with a continuing share of the profits to all parties.

In comparison the wider deal struck with Gupta included a power purchase guarantee for a loss-making aluminium plant in Lochaber in the Highlands – a guarantee totalling an eye-watering £586million. That commitment was kept secret for two years until it was revealed following a Freedom of Information request.

As Scottish Liberal Democrat economy spokesman Willie Rennie put it at the time, "It looks like the Scottish Government have been taken for mugs by the GFG Alliance with financial backing worth £586million in return for a handful of extra jobs."

I know that the steel industry in Scotland would have been in a completely different shape if my plan had gone ahead. The planned business would have been a profitable concern now, including supplying steel plate for wind turbines in much-needed renewable energy generation.

Could have and should have. Words that still stick in my throat. There has been much discussion – and rightly so – about the Scottish Government's record with building ferries. But their largely unnoticed failure to provide a better future for Scottish steel and the Lochaber smelter raises many more unanswered questions.

Looking back, I will always wonder why oh why did they make that decision?

And the mysteries continue.

In July 2024, once again the Dalzell plate mill was mothballed by Liberty Steel and all 116 staff sent home on 80 per cent salary. This was primarily due to lack of financial support regarding future slab purchases by Liberty, who I met to try and find a solution, without success.

I have been in frequent contact with both the UK and Scottish Governments and spoken to numerous MPs and MSPs and offered a business plan solution to restart the mill at a time when thousands of tonnes are required for numerous industries, primarily wind towers, defence infrastructure and bridge building.

Yet I continue to watch with incredulity as the orders for those sectors – running into thousands of tonnes – are placed in France, in Denmark and in Korea. Everywhere it seems, apart from right here in Scotland.

So much of this plate could be rolled at Dalzell if competitively-priced slab could be supplied from Scunthorpe, which has recently been given a lifeline by the UK Government.

I have now been in our steel industry for 50 years and the lack of support for Dalzell, taking all factors into consideration, is a shocking lack of foresight by all parties.

29

NEVER JUST ANOTHER SATURDAY

ALTHOUGH FOR 23 YEARS I SPENT SATURDAY afternoons perched in directors' boxes up and down the country, I was still going through exactly the same emotions as every other Rangers fan. Winning was everything. Losing was inevitably followed by a fan and media pile-on, lots of questions, fingers being pointed and some painful reflection. Not surprisingly, I was the one, supposedly, with all the answers.

There is always an expectation at Glasgow Rangers and, of course, at Celtic, that at weekends, certainly, nothing other than a victory will ever be acceptable. Across two incredibly successful decades I have Rangers games that I cannot forget – and a few that I wish I could.

Here, I've picked out eight matches that sparked vivid memories. Some we won, some we lost but each one was special to me and had some additional meaning to the familiar mantra of 'just another Saturday'.

Rangers 2 Celtic 2, October 17, 1987

In hindsight, my leanings towards Ibrox were evident quite early on. Growing up as an Ayr United fan my father had taken me to Ibrox on numerous occasions during the early 1960s to watch some of the club's legendary European nights. It was the days of Eric Caldow, Bobby Shearer and Davie Wilson. They were magical occasions and the match programmes were like treasure, never rolled up and every word pored over for days afterwards. I remember going with my wife Louise to a Rangers friendly at Ibrox against Everton in August 1971. We were both young but I think that was when I realised that Rangers were 'my big team'. Rangers News launched the same day.

The next occasion, prior to my purchase of the club, was a game that is still talked about. The scoreline of Rangers 2 Celtic 2 would indicate an exciting but run-of-the-mill Old Firm encounter, if there could ever be such a thing, but that description doesn't even come close. It was rapidly labelled 'the shame game'.

Graeme Souness and I had become friends and he had asked me if I wanted to come as his guest. I said 'yes' and he asked me if I would mind picking up his wife Danielle and their kids at their home in Edinburgh and bringing them through to Ibrox.

As I sat in the Ibrox directors' box I couldn't believe that so many Celtic fans were allowed into the main stand and that a cordon of police were dispatched to keep supporters apart.

The match began at 100mph and in 17 minutes Celtic's Frank McAvennie and Rangers goalkeeper Chris Woods were both sent off after clashing. Defender Graham Roberts took over in goal and Celtic scored twice, the second an own goal by Terry Butcher.

Incredibly Butcher was then sent off for a second yellow card but nine-man Rangers came roaring back with two goals, sparking scenes of utter chaos at the end. I probably sat open-mouthed through most of the game but the scenes at the final whistle really were extraordinary. Within days, the Procurator Fiscal had demanded a police inquiry. Butcher and Woods were found guilty of breach of the peace, while McAvennie was found not guilty and Roberts not proven. I was not even close to owning the club yet but that game definitely stirred something deep inside.

When we finally got back to Edinburgh, Graeme and Danielle, myself and Louise certainly had much to talk about over dinner at Cosmo's.

Rangers 2 Aberdeen 0, May 11, 1991

I don't think I realised how much this game had meant to me until I started compiling the list. Just a couple of weeks earlier I had told the footballing legend and my close friend Graeme Souness that he was not welcome to stay on as our manager until the end of the season.

With three-in-a-row on the line it seemed ludicrous but he had just dropped the bombshell that he was going to be the new Liverpool manager. He said he would be happy to see out the final weeks culminating in a title decider at Ibrox.

I'm sure it would have been a nice way for him to wave goodbye to Rangers but I told him, "No. Please just go now." He knew me well enough to know that it was pointless to argue. It wasn't planned and I don't know who was more shocked, him or me.

He left immediately and Walter Smith told me that he would be 'honoured' to take charge. I hoped there would be a smooth transition but it was not an easy few weeks. Momentum had been lost. We were beaten at Motherwell on the run-in and that meant the final game of the season, at home to Aberdeen, had become a league decider.

In 1991 Aberdeen were a tough team packed with international players and I was unusually nervous, more than I had ever been before. Aberdeen were actually top of the league going into the final game and were confident of a victory. I asked myself whether or not I should have left things exactly as they were until the end of the season, as Graeme had offered. This winner-takes-all match was probably down to me letting Graeme go but I didn't dwell on it for long. It was completely out of my hands.

I arrived early at the stadium and almost instantly could feel something special was brewing that day. The fans – thousands of them milling around the main stand – seemed up for it, the players, a few who were even injured, were definitely up for it and I have never, ever heard or seen Walter more determined to win a game of football. The result was never in doubt. Mark Hateley scored twice – one of his goals a magnificent header that sent the stadium into a total frenzy.

At the final whistle, I celebrated with everyone else but behind the cheering and clapping no one would know what I was privately thinking, 'Yes, of course I had done the right thing in letting Graeme go.'

Monaco 0 Rangers 1, September 20, 2000

As glamour goes, there are few places in the world as glitzy as Monaco. However, the principality's football team – despite always being smattered with a host of star names – have never attracted the support they probably deserve.

And that's what transpired when we rolled into town on Champions League business. I have such fond memories of this game. The crowd was around 12,000 and 11,000 of them had travelled from Scotland. I took several people as guests to the match, including Sean Connery. We stayed in the Martinez Hotel in Cannes which is always fully booked for the film festival. The match was an hour's drive away.

We arrived at the Louis II Stadium early and I briefly left Sean to catch up with our manager Dick Advocaat. Dick told me that he was going to try something different that night.

His plan was to play Tugay as a sweeper behind the back four and it worked perfectly. AS Monaco were worthy French champions with so many world class players but we deservedly won 1-0 through a fantastic shot from Giovanni van Bronckhorst, who would later manage the club.

Incredibly there were no food outlets or catering so when we took our seats for the game both Sean and I were pretty ravenous.

At that point I looked behind us and we saw Prince Rainier and his son enjoying hospitality in a private box. They had a chef in there with them and I squinted and did a double-take. It was David Wilson – chef at the Peat Inn in St Andrews, Scotland's first Michelin Star holder and, of course, a Rangers diehard. He clocked us and gave us a wink. No idea how he pulled that gig off but thank goodness he had. Sean and I put on our best 'we're starving' faces and five minutes later, two of the finest baguettes I have ever tasted arrived, courtesy of David and one of his waiters.

It was the perfect start to what turned out to be a perfect evening.

Red Star Belgrade 3 Rangers 0, November 7, 1990

The result was instantly forgettable but the epic journey there and the wall of noise and atmosphere was unlike anything I have experienced anywhere else in world sport.

I flew from Edinburgh to Jersey to collect my boys David and Keith, who were 18 and 15 at the time and on holiday with their mum, and to take them to Yugoslavia. I knew there was an element of risk going because there was so much political tension in the region but they were desperate to attend.

We arrived in Belgrade and it was obvious from the second we opened the jet doors that this would not be an ordinary European football night. This massive, heavily-guarded black saloon, complete with outriders, came right on to the Tarmac and drew to a halt at the foot of the steps.

We all jumped in and were driven through the heart of the city where every Red Star fan looked just wild. We finally arrived at the Rajko Mitic stadium and what greeted us there was like something out of a Mad Max-style, post-apocalypse movie. At least a dozen fires had been lit in the area around the ground and public meetings were being held. The crowds were wound up long before the game. Thousands of Red Star fans were chanting and when the car finally dropped us close to the entrance, I have never been so relieved.

I know Ibrox and Celtic Park can sound intimidating for big games but what we saw and heard that night was unbelievable. There were 82,500 in the ground. When the teams emerged from the tunnel it was a vast wall of noise and it never let up. Ally McCoist said he had never experienced anything like it.

The Red Star team, who that year went on to win the European Cup, were formidable. They had the genius of Robert Prosinecki, who later played for both Barcelona and Real Madrid, and Sinisa Mihajlovic and it was no surprise that they were three goals up with 15 minutes still to play. Graeme said later that Prosinecki had made the difference.

On the way out of the stadium our driver and security team

were joined by two men with loudhailers who used them to scream at the crowds to get out of our way. Graeme and the team needed a similar escort when they finally left an hour after the final whistle.

Despite McCoist scoring at Ibrox in the return leg, Red Star scored too and went on to win 4-1 on aggregate. It was no surprise that they won the European Cup that season.

Rangers 2 Marseille 2, November 25, 1992

This was just a magnificent occasion that Rangers fans would cherish for years afterwards. It was effectively the first Champions League game in Scotland of the modern European era. Campbell Ogilvie, one of our country's finest football administrators, had done an incredible lobbying job to reinvigorate the European competition. He is probably the architect of all we see now in the highest echelons of football, including special matchballs and the stirring anthem that still sounds so special before kick off.

On the Tuesday evening before the game we had entertained flamboyant Olympique de Marseille president Bernard Tapie in the Blue Room at Ibrox and he was a highly-interesting character.

He began his life as the son of a plumber in Paris but he was a born businessman, hugely ambitious and in his adult years served as an MP, and an actor and singer. He became a major shareholder in Adidas.

We sat together for the game. Charismatic doesn't come close. He oozed charm and held centre stage in the Blue Room prior to kick off.

His team was incredible. Barthez, Boli, Sauzee, Desailly, Boksic, Deschamps, Voller – everyone a household name and I think we felt honoured just to be part of the occasion. In 1992 we were primarily a Scottish team because of the three-foreigner rule but we also had injuries to contend with and Ally McCoist in particular would prove to be a huge miss.

Marseille were outstanding for the first hour of the game and were two goals ahead but an amazing header by Gary McSwegan and a Mark Hateley equaliser gave us an unlikely but very welcome 2-2 draw.

Sadly, I never made the return game, which ended up 1-1, because Louise was too ill by that time. It was a fine performance. Sauzee scored for them and Ian Durrant equalised. We were in the game until the final whistle and when Marseillie went on to win the Champions League were realised just how far above our weight we had punched.

When Tapie was eventually jailed for match fixing I think we all looked back, analysed our two games and wondered, what might have been?

FC Copenhagen 1 Rangers 2, August 27, 2003

I rarely let emotions show but those closest to me knew I was particularly nervous before this Champions League qualifier. And I'm sure my sense of relief when it was over told its own story.

We just had to win. It was as simple as that. Our financial situation wasn't precarious but things were tight that season and Alex McLeish knew exactly what was at stake. This was a £10million game of football.

On the day of the game I flew from Edinburgh to Copenhagen with my boys, Sean Connery and the business journalist Jeff Randall, then with the BBC, who had become something of a Rangers fan.

We had lunch in the Tivoli Gardens then just before kick off I had to have words with Barry Ferguson who seemed more concerned about negotiating a win bonus for the players. I urged him to think about nothing other than winning the game.

Then as I walked into the dressing room with Sean to wish the boys all the best, Ronald de Boer shouted at Sean, "Hey, I watched your last film. It was shit." He was referring to The League of Extraordinary Gentlemen.

Half the team, who were of course pumped up knowing what was at stake, burst out laughing. One or two others just looked a bit sheepish. Here was this global superstar trying to give them a pre-match gee-up and he's getting it tight from one of the players. I must confess I was a bit embarrassed by it. But Sean wasn't precious. He took the dig well, smiled then gave Ronald a mouthful back.

The players, of course, went on to win. Mikel Arteta was outstanding in midfield, scored the opening goal before Shota Arveladze grabbed the late winner. They got their win bonus and it seemed that Barry Ferguson had played his final game for Rangers – only to then return at a later date.

One abiding memory from the game was watching our defender Henning Berg stifle their lightning-quick winger Zuma. I later asked Berg how he had done it and he told me, "You don't run with him, you anticipate and run to where he is going."

Willie Miller was another master at that.

Zenit St Petersburg 2 Rangers 0, UEFA Cup Final, May 14, 2008

More than six hours after the game had finished, I sat quietly on a chair outside my ground-floor hotel room near Manchester. It was 4.30am, dawn just breaking. I was alone, a final glass of wine in my hand, and reflecting not only on the disappointment of losing a European final but my time with Rangers and my life in general.

I was so proud of what we had accomplished that season with a team that, on paper certainly, had no business being within 90 minutes of a European trophy. It is almost certainly the case that Rangers will be the team with possibly the lowest-ever wage bill ever to appear in a final.

Weeks earlier, after Nacho Novo had scored the winning penalty against Fiorentina in the semi-final, the fun and games began with tickets. I honestly didn't know that I had so many close friends and relatives. We could have had 200,000 in the stadium that night

Of course my entire family went down to Manchester for the game. I flew on the day of the match and checked into the hotel where the team were staying. I had been in contact with the Zenit coach Dick Advocaat during the build-up to the game. Dick and I had always enjoyed a good friendship – we actually spent one Christmas together in Scotland – but we both had more important things to deal with as kick-off drew close. I think we shook hands and promised to catch up afterwards.

Inside the stadium I shook hands with Denis Law who had been my idol growing up and I met so many famous faces from the world of football and showbusiness. I was aware of the scenes outside the stadium, in Manchester city centre, where fans clashed but we could only focus on what was happening on the pitch.

In the end the game was a crushing disappointment – just one step too far for our team who had battled so brilliantly to get to the final but that evening we were leggy and simply ran out of steam. Dick had a squad that was assembled for millions, he had prepared them well and it showed.

In the end how could I not be proud of Walter and the players. They had exceeded all expectations. Our fans knew it too.

Kilmarnock 1 Rangers 5, Saturday May 10, 2011

It might seem like an odd game to put on this list because in hindsight the ramifications were so enormous but the memories of this are so strong. This was a life-changing game for me.

I remember sitting at home – so relieved that my time was over – and watching scenes from Rugby Park, in particular Craig Whyte clearly revelling in his new status as owner of one of the world's greatest football clubs.

It was a rampant Rangers that won the league that day and there was Whyte lapping up the adulation. It didn't stop there either. Hours later he would be celebrating most of the night at a function in the Hilton Hotel in Glasgow with newly-acquired 'friends' in the media.

But at home in Edinburgh I sat there reflecting, blissfully unaware of any impending catastrophe and telling myself that the club was now in good hands. I had done the right thing. Little did I know.

Of course I had medical issues, in the form of my aneurysm, which had been weighing on my mind and what Craig Whyte perhaps didn't know at that point was that Walter would be leaving and this would be his final game. It was an incredible finale to his time at Rangers.

The baton was being passed and I was handing over the club, supposedly debt-free with a legal offer document confirming that £5million a year would be spent on players. Why wouldn't I feel satisfied that I had done the right thing?

The rest, of course, is history.

30

THE FUTURE AND
THE PAST

THE FUTURE OF SCOTLAND WORRIES ME MORE THAN
the future of Murray Capital. I don't think it is too harsh to say that
in 2025 our best export is talent.

There seems to be a massive lack of opportunities for young
people after they leave university and they have no option but to
seek a living elsewhere in the world.

It is a repeat of what happened in the 1970s when the phrase
Brain Drain was first used.

Doctors, nurses and dentists use the benefit of their Scottish
university education to find well-paid employment abroad. But
surely when we have such chronic staff shortages in the NHS it
would not be unreasonable for students to enter into mandatory
12-month or two-year contracts to help repay the education
they have received. That would alleviate the staffing issues. After
the contract is completed, they would be free to pursue a career
elsewhere if they chose to do so.

Our country has a real problem. In my lifetime the population has risen just three per cent, while in Wales during the same time span, the figure is 20 per cent and in England, the population has risen almost 30 per cent.

The Scottish Government, which has ambitions to become the greenest country in the world, does not own any onshore or offshore wind farms and, in fact, 92 per cent of our windfarms are foreign owned.

As it stands, 99 per cent of Scottish salmon farming is foreign-owned, 70 per cent of the whisky industry is foreign-owned, our main three airports at Edinburgh, Glasgow and Aberdeen are all foreign-owned, and outwith Royal Navy work, there is no active shipbuilding and no active steel manufacturing industry.

It's a damning indictment of modern Scotland that would never be allowed in other countries.

For me business has always been about seizing opportunities and getting the right people to work on them.

I like to think I am normally good at getting the right person. In my experience the original idea is normally right, it's the people that sometimes don't deliver.

We spot the idea then need a person to run it, or the person comes to me with the idea. I've got an open mind about how it comes in the front door. There is no bible of business planning that tells you how to do it. It's gut instinct and you can get it right or you can get it wrong.

You meet people and you think 'I like the cut of his jib' – 'would you like to come and work with us?' People you have met in life, and you know a wee bit of their background, their history. If there was a good guy in another company, you would just go and headhunt him.

To my mind, it's instinctive. The things in my business life that have gone wrong, in the main, were outwith my control. If somebody can't head a ball in Kaunas and my bank goes bust, it doesn't matter how clever I am. Those things were totally outwith my control.

You must always be honest with yourself. I hate people who say, 'It was his fault.' No, it's a pyramid with one at the top, then two, then four. The person at the top gets paid the most and takes the most responsibility.

If someone senior working for me makes a costly mistake I ask, 'How did we get here?' Then it's, 'I'm sorry but this is a warning, don't do it again.'

You have to give someone a chance – you don't say 'you're out.' You've got to go through a process of trying to help them through it. You might have a person who's drinking in the morning before he or she comes into work or they've got marital problems. The one thing is you don't kick someone when they're down. I wouldn't do that. You've got to treat people as you would like to be treated yourself.

But if someone is stealing or there's repeated mismanagement or they're mistreating people; it's not debatable – you're going. They go and you don't deal with them again. When a relationship breaks down, I always say, don't revisit the scene of the crime. It's then all just negative energy and if you do, you'll fall out with the person in 10 minutes.

You learn from your previous mistakes, don't you? I think in life you can make a mistake once but if you make the same mistake twice you deserve what you get. I have been in business for 50 years, I probably made money in 42 of them.

So, I've got half a clue. To use a cricketing expression, my batting average was solid. When I think back it was quite a rise for a business that started out with me being a trader, effectively a broker holding no stock, to a business of substantial scale and being one of the biggest of its kind in the UK. At some point in everyone's life they can hit a brick wall and at that juncture you can either go left, the wrong way or turn right and go the right way with the results that follow.

When you are in business your approach has to be professional. When I'm on duty, I'm on duty. I never drank alcohol on a match day at Ibrox when I was Rangers chairman because I was at work. I would arrive early, about 11am, go into the manager's room downstairs and have a chat with Walter Smith or Dick Advocaat or whoever was manager at the time, before going upstairs to have lunch. As I mentioned, I was never allowed in the dressing room within an hour of the game after the infamous David Robertson incident in 1992.

I rarely go to football matches now. I look at my life in stages. That was my time then. I am happy and relaxed in Perthshire. I have a flat in Edinburgh. Grandchildren come for their breakfast on a Sunday. Thankfully, they're all sports-daft. My two grandsons regularly attend Murrayfield and play school rugby at Strathallan. My two granddaughters are both very sporty, playing cricket and hockey at Fettes College. We've totally encouraged that as a family. I'm a bit old fashioned; healthy body, healthy mind and it runs in the family. That's just the way I've been brought up.

People sell their businesses quicker now. I waited but then when I did sell, I was selling the business to buy other ones. I think a lot of people sell to get out. I know of people who retire at 55 but now here I am at 73 and I'm not retiring.

What I don't understand with family businesses – and I know a lot of them – is the attitude of the founder fathers. They think they're Walt Disney and that they'll live forever. What's the point of building a business and saying, 'You can take over now, son, now you're 64.' What's the point? Basically, the founder is to blame. You've got to hand over the baton to give the guy a chance to make his own mark.

I have done that with David who I think is highly respected. He handles himself well, he's educating himself all the time, he does courses, he attends seminars, he's learning all the time. That was something that I wasn't that good at.

He has integrity and believes in people first, balance sheets second. We celebrated 50 years in business in 2024 and David proudly told me, and anyone else that would listen, that I have been a hard act to follow. He will be, too. He has learned to become his own man and is already planning for the next generation and how our family business will evolve.

David has said to me so many times, "I've tried not to be like you. You are unique, operating at your peak in a different era and there is no point in me trying to replicate that."

We both agree these are very different times and what I accomplished during what he calls the 100mph 70s, 80s and 90s just could not happen today. David will make sure Murray Capital has a very different and much more measured trajectory.

I quickly grew our metals business in oil, gas, manufacturing and shipbuilding – at one point with thousands of employees – but the majority of those sectors are now history.

David's business, and our family name, is now about investment and no bank debt. Fingers in different pies. And his biggest challenge is to work out how we continue to thrive in a climate of endless tax changes.

Essentially we reinvest in real estate and in private companies. The Murray name will live on and we all must ensure our foundation continues to go from strength to strength.

If there is one characteristic that I could pass on to both of my sons it would centre around resilience and dealing with whatever is thrown at you. Being optimistic in times of darkness is something that became a bit of a mantra for me and until you've been through a life-changing moment such as the car crash or the global financial meltdown you never know how you are going to respond.

David says I have finally settled into becoming his ideal chairman – more advisory and less hands-on. If he needs advice, I'm there, and still always 24 hours a day. That will never change.

David also says that he's glad my Rangers days are in the past. He is a huge fan of the club and still goes to as many games as he can but he is convinced that if my involvement with Rangers hadn't happened, we would have achieved £1billion in revenues.

Maybe but I still wouldn't have changed a thing.

———

Looking back, there are some huge things that happened to the business along the way – the Bank of Scotland selling to Halifax, not taking the money from Jack Petchey and selling Rangers, borrowing too much money. In hindsight one might have done it differently but at the time it just seemed the right thing to do. It's all very well somebody saying I borrowed too much money but what would they have done in that position? So many people wouldn't have got to the starting line to be in that position.

One of the key things about my approach to business is that I have mainly kept it private – no stock exchange involvement and few external investors. I did have some external investment when Angus Grossart sold 10 per cent of the business in 1982 for £1.5million.

Even selling 10 per cent meant that I had a different type of responsibility to shareholders: who were pension and investment funds. I had no problem with it, but you were far more accountable, and I found it not what I had been used to. So, several years later I decided to buy them all back out again. In those days I was my own man, I could make my own decisions and make my own mistakes and not be over-penalised in some sense. Sometimes you get more attention when you don't make money in a year than when you make money but that's the nature of the media and that goes with the ticket. I have no inkling to become a public company and I don't think I was a public company animal.

If your approach is like mine then it is so important to have the right advice in your business. I had Jim McDonald, my finance director, before and I have my son, David, now. Jim held me back at times. He would say, "You cannae do that, son, you cannae do that." And as I wrote earlier, I respected Jim. I owe a lot to Jim McDonald because he set good ground rules. When Jim decided for his own reasons 20 years ago to retire, I lost a bit of his discipline perhaps. As I got older and stronger, I thought I could do anything, but Jim held me back. I needed to be held back at times. David provides that role today and is always quick to point out, "Dad, you can't do that. It's a different world now."

In the early days I would listen quite a bit to Angus Grossart because he was a very astute, very professional manager of money. His business did a lot of flotations of Scottish companies and I just enjoyed his company. He unfortunately passed away in 2022.

I believe I've got a good nose for business opportunity and spotting where things can go wrong – I have been through three recessions, after all, and I hope that I got more things right than not. Thankfully I'm also still in the game at the age of 73 having started at nearly 21. There are not many first-generation business founders that have created the kind of legacy I have, after having had to leave school because your father couldn't pay the fees.

I was in a generation of people who started their own businesses but today for many of this younger generation it's a whole different belief. Plenty of top entrepreneurs did not go to university. They started a business and built it up from the bottom.

I think we are creating an era of kids today who would rather go and work for somebody than start their own business. I don't see as many budding entrepreneurs, It's different now. Is the next generation as hungry as ours was, unless it's through necessity?

There are a multitude of tech ideas but there is also a style of selling early, of cashing in. I think it is a completely different business environment. David has a better handle on the current situation than I have. He is in business groups, attending meetings and seminars. I'm primarily in the steel business and I'm the chairman of the company.

One of my proudest moments happened only a few weeks ago when David received the Family Business of the Year award on behalf of Murray Capital, where he is MD, at the 2025 British Business Awards.

David said it was in recognition of our family's resilience, dynamism and ambition for more than 50 years. That's a tribute to so many good people across so many years. The future is definitely in safe hands.

Raising money is completely different today. The main banks are not the lenders they once were and there are a lot of secondary banks that have arrived in Scotland. If you want venture capital funding today, it's double digit interest rates so it's a completely different environment.

I believe that has put a lot of people off starting their own business. I don't think this younger generation would put off holidays, drive through the night, go through the pain, go without things, not have a holiday for a couple of years.

Today it is 'at this time we go to Spain, at Christmas we go there...' For me that wasn't on the agenda. It was how do we start a business; how do we work?

I remember playing a game of rugby one night and then going and getting a lorry and delivering some stainless steel down at Prestonpans at 10.30pm. I really don't think people would go that extra mile today.

You have to see the opportunity; you have to read the market and do what it takes to deliver it. If you want one steel pipe, one plate, one beam, a steel mill won't make that for you. There is a minimum 20 tonnes order.

So, we would bulk buy – a steel mill would like us because they were rolling steel for us every week when a company might only buy from them at mill quantities three or four times a year. We would think of buying 2,000 tonnes of plate for stock and that's a good rolling for a supplier. That gives them economies of scale where they don't have to stop-start, stop-start. Let's roll one-inch plate for Murray's for two days. That was a gap in the market that we saw and took on.

People talk about my drive but I couldn't afford to fail. You've got people relying on you. Even to this day there are people relying on me making decisions – though not to the extent of a few years ago.

You have to succeed through adversity. There are about five or six reflective moments in my life. I'm at Fettes and my father can't pay the fees, my mother and father split up. I go to Broughton School.

I then start in the metal business at the age of 17. I meet Louise when she's 16, still at school. I go to her parents' anniversary dinner and I don't even have a suit; I borrow one.

Then I lose my legs, then there's recessions, then my father dies when I'm 24 and then Louise passes away, aged 39, and my sole concern is guiding two teenage boys in their future life. My mother later died and to cap it all, I had major surgery after my aortic aneurysm. All of that has made me resilient.

People talk about determination but I put a pair of metal legs on every day. No option. I've got to do it. People rely on me. I'm just used to it now.

Why look back and say, 'I wish, I wish?' I don't think I've ever had time to feel sorry for myself because I had big support from my family. I'm proud of my boys and what they have achieved in life so far. I'm pleased that they're married and settled, involved in the family business and I have four happy and healthy grandchildren. I do consider myself a lucky man.

I hope that any of the mistakes I have made are honest mistakes.

You don't need to go to church to be a good Christian – it's about being a good person, doing the right thing. We went through a difficult time with the business but there was nobody who wouldn't deal with me – we paid our bills. Who took the biggest hit? It was the bank and me.

But you shouldn't go into business if you haven't got determination. It is not for the fainthearted. You can't make money every week, every month without taking the odd blow.

If you get knocked down – and I did, repeatedly – you've got to get back up again. I have done that my whole life… repeatedly.

Special thanks to
Bruce Waddell

Thanks to
Ken Symon
Douglas Alexander